A DAY
IN THE LIFE

The Unofficial
and Unauthorised Guide
to 24

A DAY
IN THE LIFE

The Unofficial
and Unauthorised Guide
to 24

By Keith Topping

First published in England in 2003 by

Telos Publishing Ltd
61 Elgar Avenue, Tolworth, Surrey, KT5 9JP, England
www.telos.co.uk

Telos Publishing values feedback. Please e-mail us with any comments
you may have about this book at feedback@telos.co.uk

ISBN: 1-903889-53-7
Text © 2003 Keith Topping
Cover © 2003 Dariusz Jasiczak
The moral rights of the author have been asserted.

Internal design, typesetting and layout
by Arnold T Blumberg
www.atbpublishing.com

Printed in England by
Antony Rowe Ltd
Bumper's Farm Industrial Estate
Chippenham
Wiltshire
SN14 6LH

1 2 3 4 5 6 7 8 9 10 11 12 13 14 15

A DAY IN THE LIFE

is dedicated to

the *very* legendary

Ian Mond

and

Geoffrey D Wessel

12:00 1:00 2:00 3:00 4:00 5:00 6:00 7:00 8:00 9:00 10:00 11:00 12:00 1:00 2:00 3:00 4:00 5:00 6:00 7:00 8:00 9:00 10:00 11:00 12:00

The author wishes to present bouquets of sincere best wishes to the following friends and colleagues for their encouragement and contributions to this book: Ian Abrahams, Di and Bernie Atkinson, Sean Brady, Matt Broughton, Neil Connor, Andy Cowper, Martin Day, Diana Dougherty, Clay Eichelberger, Jeff Farrell, the Godlike Genius of Jeff Hart, Tony and Jane Kenealy, Michael Lam, Phil McConerty, Whistling Jock Purcell and Chrissy Cornish, Jim Sangster, Paul Simpson, Kathy Sullivan, Colin Topping, Graeme Topping, Lily Topping, Nick Wallace and Maggie Walsh.

Also a necessary, and long-overdue, shout-out to Ted and Len, Beth, Tom and Ed, Michael, Marcus, Fran, Samantha and Trish, Keef, George, Bill, Rhys and Sarah.

My additional thanks go to Kirstie Addis, who was instrumental in getting *A Day in the Life* airborne in the first place and, especially, to David Howe and Stephen James Walker, who *kept* it airborne when it looked like crashing and burning. Also, to Arnold Blumberg, Darius Jasiczak and Roger Anderson. And to the ever-wonderful Susannah Tiller. For, you know, *stuff.*

A special acknowledgement for my friend Jim Swallow and his fabulous comment when I told him that I'd been commissioned to write *A Day in the Life*: 'Are they giving you just the one day to write it in?' Ah, thereby hangs a tale, matey...

INTRODUCTION

12:00 1:00 2:00 3:00 4:00 5:00 6:00 7:00 8:00 9:00 10:00 11:00 12:00 1:00 2:00 3:00 4:00 5:00 6:00 7:00 8:00 9:00 10:00 11:00 12:00

MIDNIGHT TO MIDNIGHT

*'Right now terrorists are planning to assassinate a Presidential candidate.
My wife and daughter have been kidnapped. And the people I work with may be involved.
I'm Federal Agent Jack Bauer. And this is the longest day of my life.'*

What follows, constitutes a brief history of time.

It was November 2001, and I was taking a well-deserved holiday in Los Angeles, having recently completed work on my *West Wing* book *Inside Bartlet's White House*. Whilst there, I used the opportunity to catch up on the, post-September 11th, television season's debut shows. Let's ignore, for a second, how spectacularly sad it is for someone *on holiday* to spend much of their time watching TV. Anyway, one show, in particular, looked really interesting. It was the third episode of a new Fox drama series called *24*. Some friends had already alerted me to the ingenuity of the concept and it all sounded *very* clever. An entire season taking place over 24 one-hour episodes, in virtual real time. (The clock continued to run even during the commercial breaks.) The timescale was to span one complete day - midnight to midnight - in the life of a US Federal agent. His task was to attempt to stop a determined and complex cabal of international terrorists from assassinating an African-American Presidential candidate on the day of the California primary election. At the same time, the agent also has to deal with the kidnapping of his teenage daughter and, subsequently, his wife. And, to cope with all sorts of other outrageous malarkey and dodgy shenanigans besides.

Back in England, I spent a lot of the winter of 2001 telling anyone whom I thought might be in the slightest bit interested about this great new show. And about how, when it turns up over here, *you gotta see it*. The last time I got this excited about a new import, it was over *The West Wing*. The time before that, it was *Buffy the Vampire Slayer*. Finally, in February 2002, the BBC announced that it had acquired the first UK broadcasting rights to *24*. Within about three weeks of the series' debut on BBC2, in March, *everyone* (and their dog) was talking about this show. It's always nice, if somewhat irritating for others, to be able to say that you were there first.

So, this is *A Day in the Life*. Of Jack Bauer, that is. Bauer, as played stoically, though with occasional moments of manic ultraviolence, by the very magnificent Kiefer Sutherland, is the key to *24*'s ultimate success. An everyman-yet-superman flawed hero, facing insurmountable odds and determined and well-resourced foes. Someone with only his wits, his integrity, his plethora of way-cool gadgets and his abilities as an armour-plated one-man killing machine to keep him going. Actually, what many of *24*'s more intellectual critics and viewers seem to have missed is that, at *24*'s heart, is an underlying fantasy. Basically, this is the story of an overworked, stressed-out, middle-management stooge who gets, for one day, to live out all of our dreams and demonstrate his massively under-appreciated skills to his bosses, and to the world at large. Seen in this context, Jack Bauer becomes a prototype for a new age, a middle-class hero.

24 has been a television industry phenomenon. We've never seen anything quite like this before. It's got literally *everything* that a successful modernist thriller should have. Conspiracy theory, political intrigue, occasional flashes of jet-black humour, fashionable Los Angeles locations, a stellar cast of mainly little-known supporting actors and, especially, testosterone coming out of its nostrils.[1]

That's chiefly why I wanted to write this book. In my eyes, *24* is *extraordinary*, dangerous, high-octane, sexy television, cleverly put together to maximise the breathlessly clock-watching nature of its scripts. It is constructed like *Die Hard* meets James Bond meets *JFK*, featuring elements drawn from everybody's favourite TV shows and movies from the last couple of decades. Like many modern American television series (*Buffy the Vampire Slayer*, *Stargate SG-1* and *The X-Files* being three excellent contemporary examples), *24*'s creative team seem to revel in knowingly sampling exterior texts into their work. To, as it were, wear their source material like a badge of authenticity. They do this, seemingly, in the firm belief that their audience are sussed enough to know what they are watching an homage to. And, to join in the production team's celebration of that twilight world between parody and tribute. Intellectual parallels crop up all over *24* in a mix of knowing allusions and visual references. It's clear that the producers have, whether consciously or unconsciously, defined their audience as a collective mass of people who have, more or less, the same video and comic collection as they themselves do.[2]

Importantly, *24* also has a interesting audience demographic with something of an intellectual crossover with *The West Wing*. (A similar political theme marbles both shows and it was no surprise, whether by accident or design, that in Britain at least the two were scheduled to follow one another on Sunday nights.) There is also a shared audience with series like *The X-Files* (all the Black Helicopter-crowd just *love 24*). Put simply, all sorts of different people watch *24* and for many different reasons. But, ultimately, for one reason only. It's *fantastic* telly. 'It creates a level of angst that a lot of shows don't,' notes Kiefer Sutherland, and he's absolutely right.

12:00 1:00 2:00 3:00 4:00 5:00 6:00 7:00 8:00 9:00 10:00 11:00 12:00 1:00 2:00 3:00 4:00 5:00 6:00 7:00 8:00 9:00 10:00 11:00 12:00

HEADINGS

REAL WORLD JUNCTION The obligatory interaction between the world that *24* occupies, and the one that the author and his readers do. Unless, of course, you know different.

L.A. STORY A guide to La-La Land, featuring extensive

· ·

1 The BBC's digital channel BBC Choice ran a 60 minute Jonathan Ross-fronted documentary in August 2002 called *24 Heaven* to coincide with the first UK broadcast of the first season's finale. This included interviews with many of the cast and crew, and contributions from some of *24*'s celebrity (and non-celebrity) British fans. As *Top Gear* presenter and chat show host Jeremy Clarkson - a highly vocal and passionate fan of the series - noted, *24* works largely because it is: 'Pure, unadulterated plot.'

2 Movie influences on the general concept of *24*, besides John Tiernan's *Die Hard* (1988) and Oliver Stone's edgy *JFK* (1993), appear to include two further, and glorious, examples of US cold-war paranoia and cynicism: John Frankenheimer's *The Manchurian Candidate* (1962) and Alan J Pakula's *The Parallax View* (1974). The epic chase sequences of William Friedkin's *The French Connection* (1971) and Peter Yates's *Bullitt* (1968) would appear to have been hugely influential on the visuals of the series. Also, *Patriot Games* (Phillip Noyce, 1992) in which a federal agent, called Jack, tries to stop a political assassination by a terrorist with a specific revenge agenda against the agent and his family. Another, perhaps even more obvious, debt is owed to John Badham's *Nick of Time* (1995, starring Johnny Depp and Christopher Walken). This takes place in virtual real time and features a complex plot that concerns a daughter's kidnapping and an attempted political assassination. Mike Figgis's *Timecode* (2000) also shares many experimental thematic links with *24*.

notes on geographical references and the filming locations used. 'This is a show that made Angelenos proud that television knew all about its grim and banal recesses,' noted *the Independent*. 'After more than 90 years of [Hollywood] using L.A. as a backdrop, here is a work that makes the odious, endless, beguiling place fresh as morning.'

COOL GADGETS

'The gadgets are great,' notes Carlos Bernard, who plays Tony Almeida in *24*. His view is shared by many male viewers, for whom *24* is like a weekly dose of technological pornography. Strangely, one of few people who isn't a huge fan of the show's penchant for Bondian-style gadgets is Kiefer Sutherland. Mainly, he admits, because of the weight of carrying all of them around with him. 'I hope people like the gadgets,' he adds, 'because they were an incredible pain in the butt for me.'

REFERENCES

Pop-culture, 'Generation X' and general homages to all things esoteric.

POINTS AT WHICH KIM/TERI NEED A SLAP

Lots of *24* fans don't really like Jack Bauer's daughter, Kimberly, very much. They reckon she's a saucy little minx with the IQ of a mollusc. This author, actually, isn't one of them. He considers that young Ms Bauer displays considerable courage and occasional maturity far beyond her tender years during the course of this most difficult of days. On the other hand, there *are* a few occasions when he'd quite like to hit her repeatedly on the head and he feels that he's not alone in this. Indeed, noted TV critic Robert Bianco, in *USA Today*, has, on several occasions, nominated Kim for an award celebrating *The TV Teenager you'd Most like to Slap*. And, as for her mother... okay, she's having a *very* traumatic 24 hours. But *whine, whine, whine, whine, whine...* Marge Simpson can get away with it, love. Her husband's a fat, balding failure. Yours is James Bond. *Get over it.*

Just so we're absolutely clear about this, the author wishes to stress that whilst, on occasions, he'd like to give the characters of Kim or Teri a slap, he certainly has *no wish* to extend this to Elisha Cuthbert and Leslie Hope. These are the two extremely talented ladies who play Kim and Teri, respectively. It's a considerable coup for any actor to give a performance that produces an emotional response in the audience. Even, perhaps *especially*, a negative one. It's a tribute to both Elisha and Leslie that we, as viewers, care enough about Kim and Teri that we feel *anything* regarding their situation. Excellent work, ladies.

LOGIC, LET ME INTRODUCE YOU TO THIS WINDOW

A section that, *gleefully*, details the mistakes, the continuity errors, the geographical absurdities, and all of the bits of the plot that simply don't make sense. Plus, anything whatsoever to do with sudden bouts of amnesia for dramatically shaky reasons.

QUOTE/UNQUOTE

Samples of the dialogue that it's worth replaying the DVD for.

Other categories appear from time to time. Most of them should be fairly self-explanatory, **Sex and Drugs and Rock 'n' Roll**, for instance. **Critique** details what the press made of it all. **Comments** from the cast and crew have been added where appropriate. Each episode concludes with a review and copious notes on continuity and other assorted trivia.

So, the clock is ticking and we have much ground to cover before the day is over. Welcome to the world of international terrorism, political manoeuvring and dysfunctional family values. Use whatever means you have at your disposal to achieve your aims. And trust no one.

Tick, tick, tick...

Keith Topping
His Gaff
Merrie Albion
November 2002

THE CAST

12:00 1:00 2:00 3:00 4:00 5:00 6:00 7:00 8:00 9:00 10:00 11:00 12:00 1:00 2:00 3:00 4:00 5:00 6:00 7:00 8:00 9:00 10:00 11:00 12:00

UNUSUAL SUSPECTS

Kiefer Sutherland (Jack Bauer): The absolute spitting image of his actor father, Donald,[3] Kiefer William Frederick Dempsey George Rufus Sutherland is the grandson of former Saskatchewan Premier Tommy Douglas.[4] Born, in London, in December 1966,[5] Kiefer's mother, Shirley Douglas, was also a fine actress.[6] Kiefer lived with her and his twin sister, Rachel, in Toronto after his parents divorced when he was seven. Following a rebellious-teen phase,[7] his first acting appearance was in a tiny role in *Max Dugan Returns* (1983). He came to wider public attention as adolescent tough Ace Merill in *Stand By Me* (1986) and as the teenage vampire gang-leader, David, in *The Lost Boys* (1987), the film which cemented his burgeoning star-status. A member of the so-called 'Brat Pack' along with fellow young actors and friends like Charlie Sheen, Emilio Estevez and Lou Diamond Phillips, more ensemble movies followed. These included the smash hit Western *Young Guns* (1988) and its sequel (1990), and *Flatliners* (1990), in which he co-starred with Julia Roberts, with whom Sutherland subsequently became romantically involved. The last-minute cancellation of the couple's planned Hollywood wedding, in June 1991, was headline fodder for the tabloids for some months afterwards.[8]

'The first 10 years of my career, I was involved in a lot of hit films,' Kiefer says. 'I was very fortunate for that. I was probably too young to realise *how* fortunate. I didn't take complete advantage of it.' After the Roberts debacle, he spent much time on a ranch in Montana and competed in rodeos, twice winning the US Team Roping Championship. On returning to Hollywood, Sutherland has, like his father with whom he has acted on several occasions (notably in 1996's *A Time to Kill*), shown a willingness to vary his work. From comedy - a strait-laced FBI agent trying to deal with flaky fugitive Dennis Hopper in *Flashback* (1990) - to serious drama - a venal, redneck, by the book Marine, in *A Few Good Men* (1992). He was an effective and empathic lead in *The Vanishing* (1993), a lively Athos in *The Three Musketeers* (1993) and made a creditable directing debut on the TV Movie *Last Light* (1993), in which he also starred as a condemned killer. Other important films include: *Crazy Moon* (1986), *Bright Lights Big City* (1988), *1969* (1988), *Renegades* (1989), *Twin Peaks: Fire Walk With Me* (1992), *Freeway* (1996), *Dark City* (1998), *The Right Temptation* (2000), *Beat* (2000) and *I Fought the Law* (2001). Twice married and divorced,

• •

3 Donald Sutherland's impressive CV includes several of this author's favourite movies: *Dr Terror's House of Horrors, The Dirty Dozen, MASH, Klute, Don't Look Now, The Eagle Has Landed, The First Great Train Robbery, Murder by Decree, Backdraft, Buffy the Vampire Slayer* and *JFK* not least amongst them. During the 1960s, Sutherland was a British TV regular; he played the voodoo god Dwumbala in an episode of *The Champions*, for instance, and also appeared in series like *Man in a Suitcase* and *The Saint*.

4 Douglas was the leader of the first elected socialist government in North America and was the father of Canada's National Health Service.

5 Within two months of Kiefer's birth, his father was filming a memorable guest appearance in the seminal *The Avengers* episode 'The Superlative Seven'. In this, Donald Sutherland plays a Central European terrorist involved in a fiendishly complex kidnapping plot. *Plus ça change, plus c'est la même chose.*

6 Readers may remember Shirley as Mrs Starch, the piano teacher in *Lolita*, Laura in *Dead Ringers* and as the voice behind Infectia in *The Silver Surfer* cartoon series.

7 Sutherland freely admits that his school nickname, 'Reefer', wasn't *just* because it rhymed with Kiefer.

8 'I felt bad for us both,' Kiefer told *Radio Times*, 'but we asked for it.'

Kiefer has a 14 year old daughter, Sarah Jude.

Dennis Haysbert (David Palmer): Born in June 1954, Dennis Haysbert grew up as the eighth of nine children in San Mateo, a town in Northern California not known for its ethnic diversity. His father worked in security for United Airlines, but Haysbert didn't travel much as a child. Travelling was something rich people did. Six foot four inches tall and a star football player and athlete in high school, Dennis was pushed toward cultural pursuits by his mother. At 13 he walked into the rehearsal of a high school play and decided, 'I could do that.' At the time San Francisco was a hotbed of African American politics, with the Black Panthers active across the San Mateo Bridge in the East Bay. 'I never wanted to venture over the bridge,' says Haysbert. He graduated from the American Academy of Dramatic Arts in the late 1970s and began his acting career on TV shows like *Scarecrow and Mrs King*, *The Fall Guy*, *Magnum, P.I.*, *The A-Team*, *Buck Rogers in the 25th Century*, *The Incredible Hulk* and *Laverne & Shirley*. His first movie was *A Summer to Remember* (1985). He subsequently appeared in *Major League* (1989) and its two sequels, *Navy SEALS* (1990), *Love Field* (1992), *Heat* (1995), *Insomnia* (1996), *Absolute Power* (1997), *The Thirteenth Floor* (1999), *Random Hearts* (1999) and *Love and Basketball* (2000). He also played Dr Morris in the TV series *Now and Again*. 'African-Americans are usually cast as drug-addicts, criminals or judges,' Haysbert told *The Guardian*. 'It's a pleasure to be portraying something a little different.' Haysbert's heroes include former Presidents Jimmy Carter and Bill Clinton, and Colin Powell 'who I wish *would* run for president,' he notes.

Sarah Clarke (Nina Myers): Often credited on-screen under her middle name, Lively,[9] Sarah was born in St Louis. She is probably best known in the US for her appearance in an award-winning advert for the VW Jetta and also in adverts for the supermarket chain K-Mart. Sarah wasn't interested in acting when she studied Italian and fine arts at Indiana University but, having spent a year in Bologna, she got inspired. 'I didn't really get the bug until I had to acclimate to a new culture and let go of my identity as an American,' she told the *Detroit News*. Returning home after college, Sarah worked as an architectural photographer and took acting lessons for free in exchange for shooting photos for a community arts centre. Sarah's first movie was *Pas de Deux* (1999) for which she won an Outstanding Performance Award at the Brooklyn Film festival. Between roles, Sarah temped for a law firm and worked at a furniture store in New York to pay the bills. Her acting CV includes appearances in *Sex and the City*, *The Accident* (2001) and *Emmett's Mark* (2002). During the filming of *24*, Sarah became engaged to her co-star Xander Berkeley.

Leslie Hope (Teri Bauer): A native of Halifax, Nova Scotia, Leslie was born in May 1965 and got her initial break playing Linda Martin in *Knots Landing*. A founding artistic director of The Wilton Project, a theatre group in Los Angeles, Leslie has also appeared in *Dragonfly* (2002), *Sanctuary* (2001), *The Spreading Ground* (2000), *The Life Before This* (1999), *Shadow Builder* (1997), *First Degree* (1995), *Schemes* (1995), *Cityscrapes: Los Angeles* (1994), *Doppelganger* (1993), *Talk Radio* (1988), *Love Streams* (1984), and on television in *The Outer Limits*, *Star Trek: Deep Space Nine*, *Early Edition*

9 She is credited as Sarah Lively in *The Accident* and on her appearance in the TV series *Ed*.

and *SeaQuest DSV*. An outspoken advocate of equality within the industry, Leslie complained bitterly to *The Guardian* at the Monte Carlo television festival that she believed the second season of *24* could be diluted by 'beautiful women in their 20s' on the orders of nervous network chiefs. 'Fox is owned by Rupert Murdoch,' she noted. 'The business is all about money. The tone of the show might shift into other areas. I'd be concerned about that.'

Elisha Cuthbert (Kimberly Bauer): Whilst touring the world as a correspondent and presenter on the award-winning factual children's TV series *Popular Mechanics for Kids*, Elisha Cuthbert impressed then-First Lady Hillary Clinton. Cuthbert was subsequently invited to Washington for a meeting at the White House. 'I was lucky,' Elisha has noted. 'I found what I wanted to do when I was 11.' Born in November 1982, in Calgary, Elisha made her acting debut as Sarah in *Dancing on the Moon* (1998) at the age of 15. She also played Katlin in *Lucky Girl* (2001), Katherine Winslowe in *Believe* (2000) and Nicole Stone in *Airspeed* (1998), and appeared in *Nico the Unicorn* (1998), *Who Gets the House?* (1999), *Old School* (2002), the Nickelodeon series *Are You Afraid of the Dark?* and *Largo Winch*. She *hates* being asked 'What's Kiefer Sutherland like?'

Penny Johnson Jerald (Sherry Palmer): A very familiar face on US television, Penny Johnson graduated from famed New York school of music, Juilliard, before moving to Los Angeles to become an actress. She played Laura Harmon in *Deliberate Intent* (2000), Roscoe Dellums in *The Color of Friendship* (2000) and Laney Roosevelt in *Road to Galveston* (1996). Her movies include: *Swing Shift* (1984), *Kaleidoscope* (1990), *Goin' to Chicago* (1991), *Fear of a Black Hat* (1993), *What's Love Got to Do With It?* (1993), *Automatic* (1994), *Death Benefit* (1997) and *Absolute Power* (1997). She featured as Beverly Barnes in *The Larry Sanders Show*, though she's probably best known to viewers for her recurring role as Kassidy Yates, Captain Sisko's love-interest in *Star Trek: Deep Space Nine*. Her other TV appearances include *General Hospital*, *The Paper Chase*, *The Practice*, *The X-Files*, *ER*, *Parker Lewis Can't Lose* and *Hill Street Blues*. During the 90s, Penny also worked as a script supervisor on *Clubhouse Detectives*, *Seasons of the Heart* and *Love Kills*. 'When I'm out in public, people come up to me and say, "Oh my gosh, you're the J.R. of *24*,"' Penny notes. The Sherry Palmer mystique has even infiltrated her home. 'My daughter, Danyel, is an avid fan. When she's in her room watching, I can hear her from upstairs yelling, "Mom, you didn't!"'

Carlos Bernard (Tony Almeida): Born Carlos Bernard Papierski in Evanston, Illinois, Carlos's first big break was appearing as Chajén in *The Killing Jar* (1996). He played Chico Escovedo in *Vegas, City of Dreams* (2001), Ronaldo Alvarez in *Mars and Beyond* (2000) and Rafael Delgado in the series *The Young and the Restless*. His CV also includes appearances in *Babylon 5: A Call to Arms*, *National Lampoon's Men in White* (1998), *Sunset Beach*, *Silk Stalkings*, *F/X: The Series* and *Walker, Texas Ranger*. Concerning his 'evil' facial hair (the goatee patch of chin stubble which, apparently, convinced many viewers that Tony was the CTU mole from the first episode), Carlos notes: 'I shaved it off the day that we finished shooting.'

BEHIND THE CAMERA

12:00 1:00 2:00 3:00 4:00 5:00 6:00 7:00 8:00 9:00 10:00 11:00 12:00 1:00 2:00 3:00 4:00 5:00 6:00 7:00 8:00 9:00 10:00 11:00 12:00

BEHIND THE CAMERA

24 co-creator Joel Surnow had previously written for shows like *WiseGuy, The Equalizer, Miami Vice* and the animated *Bill & Ted's Excellent Adventure* series. He was also a consultant and director on the excellent *La Femme Nikita* where he worked extensively with writer Robert Cochran. Cochran, himself, had a similar crime/military-fiction background to Surnow, scripting episodes of *JAG* and *L.A. Law* and co-producing *The Commish*.[10] Michael Loceff was also one of the regular writers on *La Femme Nikita*.

Cyrus Yavneh's previous production work included TV movies like *Town and Country, In the Army Now* and *The Woman Who Loved Elvis*. After graduating from Princeton, Howard Gordon and his partner, Alex Gansa, wrote for *Spenser For Hire, Beauty and the Beast* and, most notably, *The X-Files*. Subsequently, as a solo scriptwriter, Gordon's hugely impressive CV includes contributions to *Angel, Buffy the Vampire Slayer* and *Strange World*. London-born director Stephen Hopkins previously worked on *Under Suspicion, Tube Tales*, the *Lost in Space* movie, *Blown Away, Predator 2* and *Crossworlds*. He was Russell Mulcahy's assistant director on the 80s cult classic *Highlander*.

Robin Chamberlain's CV includes *MacGyver, Wanda Nevada* and *Get Real*. British novelist Andrea Newman can lay claim to a genuine television first when her adaptation of her own *A Bouquet of Barbed Wire* brought one of TV's last taboos, incest, into the public domain in 1976. The mini-series, starring Frank Finlay and Susan Penhaligon, was an enormous hit on both sides of the Atlantic. Work on *MacKenzie* (another self-adaptation), *The Frighteners*, the hugely popular *A Sense of Guilt* and *Imogen's Face* followed before Andrea moved to the US to write for *Felicity*. Paul Gadd had previously worked on *Born on the Fourth of July* and *Northern Exposure*. Michael Chernuchin was a scriptwriter on *Bull, Law & Order* and *Homicide: Life in the Streets*. Tony Krantz was a producer on *Mulholland Drive, Sports Night, Mosaic, Felicity* and *Wonderland*.

With more than 40 Oscar and Emmy nominations for his productions, and as recipient of 2001's Producers Guild of America's *David O Selznick Lifetime Achievement Award*, Brian Grazer is one of the most prolific producers in Hollywood. His films and TV series include: *Splash, Kindergarten Cop, Ransom, Apollo 13, The Nutty Professor, Bowfinger, Stealing Harvard, A Beautiful Mind, The PJs, Mercury Rising, Fear, Backdraft, The Doors, Parenthood* and *Spies Like Us*. His voice can be heard in *The Simpsons* episode 'When You Dish Upon A Star' which also featured his partner in Imagine Films Entertainment, Ron Howard.

Born in Duncan, Oklahoma as part of a famous acting family (his father Rance, mother Jean and brother Clint all regularly appear in his movies), Ron Howard featured in his first film, *Frontier Woman*, aged 18 months. As a child-actor, he appeared in *Lassie, The Twilight Zone, The Fugitive* and *The Music Man*, and was the precocious Opie on *The Andy Griffith Show*. He then moved from Mayberry to Milwaukee to play Richie Cunningham, in *Happy Days*. His movies include *The Wild Country, American Graffiti* and *The Shootist*, for which he received a Golden Globe nomination. But his dream was always to be a director. After high school, he attended a film programme at the University of Southern California. His first two movies, *Eat My Dust!* and *Grand Theft*

10 Cochran and Surnow also worked together on *The Commish*, and for one season, on the soap-opera *Falcon Crest* where they first encountered a young Leslie Hope.

15

Auto, both financed by Roger Corman, were made whilst Howard was still in *Happy Days*. Subsequently he became one of the most successful directors of the 80s and 90s, his films including *Splash*, *Cocoon*, *Parenthood*, *Backdraft*, *Apollo 13*, *Edtv*, *A Beautiful Mind* (for which he won an Oscar) and *How the Grinch Stole Christmas*.

CRITIQUE Even before the series had been broadcast, columnists and reviewers were falling over themselves to predict great things for *24*: 'Although there are only two main story lines, each episode has no fewer than six stories to keep track of,' noted Aaron Barnhart after seeing an advance preview. 'Full of suspense and action-packed, there's a lot going on in *24*, but you have to pay attention to truly appreciate it. I predict *24* will have a lot of viewers' undivided attention this fall.'

DID YOU KNOW? Although impressed enough with the *24* concept to pass over several similarly-themed ideas in its favour, Fox were so nervous about the viewer commitment required for the series to work fully that they, initially, only ordered 13 episodes. As Cheryl Klein perceptively noted on *zap2it.com* four months before the series debut, each episode had to inform both previous and future episodes in the tightly woven plot. But, as with most TV shows, the crew had started shooting the early episodes before the writers have even scripted the later ones. In effect the series was, from day one, playing an intellectual game of catch-up with itself. And, as a consequence, also with its audience. When Joel Surnow pitched the initial premise to Robert Cochran, Klein noted, Cochran agreed that it was an absolutely brilliant idea. He then added: 'It's also impossible. Don't *ever* bring it up again!' At the *Television Critics Association Press Tour* in Pasadena, in July 2001, Kiefer Sutherland noted: 'The [plot] device was not the most attractive thing to me at first. I thought the characters were really well developed.'

24 - Season I
(2001-2002)

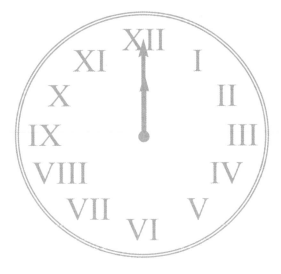

The following takes place
between midnight and midnight
on the day of the California Presidential Primary.

24 Season I (2001-2002)

Real Time Productions/Imagine Television/ 20th Century Fox Television

Created by Joel Surnow, Robert Cochran

Co-Producer: Robin Chamberlain (2-24), Michael Loceff (2-24)

Producer: Cyrus Yavneh, Andrea Newman (2-24)

Associate Producer: Bob Johnston (1), Paul Gadd

Consulting Producer: Michael S. Chernuchin

Executive Producer: Brian Grazer, Tony Krantz, Joel Surnow, Robert Cochran, Ron Howard[11]

Co-Executive Producer: Stephen Hopkins, Howard Gordon (2-24)

Script Supervisor: Tracy E. Zigler

Script Coordinator: Jessica Abrams (2-24)

Original Music: Sean Callery

Regular Cast:

Kiefer Sutherland (Jack Bauer)

Leslie Hope (Teri Bauer)

Elisha Cuthbert (Kim Bauer)

Sarah Clarke (Nina Myers)

Dennis Haysbert (Senator David Palmer)

11 Uncredited.

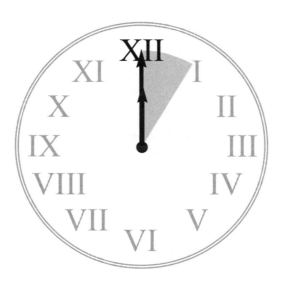

12:00 MIDNIGHT – 1:00 A.M.

12:00 1:00 2:00 3:00 4:00 5:00 6:00 7:00 8:00 9:00 10:00 11:00 12:00 1:00 2:00 3:00 4:00 5:00 6:00 7:00 8:00 9:00 10:00 11:00 12:00

12AM

1 12:00 MIDNIGHT – 1:00 A.M.

US Transmission Date: 6 November 2001 (Fox)[12]
UK Transmission Date: 3 March 2002 (BBC2)
Writers: Robert Cochrane, Joel Surnow
Director: Stephen Hopkins
Cast: Carlos Bernard (Tony Almeida), Penny Johnson Jerald (Sherry Palmer) Mia Kirshner (Mandy), Michael O'Neill (Richard Walsh), Xander Berkeley (George Mason), Rudolf Martin (Martin Belkin), Richard Burgi (Alan York), Daniel Bess (Rick), Matthew Carey (Dan), Jacqui Maxwell (Janet York), Karina Arroyave (Jamey Farrell), Tanya Wright (Patty Brooks), Devika Parikh (Maureen Kingsley), Gary Murphy (Vincent), Jeff Ricketts (Victor Rovner), Karen Kim (Flight Attendant), Petra Wright (Flight Attendant), Ward Shrake (German Airline Passenger)[13]

OTHER TRANSMISSION DATES Canada, 6 November 2001. Bulgaria, 10 January 2002. Iceland, 17 January 2002. Denmark, 3 February 2002. Brazil, 1 March 2002.

4:00 P.M., Kuala Lumpur: As Federal Agent Rovner transmits important data on his computer, there is a sinister knock on his door.

12:02 A.M.: Los Angeles: Richard Walsh is head of the shadowy government agency, the Counter Terrorist Unit (CTU).14 He receives a telephone call suggesting that a black presidential candidate, Senator David Palmer, is being targeted by assassins. Palmer, meanwhile, is on the balcony of his Los Angeles hotel room writing a speech with Patty, his campaign manager. Today will be the day of the California Presidential Primary Election.

12:03: Sultry teenage-*sexbomb*, Kimberly Bauer, tells her father, Jack, that she's glad he has recently moved back in with her mother, Teri. After Kim goes to bed, Jack and Teri talk about how Kim seems to enjoy playing her parents off against each other. They then discover that she has sneaked out of the house. Finding her will have to wait, however. Jack receives a call from his co-worker at CTU, Nina Myers, who tells him that Walsh has called him to a meeting.

POINTS AT WHICH KIM NEEDS A SLAP A pouty opening scene playing chess with her father, which is all very *me, me, me*. Later evidence (telling a pack of lies to Rick about her father being dead for no other reason that to illicit sympathy), confirms Teri's, half-spoken, assessment of her daughter as a right manipulative little madam.

12:07: Kim and her friend, Janet, are on their way to meet two boys, Dan and Rick. They arrive at a furniture store, break in, have a party, and trash the place.

· ·

12 This episode was originally scheduled for broadcast on 30 October 2001. It was postponed, by a week, due a variety of network scheduling changes brought about as a direct result of the attack on the World Trade Center, and the Pentagon, on 11 September.
13 Uncredited.
14 It is never made entirely clear within the series whether the CTU is supposed to be an autonomous agency in its own right, or whether it is a branch of either the FBI or, more likely, the CIA. References to Jack being a 'federal agent', or to 'the agency' don't help to clarify matters.

FREEZE-FRAME A pair of Kim's purple knickers are briefly visible, hanging out of a drawer in her room.

CIGARETTES AND ALCOHOL Vincent, Kim's ex-boyfriend, is in his bedroom with a friend, surrounded by empty cans of beer. Party on, dude. Rick has a six-pack at the furniture store to get the party going.

12:09: At CTU, Jack meets with Nina and fellow agent, Tony Almeida, whilst waiting for Walsh. TV reporter Maureen Kingsley announces that Senator Palmer is widely expected to win today's election. Walsh tells Jack, and his colleagues, that a foreign power - or possibly a hate group - intends to make an attempt on Palmer's life.

THE CONSPIRACY STARTS AT CLOSING TIME In private, Walsh confides to Jack that there may be a mole within the CTU itself and that District Director George Mason is on his way to give Jack further information. Jack should, Walsh continues, trust no one.

12:22: Patty receives a call from a German photographer, Martin Belkin, currently on a flight to Los Angeles, who has an appointment to meet Palmer at breakfast.

SEX AND DRUGS AND ROCK 'N' ROLL Teri finds three joints in Kim's room and calls Jack who suggests that Teri should investigate Kim's e-mails. Unfortunately, they don't know her password. Meanwhile, at the furniture store, Dan and Janet have rather noisy sex on a display bed.

12:25: Mason tells Jack that the assassin is likely to be German whilst suggesting that Palmer is no friend of the agency. Suspicious, Jack shoots Mason with a tranquiliser dart. Jack believes that Mason has misappropriated seized drug-money. He coaxes Nina into procuring blackmail information from Mason's bank account.

12:38: Alan York, Janet's father, calls Teri. He doesn't know where his daughter is, he says, and suspects that the two girls are together. Nina asks Tony to hack Mason's account. Tony grudgingly asks if Nina is still sleeping with Jack. He resents Jack for previously uncovering members of CTU who were involved in illegal activity. But he does what Nina asks.

POINTS AT WHICH KIM NEEDS A SLAP Jack gets the unit's hacker, Jamey Farrell, to discover Kim's e-mail password: LIFESUCKS. Teenagers, don't you just *love* them?

REFERENCES Posters on Kim's bedroom wall include the bands Green Day and Coldplay and rapper 2Pac Shakur. Martin claims to have met Princess Diana (1961-97). There's a dialogue allusion to 10CC's mid-70s hit 'I'm Mandy, Fly Me'. Kim's organiser has various Goth-style stickers on the cover, including one of a snake. Inside, a briefly glimpsed note reads 'Jamie luvs Bill.' Mandy is reading the in-flight magazine *Traveller*.

12:43: Martin chats to a beautiful woman sitting next to him on the plane. Palmer takes a break from his speech to spend time with his wife, Sherry. Maureen Kingsley calls for a response to an incriminating allegation that she intends to air in the morning. Having read Kim's e-mails, Teri calls Alan with the likely location of the girls.

BUSTED! Kim, Janet, Dan and Rick are about to drive to a party, when Kim sees various text-messages that her mother has left on Kim's mobile phone. She wants to go home, knowing that she's in trouble. Dan offers to drop her off.

THE MILE HIGH CLUB Martin and his new friend, Mandy, have fabulous (if somewhat cramped) sex in the plane's toilet.

QUOTE/UNQUOTE Nina, after discovering that Jack has tranquillised Mason: 'I thought you wanted to get your life together? You think this is *helping*?'

12:52: Jack finds evidence against Mason and wakes him up to say that if Mason doesn't tell him from where he got the information about the intended Palmer hit, Jack will reveal Mason's corruption. Mason tells him, then leaves. Mandy steals Martin's wallet then, casually and efficiently, plants a bomb on the plane, and escapes by parachute seconds before the aircraft explodes.

L.A. STORY The Bauers live in the Pacific coastal suburb of Santa Monica, one of the most sought-after places to live in the L.A. area.[15] Teri and Alan drive to the San Fernando Valley to find the girls. 'The netherworld known as the 818 area code' according to Cordelia Chase in *Angel*, the Valley is a collection of suburbs just across the Santa Monica mountains from Hollywood which includes Sherman Oaks, Van Nuys, North Hollywood, Burbank, Northridge and Reseda. It will be most familiar to readers as the suburban wasteland of strip malls and fast-food diners as depicted in movies like *Magnolia*, *Buffy the Vampire Slayer*, *Anywhere But Here*, *Pulp Fiction*, *Short Cuts*, *Two Days in the Valley* and *Go*. Or, perhaps for older readers, as the regular filming location for *The Rockford Files*.[16] David Palmer's suite is in The Standard Hotel, at 8300 Sunset Boulevard opposite the classic art deco-style Argyle Hotel which can be seen in many shots from Palmer's balcony.[17]

12:57: Tony tells Jack that a 747 has exploded over the Mojave Desert. Kim is distressed when Dan deliberately goes in the opposite direction to her home.

• •

15 Approximately 15 minutes drive from Downtown L.A. - *in theory*, something that should be applied to *all* approximations in connection with Los Angeles travel - Santa Monica is also famous for its pier, the magnificent state beach and the Third Street Promenade retail and restaurant area. Not forgetting the numerous bars on Santa Monica Boulevard itself, as immortalised in Sheryl Crow's 1996 hit 'All I Wanna Do'. Santa Monica has certainly changed a vast amount since Raymond Chandler used it as the setting for *Farewell My Lovely* and described it as resembling a giant funfair.

16 Amongst the valley's more dubious claims to fame is as the capital of the US's booming porn movie industry, which is often said to be a not insignificant part of the local economy. For an amusing fictionalised study of the valley's porn trade, see Paul Thomas Anderson's film *Boogie Nights* (1999).

17 Possibly the most famous street in the world, Sunset Boulevard runs right through Hollywood into West Hollywood where it becomes the even more legendary Sunset Strip, a fantastic two mile conglomeration of chic restaurants, hotels and night-clubs. This is home to The Comedy Store, the Whisky-a-Go-Go, the Roxy and the Viper Room. And, most notoriously, the Sunset Hyatt Hotel, the staging area for the wild and lurid antics of several generations of rock stars from Led Zeppelin, The Rolling Stones and The Who onwards. A flavour of the Hyatt's extremely colourful past can be glimpsed in Cameron Crowe's seminal *Almost Famous* (2000).

LOGIC, LET ME INTRODUCE YOU TO THIS WINDOW Each *24* episode is supposed to take one hour in real time, but in actuality, three minutes are gradually added to the timer during the various US commercial breaks. Thus each time the clock hits :00 at the end of an episode, it's actually three minutes to the hour. This subsequent time is used for the credits, further commercials, and scenes from the next episode. In the UK, *24* is broadcast on the BBC which is commercial-free. Because of this, episodes do *not* run in real time, *per se*. Thus, the caption 'Events occur in real time' was removed from the opening credits by the BBC.

How, without the aid of rocket propulsion, does Janet drive from Santa Monica to Van Nuys - approximately 20 miles - in just over six minutes? At the end of the episode, Dan's truck is still, clearly, driving through the Valley (note the 818 area-code sign, for instance). However, Kim says 'Turn here, I live on 10th,' suggesting that they're back in Santa Monica. Seventy nine seconds after the aeroplane has exploded, Tony tells Jack that 'preliminary sources' suggest the cause of the explosion was a bomb. How can they tell *that* quickly? Who was knocking on Rovner's door in Kuala Lumpur? If it was any of the organisation involved in the assassination plot who were attempting to stop him from transmitting vital information back to the US, then why do they bother to knock? There's no station ID on Maureen Kingsley's *Late Night News* broadcast as there are on all US TV news shows. Given the meticulous planning that has gone into much of the conspiracy, isn't using a pair of waste-of-space losers like Dan and Rick rather slapdash? Dan, seemingly, *does* work at the furniture store and both Janet's and Kim's e-mails mention him, and his work location, specifically by name. This has, therefore, left a trail of evidence that could easily be followed after the operation had ended even if both of the girls were dead, as seems to have been the plan from the outset. Of course, it's perfectly possible that Gaines never intended Dan and Rick to survive long enough to spend their $20,000 as well. But later evidence suggests that both Melanie and Frank knew about Dan and Rick's connection to Gaines too.

Then there's the whole deal with blowing up the plane. It's big, it's attention-grabbing and it's very exciting. It also makes *absolutely no sense whatsoever*. The rationale for it within the plot is that the terrorists need to acquire an ID card from the photographer. So, they go to all of the effort and expense of picking his pocket whilst he's on a plane and then blowing up the plane to *hide the theft*. Wouldn't it have been far simpler just to have waited until he arrived at LAX, picked him up outside the airport and bumped him off in a quiet back alley? Then, to have hidden the body and stolen the ID card that way? Isn't it also going to look a bit suspicious when this photographer, who has been *very publicly and obviously dead* for seven hours (he's on the plane's passenger list, after all), suddenly turns up alive and well to photograph the Senator at breakfast? Not only that, but the blowing up of the plane automatically sets the entirety of American law enforcement on the terrorists' trail several hours before they attempt to commit the crime that they are *really* planning. Bear this in mind for later in the season - these terrorists are, basically, *stupid*. If you work from that premise then a lot of their plan becomes much easier to rationalise.

'YOU MAY REMEMBER ME FROM...' Daniel Bess was in *Not Another Teen Movie* and *Firefly*. Xander Berkeley's massive CV includes appearances in *Wolf Lake*, *Shanghai Noon* (as Marshall Van Cleef), *Phoenix*, *Amistad*, *Apollo 11* (as Buzz Aldrin), *Heat*,

Apollo 13 (as Henry Hurt), *A Few Good Men*, *Terminator 2: Judgment Day*, *The Grifters*, *Straight to Hell*, *Sid and Nancy*, *Mommie Dearest*, *The Adventures of Brisco County Jr.*, *Miami Vice*, *The A-Team*, *Tales of the Gold Monkey* and *M*A*S*H*. Jacqui Maxwell played Summer in *Gilmore Girls*.

Columbian-born Karina Arroyave appeared in *In Too Deep*, *Falling Down*, *Dangerous Minds* and as Bianca Marquez in *As the World Turns*. Matthew Carey played Tony Santos in *L.A.X*, and also appeared in *Junk* and *Family Rules*. Jeff Ricketts played Malcolm in *Chance*. His movies include *Spoof! An Insider's Guide to Short Film Success*, *The Prime Gig*, *Holes* and *Psycho for Milk*. Karen Kim was in *An American Daughter* and *Sherman Oaks*. Rudolf Martin played Dracula in *Buffy the Vampire Slayer* and Vlad the Impaler in *Dark Prince: The True Story of Dracula*. He was Raoul in *Bedazzled*, Gilbert in *Punks* and Anton Lang in *All My Children* and appeared in *Swordfish*. Mia Kirshner played Catherine in *Not Another Teen Movie* and Ruby in *Wolf Lake* and appeared in *Saturn*, *Johnny's Girl* and *Exotica*. Devika Parikh was Bonnie in *The West Wing*. Her movies include *Book of Love*, *Caught* and *Judgement Day*.

Tanya Wright was Tanya in *The Cosby Show*, and appeared in *Parker Lewis Can't Lose*, *Mutiny* and *Moesha*. One of this author's favourite actors, Michael O'Neill, plays Ron Butterfield in *The West Wing* and was in *Traffic*, *The Mod Squad*, *The Legend of Bagger Vance*, *Sea of Love*, *Roswell* and *The X-Files*. Petra Wright appeared in *My Daughter's Tears* and *Cowboy Jesus*. Richard Burgi was James Ellison in *The Sentinel*, Captain Hunter in *The District* and Phillip Collier in *Days of Our Lives*. Ward Shrake was in *American Girl*, *Totally Blonde*, *Bundy* and *S Club 7 in Hollywood*.

BEHIND THE CAMERA Composer Sean Callery previously worked on *La Femme Nikita*, *Blowback*, *Star Trek: Generations* and *Se7en*.

NOTES 'We have reason to believe that, by the end of the day, an attempt will be made on David Palmer's life.' Barely a shot or a line of dialogue is wasted in this, one of the finest opening episodes of *any* TV series in recent memory. A testosterone-soaked, adrenaline-pumping, kaleidoscopic white-knuckle ride into 24-carat paranoia. The episode is streaked with vivid imagery and startling set pieces that will live long in the memory of every viewer. Aided by Stephen Hopkins's dazzling quick-cutting techniques and imaginative use of split-screens (inspired by movies like *The Thomas Crown Affair*, *The Boston Strangler*, *Carrie* and *Bullitt*), it's fair to say that *24* doesn't so much hit the ground running, as sprinting with vapour-trails behind it.

Jack's home telephone number is 310 555 3067,[18] and his car licence plate is 4RHI384. Jack also surfs. Kim says the Bauers live on 10th Street, in Santa Monica, which appears to be approximately a six minute drive from CTU headquarters. Passwords used for Internet connections from the Bauer's number, apart from LIFE-

18 Ever wondered why 555 is used as a telephone prefix in many US films and TV series? When exchange-names were part of phone numbers, digits also corresponded to letters, the first three signifying the exchange the caller was dialling. Unfortunately '5' was J K and L and there aren't many American place-names using a combination of those. Due to the low number of 555 codes, Hollywood was encouraged to quote them in their productions to prevent real telephone subscribers being harassed by people trying out numbers they'd heard in the movies. Now the 555 code *is* used by various service providers. Only 555-0100 to 555-0199 are set aside by Bellcore for the entertainment industry. This episode *doesn't* use one of those so, presumably, the producers visited the website *www.home.earthlink.net/~mthyen/* which lists other numbers available to movies

25

SUCKS, include KIM*B and WILD-ONE. In the recent past Jack was involved in an internal CTU investigation which culminated in the prosecution of three agents who had accepted bribes. Jack and Teri have friends called Denise and Steve. They, in turn, have a daughter called Nicki who is currently undergoing therapy. Heroin dealer Phillipe Darcet was arrested in August of last year (probably 2001) in Barcelona by a team lead by George Mason.[19] Subsequently, $200,000 was transferred from Darcet's funds to an offshore account in Aruba. Mason authorised the transaction.

The series was originally to be entitled *24 Hours* but this was changed to avoid confusion with a current affairs show on CBS. Most of the official press releases prior to *24*'s debut billed the actress playing Nina as Sarah Lively. For final transmission, however, she opted to use Sarah Clarke instead.

REAL WORLD JUNCTION The events of 11th September 2001 in New York and Washington delayed *24*'s network premiere by a week. Fox also required the cutting of shots of the aeroplane exploding at the episode's climax (though bits of fiery debris flying past Mandy can still be seen). The original pilot also contained a radically different opening scene, set in Venice instead of Kuala Lumpur. Additional minor timing changes also occurred.

SOUNDTRACK 'It's All Good' by The Fearless Freep, 'Fix and Destroy' by The Dirtmitts, Sugarcult's 'Bouncing Off the Walls', 'Compromise' by Mean Red Spiders, 'Live at E's' by Sublime, Krome's 'Chair on a Wire', 'Everything and Nothing' by Rocket Science, 'Iguaza' by Gustavo Santaolalla, The Angel's 'Destiny Complete', 'Feelin' Irie' by Jazz Pharmacy and Tricky's 'Christiansands' (at the climax). 'Break Stuff' by Limp Bizkit ('It's just one of those days') was used heavily by Fox to promote the series on trailers during October 2001.

The untransmitted version of the pilot also included Madonna's 'Ray of Light' and 'Californication' by Red Hot Chilli Peppers, but neither appear in the final episode.

CRITIQUE 'This is a huge commitment for viewers, but the signs are that it might be one worth taking (fans of the much missed *Murder One* might be particularly amenable),' noted *Radio Times*. '*24* is full of arresting images and is surprisingly dark for American television.'

Indeed, the opening episode of *24* achieved some of the best reviews of any new network drama in *years*. Matthew Gilbert in the *Boston Globe* called it 'an innovative and expertly executed hour of suspense.' Howard Rosenberg in the *Los Angeles Times* described it as 'smashing.' 'Gripping from the get-go,' added Tom Shales in the *Washington Post*. Linda Stasi of the *New York Post* bestowed special praise on Kiefer Sutherland. 'He's so good, it's like he's not acting.' John Corman in the *San Francisco Chronicle* also enjoyed Sutherland's performance, but gave the show itself only a lukewarm review: 'It's a pleasingly glossy production with a gimmick [that] it doesn't really need and a star it couldn't afford to lose,' he wrote. Antonia Zerbisias in the *Toronto Star*

and TV shows. The area code 310, on the other hand, *is* a real Los Angeles code. It covers several suburbs including West Hollywood, Santa Monica, Beverley Hills and Malibu.

19 It is never specifically stated on-screen on which date, or even in which year *24* takes place. 5th March 2002, with its real-life California Primary election, would seem to be as good a bet as any. See, also, **Dating *24***.

commented that when she first saw the *24* pilot in August, she found it 'slick and surprising' and wrote 'Five Harrison Ford movies rolled into one series,' in her notes. But after the 11 September attacks and the subsequent anthrax alerts, the drama, she considered, now seemed 'trivial and simplistic.'

It was inevitable, of course, that some TV reviewers would feel obliged to comment on the sensitivity of the timing of the series debut. The *Boston Herald*'s Monica Collins was one: 'After Sept 11, this first episode of *24* was rushed back into the editing room to delete a scene of the jetliner exploding. Seems a rather superfluous exercise in tastefulness when you watch the final result.' Collins also noted that *24* was exciting and intriguing. 'Using a split-screen technique to further propel the interlocking storylines, the drama has an edgy, hip style, enveloping you in suspense and danger... I admired *24*, but I don't think I'll watch it every week. For now, I get all the thrills I can stand from *60 Minutes*.'

CAST AND CREW COMMENTS For the first episode, the production hired noted director James Foley (*Glengarry Glen Ross*) to set the visual style for the series. Sadly, a week before shooting commenced, Foley had to leave the project due to a family bereavement. His replacement, Stephen Hopkins, together with editor David Thompson, subsequently devised the concept of using split-screens in the opening episode mainly due to the large number of telephone conversations that the script had called for. 'I am obsessed with American 70s movies,' noted Hopkins. 'They do [split screen] very well. I think now that we're living in the age of computers, where we're used to looking at lots of different [information] at the same time, people might be ready to give it another go.'

'The concept is incredibly innovative,' Kiefer Sutherland told *The Observer*. 'We're approaching this as a 24-hour movie... The continuity is non-stop.'

AWARDS Cochran and Surnow's script for this episode won an Emmy at the 2002 awards ceremony.

DID YOU KNOW? The satellite, seen in the opening episode, which relays Rovner's intel to CTU, was actually stock footage taken from the movie *Enemy of the State*.

Sarah Clarke did her audition for *24* in January 2001 and didn't subsequently hear anything until March when she was flown to Los Angeles for a second interview. She was then hired on the spot, and filming for the pilot began that afternoon. Fears of an actors' strike sped everything up, so that the costuming department didn't even have time to fit Sarah for a blouse for the pilot. 'I ended up wearing my own shirt,' she told Mike Schneider. 'I don't think anybody realised that if we used that shirt, we were going to need 12 more of them for the rest of the series!'

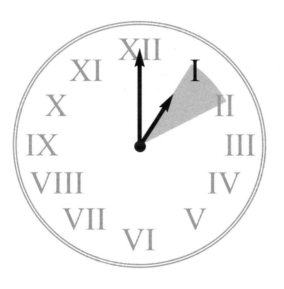

1:00 A.M. – 2:00 A.M.

12:00 1:00 2:00 3:00 4:00 5:00 6:00 7:00 8:00 9:00 10:00 11:00 12:00 1:00 2:00 3:00 4:00 5:00 6:00 7:00 8:00 9:00 10:00 11:00 12:00

2   1:00 A.M. – 2:00 A.M.

US Transmission Date: 13 November 2001
UK Transmission Date: 10 March 2002
Writers: Joel Surnow, Michael Loceff
Director: Stephen Hopkins
Cast: Carlos Bernard (Tony Almeida), Penny Johnson Jerald (Sherry Palmer), Mia Kirshner (Mandy), Michael O'Neill (Richard Walsh), Rudolf Martin (Jonathan), Richard Burgi (Alan York), Daniel Bess (Rick), Matthew Carey (Dan), Jacqui Maxwell (Janet York), Karina Arroyave (Jamey Farrell), Tanya Wright (Patty Brooks), Michael Massee (Ira Gaines), Vicellous Reon Shannon (Keith Palmer), Megalyn Echikunwoke (Nicole Palmer), Glenn Morshower (Aaron Pierce), Kim Murphy (Bridget), Scott Denny (Scott Baylor)

1:02: Mandy lands in the desert. She buries Martin's ID, attached to a homing device, before being picked up by someone in a jeep. The ID is subsequently retrieved by a motorcyclist. Teri and Alan arrive at the store to find that the girls have already gone. Kim threatens Dan and Rick with the revelation that her father is a government agent.

L.A. STORY The Palladio furniture store is said to be in Van Nuys. At the end of the episode, Jack is seen speeding along a section of the Ventura Freeway in Burbank.

VALLEY LIFE Framed by mountain ranges on both sides, the San Fernando Valley is often blanketed by an uncomfortable thick layer of smog and is, on average, approximately 20°F hotter than the Westside and beach-front communities like Santa Monica and Venice. Living in the Valley was very fashionable in the early days of Hollywood when celebrities such as Walt Disney and John Wayne had their private homes there. This trend reached its apex when many of the major movie studios based themselves around Burbank in the 1940s. What the Valley lacks in culture, it more than makes up for via a plethora of shopping malls, a phenomenon that began in Sherman Oaks in the late 1970s, with the gloriously tacky Galleria, and was ultimately immortalised by Frank and Moon Unit Zappa on the 1981 song 'Valley Girl'.

Surrounded, as it is, by four major freeways, seemingly everyone in the Valley owns a car. Because of the dominance of car-culture in the Valley, the area is said to have given birth to both the drive-in movie theatre *and* the drive-thru fast-food restaurant.

SEX AND DRUGS AND ROCK 'N' ROLL Alan finds an empty condom packet at the furniture store. This causes Teri to berate Jack when he suggests that Kim knows her limits. Dan says that Rick should have given Kim, who is becoming hysterical, a roofie - the street name for the so-called 'date rape' drug, Rohypnol.

1:09: Walsh meets Baylor, a nervous agent, who gives him a computer card that contains information concerning the plot against Palmer. An unseen assailant opens fire, killing Baylor and injuring Walsh. Walsh telephones Jack urging him to come to the Dunlop Plaza.

REFERENCES There are visual and dialogue links in Walsh's meeting with Baylor to *All the President's Men* and *JFK*. Jack alludes to the movie *Very Bad Things*. Amongst the codes that Nina pulls up is one for Four Sons Construction, a probable reference to John Ford's *Four Sons*.

THE CONSPIRACY STARTS AT CLOSING TIME Rick tries to calm Kim and alludes to an organisation ('these people') who are behind her kidnapping.

1:18: Mandy arrives at the house of a man called Gaines, who gives her a briefcase full of money and asks for Martin's ID. She says he'll get it soon. Mandy meets Jonathan who, through plastic surgery, has been transformed into a double of Martin.

LOGIC, LET ME INTRODUCE YOU TO THIS WINDOW Gaines's compound is just over 15 minutes drive from where Mandy landed in the Mojave desert. Even at its *closest* point, the Mojave is a good one hour plus drive from *any* part of Los Angeles. This would suggest that the compound is situated well out of the L.A. area. However, subsequently it's placed somewhere in the north of the Valley. The entire 'information held on the magnetic strip of a keycard' plot, although theoretically possible, stretches the bounds of credulity somewhat. Baylor says that this is the perfect way to get information in to, and out of, secure locations. That's possibly true. But it also requires some means of transferring the information onto the card whilst *inside* such a secure location in the first place.

Jack crawls across several feet of broken glass without, apparently, suffering any cuts or tears in his clothes. Is it usual federal policy for an agent to cut off the thumb of a dead terrorist to aid in identification? Tony pulls up a word-perfect transcript of Jack's telephone conversation with Nina less than 60 seconds after it has taken place. Are we, therefore, to believe that it's the job of someone within CTU to transcribe, in virtual real time, the cellphone conversations of their agents? Walsh tells Jack that Baylor assured him that Jamey could be trusted. Baylor said no such thing (to be fair, that conversation could have taken place off-screen). Of course, as we subsequently discover, she *can't* be trusted.

1:23: Jack finds Walsh who says that there were at least two shooters. A lengthy gunfight follows during which Jack and Walsh kill two of their assailants.

CLUE Tony says that he's really impressed with how convincing a liar Nina can be. By the end of the season, he won't be the only one.

1:44: The Palmer children, Keith and Nicole, arrive at their hotel. Palmer calls a meeting with one of his aides over Maureen Kingsley's allegations.

QUOTE/UNQUOTE Alan: 'It's hard to know with teenage girls whether they're angry at you, or just angry.'

SEPARATE BEDS As Teri and Alan search for their daughters, Teri mentions her temporary separation from Jack. Alan notes that his ex-wife, an Australian, left and never returned.

1:50: Secret Service agent Pierce arrives at Palmer's hotel room and admits that there is expected to be an attempt on the Senator's life sometime today. Outside, Palmer gets in his car and drives off. As Jack and Walsh make their escape, Walsh is shot again. Dying, he throws the card to Jack and tells him to have Jamey discover who is the mole within CTU.

1AM

COOL GADGETS In his car, Jack has an optical scanner which can, Jamey tells him, also transmit the information held on the keycard's magnetic strip.

1:56: Dan tells Kim that he'll hurt Janet unless Kim does as she's told. To prove his point, he breaks Janet's arm with a wheel-iron. Kim rings her mother and says that that she and Janet are at a party. Teri, furious, wants to pick up the girls herself, but Kim refuses. Teri suspects that something is wrong because Kim says 'I love you' during the conversation. Jamey gets a name from the keycard - Nina Myers.

'YOU MAY REMEMBER ME FROM...' Michael Massee's impressive CV includes appearances in *Amistad*, *Playing God*, *Lost Highway*, *Se7en*, *Murder One*, *The Crow*, *The X-Files* and *Picket Fences*. Vincellous Shannon played Archer in *Hart's War* and appeared in *The Hurricane*, *Can't Hardly Wait*, *Kangaroo Court*, *Touched by an Angel*, *Beverly Hills 90210*, *D2: The Mighty Ducks* and *Dream On*. Scott Denny was in *Urbania*, *Rudy* and *Dawson's Creek*. Megalyn Echikunwoke played Shannon in *BS**, and appeared in *Funny Valentines*. Kim Murphy was Beth in *Burning Annie*, Alex in *Campfire Tales* and Nina in *Cybill*. Glenn Morshower plays Mike Chysler in *The West Wing* and appeared in *Black Hawk Down*, *The Core*, *Godzilla*, *Air Force One*, *Under Siege* and *JAG*.

BEHIND THE CAMERA New Zealand-born cinematographer Rodney Charters previously worked on movies like *The Intern*, *M.A.N.T.I.S*, *Kiss My Act*, *Blink!*, *Conundrum*, *Car 54 Where Are You?* and *Tek War*. He also directed episodes of *Roswell* and *Hercules: The Legendary Journeys*.

NOTES 'I got hard information on the Palmer hit.' Keeping the pace going from the opening episode the second hour is, if anything, even more intense and dramatic. (This is particularly true of the lengthy and tension-soaked Dunlop Plaza scenes.) Watch these two back-to-back with a few mates, some beer and a take-away as an absolute and guaranteed cure for insomnia and boredom.

Palmer is watching footage of the aftermath of the crash of flight 221 on KRLO channel 41. The Senator was a college baseball star. The entry code for 2350 Dunlop Plaza is "91367*". Jamey has the picture of a young boy (presumably, her son) on her computer.

CAST AND CREW COMMENTS 'I feel like one of the Simpsons,' Elisha Cuthbert told the press upon learning that she would have to stick to the same wardrobe for most of the season. In a subsequent interview with *FHM* she noted that she still has the red *Boy Scouts of America* cut-off T-shirt that she wears throughout her kidnapping ordeal. 'I kept a couple for posterity but I don't think I'll ever wear them again. I've worn that thing for the last 10 months of my life.'

However media interviewers are advised not to ask Cuthbert to talk about Kiefer Sutherland. 'I hate that freaking question,' she told the *New York Post*. 'He's the coolest guy ever, but it's like, what do you mean, "What's it like to work with Kiefer Sutherland?" Why isn't it, "What's it like to work with Elisha Cuthbert?" That's what people should be asking *him*.'

SOUNDTRACK 'Did You Forget?' by Perry Farrell, 'Losing an Edge' by Rocket Science and 'Darker' by The Doves. Keith mentions that cartoon punk-band Green Day played 'The Time of Your Life' at one of Palmer's election rallies.

DID YOU KNOW? Although critics immediately fell in love with *24*, several commentators noted that viewers were seemingly concerned that if they missed one episode they would not be able to catch up. Leslie Hope told *extratv.com*: 'The fact is each episode is a self-contained unit, so you can actually jump right in at any point.' Dennis Haysbert, added that *24* itself spends ample time playing catch-up: 'There's a recap at the beginning of the show, so you really don't need to see it from day one.'

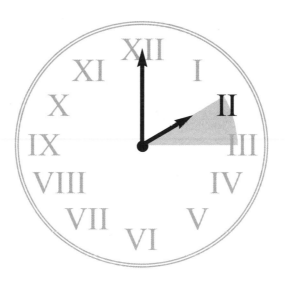

12:00 1:00 2:00 3:00 4:00 5:00 6:00 7:00 8:00 9:00 10:00 11:00 12:00 1:00 2:00 3:00 4:00 5:00 6:00 7:00 8:00 9:00 10:00 11:00 12:00

3 2:00 A.M. – 3:00 A.M.

US Transmission Date: 20 November 2001
UK Transmission Date: 17 March 2002
Writers: Joel Surnow, Michael Loceff
Director: Stephen Hopkins
Cast: Carlos Bernard (Tony Almeida), Penny Johnson Jerald (Sherry Palmer), Mia Kirshner (Mandy), Rudolf Martin (Jonathan), Richard Burgi (Alan York), Daniel Bess (Rick), Matthew Carey (Dan), Jacqui Maxwell (Janet York), Karina Arroyave (Jamey Farrell), Michael Massee (Ira Gaines), Vicellous Reon Shannon (Keith Palmer), Glenn Morshower (Aaron Pierce), Kim Murphy (Bridget), Zach Grenier (Carl Webb), Keram Malicki-Sánchez (Larry Rogow), Stephen Duvall (Rocco), Marcus Brown (Teenager #1), Joe Nieves (Teenager #2), Carmen Mormino (Businessman)

2:02: Teri calls Jack to confirm that she's heard from Kim. He is angry that Teri didn't discover their daughter's exact location.

L.A. STORY The opening shot sees Jack driving on a section of Hollywood Boulevard (a *long* way from where he was at the end of the previous episode, and only *vaguely* in the right direction toward CTU).[20] Kim and Janet escape from Dan and Rick at Van Nuys airport[21] and run into a disused warehouse. This, Kim subsequently tells her mother, is close to Platt's Auto Body dealership in North Hollywood.

THE CONSPIRACY STARTS AT CLOSING TIME Gaines is angry with Mandy for having involved her lesbian accomplice, Bridget, in the operation. Bridget has talked Mandy into demanding an extra million dollars for delivering the ID card. Gaines claims no more money is available.

2:06: Sherry reminds Pierce that this isn't the first death threat that her husband has received. Gaines calls Dan to confirm that he and Rick have captured Kim.

SEX AND DRUGS AND ROCK 'N' ROLL Dan smokes a joint but tells Rick that he doesn't intend to waste any of his stash on the agonised Janet. Ignoring Dan, Rick cooks

· ·

20 Another of L.A.'s most legendary streets, Hollywood Boulevard is usually one of the first ports of call for most first-time visitors to Los Angeles. Despite a plethora of tacky tourists stores selling junk that you'll regret buying the moment you get home, it also contains numerous genuine attractions. These include the junction of Hollywood and Vine, the location where many a budding star of the past was allegedly spotted by a big-name film director. The *Hollywood Walk of Fame* also begins at this junction. A series of metallic stars laid into the sidewalk honouring various film, TV and music celebrities, this concept was first instigated by the Hollywood Chamber of Commerce in 1960 in an effort to boost tourism. Other landmarks on Hollywood include the Capitol Records Tower building, Mann's Chinese Theatre, the rococo El Capitan Theatre, Frederick's lingerie shop, Ripley's Believe-It-Or-Not which sports a life-size Tyrannosaurus Rex emerging from the roof, and Hollywood Book City, possibly the most famous, and certainly the most labyrinthine, bookshop in the world.

21 A real location, situated on Sherman Way in North Van Nuys.

up some heroin and injects it into the traumatised girl, telling Kim that it will help to ease Janet's pain.[22]

SOCIAL COMMENT Palmer arrives at a parking lot where two black teenagers are smashing cars with baseball bats. He confronts one of the thugs, who demands $100. When Palmer won't pay, the youth tries to mug him, but Palmer fends him off easily. The other teen, recognising whom they're talking to, asks Palmer what he intends to do for them when he's President. Palmer warns that if they stay on their current path, they'll be dead before he's sworn in.

REFERENCES There are possible dialogue allusions to *The Prisoner* (this is how Dan refers to Kim on two occasions).

> **2:17:** Jack calls Nina and asks for a copy of the plane's passenger list. He also wants to talk to her in private. Jack entrusts Jamey with the information that Walsh gave him and asks her to extract as much data as possible from the keycard. Jamey confirms that the encrypted files on it definitely came from Nina's computer.

LOGIC, LET ME INTRODUCE YOU TO THIS WINDOW Aside from a couple of geographical inconsistencies (see **L.A. Story**), Data Services tell Jack that he called them about an hour ago to identify the thumb. In fact, it was only 20 minutes ago. Janet seems remarkably focused for much of the episode considering that she has a broken arm *and* that she's just been pumped full of smack. Van Nuys Airport to any part of North Hollywood: distance, approximately two miles. Yet Kim and Janet, neither of whom are wearing particularly sensible running shoes (and leaving aside Janet's broken arm and drug-addled condition for a moment), manage to maintain a 20 to 30 second advantage over Dan and Rick who are sprinting after them. These girls should be in the Olympics with a performance like that.

The memorandum on Walsh's death was posted to a CTU Internet bulletin board at 2:11AM, less than 15 minutes after Jack first told Jamey to contact Division about the deaths of two agents at Dunlop Plaza. It's almost as if someone had Walsh's epitaph already written in advance, isn't it? We'll probably never know what the job that Gaines had lined-up for Mandy in the summer was. Bet it was a good one. This episode contrives to make North Hollywood look like South Central or Compton. This author can confirm, as someone who has driven through NoHo at 2AM (indeed, it was there that I first watched this episode) that it's not, actually, *that* bad.

> **2:27:** Janet regains consciousness. When Dan and Rick venture away from the van, Kim and Janet stage an elaborate escape. After a lengthy chase, they hide in an alley where a male prostitute, Larry, covers for them, sending Dan and Rick in the wrong direction using the 'they went thataway' technique.

22 Unusually for Hollywood (and, particularly, television), the actual scene of the heroin being prepared and injected was left intact. Even more remarkably, it seems to have escaped the censor's scissors in Europe too. That's possibly because it shares none of the quasi-glamourous nature of John Travolta's trip in *Pulp Fiction*. Indeed, the scene is closer in tone and spirit to the gritty realism of the depiction of helpless addiction in *Trainspotting* (1996).

QUOTE/UNQUOTE Larry, to Janet: 'Wanna trade places with me for a while? Turn some tricks while I go snuggle with your daddy in the Hollywood foothills?'

2:39: Palmer meets Carl, an employee who, it is implied, takes care of the Senator's problems. Palmer says that Kingsley will allege that a boy called Gibson who raped Nicole some years ago, didn't commit suicide as was widely reported. Rather, he was thrown out of a window by Keith. Palmer believes that this is a lie and wants to know the identity of the source.

FASHION VICTIMS Larry suggests that Kim's designer jeans are worth $500.

2:43: Jack confronts Nina with the keycard, demanding to know who she works for. Nina says that she works for *him*. Gaines gives Mandy an extra million in exchange for the ID. They drive into the desert where Bridget recovers the ID and gives it to Gaines. Jonathan then shoots Bridget, killing her. Mandy sadly looks at her dead lover and then she and Gaines drive off, leaving the body behind.

SEX AND DRUGS AND ROCK 'N' ROLL Mandy and Bridget seem to be involved in a rather abusive S&M-style relationship (note, for example, how hard Mandy slaps Bridget and how tightly she grips Bridget's hair when they are kissing).

2:56: Jack believes that Nina is innocent and, after apologising, he asks Jamey to find out who could have hacked into Nina's account. A suspicious Tony calls Division and tells them to relieve Jack of his command.

DATING 24 On 14th January, when Nina's computer was used to access the information about Palmer, she and Jack were spending a, presumably dirty, weekend in Santa Barbara.[23] This, says Nina was 'a couple of months ago', meaning (if this isn't an approximation) that *24* is set in March, or perhaps early April.

2:57: Still frantically trying to escape from Rick and Dan, who have been held up by a fight between Larry and a drug dealer, Kim calls Teri. Kim gives her location just as Janet is hit by a car whilst crossing the road. As Janet lies motionless, Dan and Rick apprehend Kim and drag her back to the van.

'YOU MAY REMEMBER ME FROM...' Zach Grenier's CV includes *The X-Files*, *Working Girl*, *Swordfish*, *Shaft*, *Fight Club* and *Twister*. Keram Malicki-Sánchez appeared in *American History X*, *John Q* and *Buffy the Vampire Slayer*. Carmen Mormino was in *Man's Best Friend*, *One Hour Photo* and *Brimstone*. Marcus Brown appeared in *Lush*.

BEHIND THE CAMERA Cinematographer Peter Levy previously worked on *Lost in Space*, *Cutthtroat Island*, *Ricochet* and *Robbery*.

· ·

23 A beautiful affluent costal town in California approximately 80 miles north of Los Angeles. With a population of approximately 90,000 it is noted for its Spanish-style architecture, Stearns Wharf wooden pier and the relaxed shopping area, de la Guerra Plaza.

NOTES 'Are we saying Nina's a traitor?' This was the first episode of *24* that I saw and, significantly, it's an absolutely perfect jumping on-point if you've missed the first two shows. It's still early enough in the ongoing plot for easy explanations for who all of the characters are via the 'Previously on...' opening. The episode includes one of the key moments that helps to set *24* apart from the bland eye-candy that is much modern television drama: Jonathan coldly shooting Bridget in the back. Fantastic cliff-hanger too, the first of what was to become a season-long penchant for life-and-death struggles as the clock ticks ever onward.

Note that Jack has a number of tattoos which, by a curious coincidence, correspond exactly with those belonging to the actor Kiefer Sutherland. (This author particularly admires the dagger motif on his right arm. Well classy.) Jack's authorisation code to get Data Services to identify a dismembered thumbprint is 4393-CTU. Palmer's opponent in the primaries is called Hodges (probably named after one of the series' Production Assistants, Jennifer Hodges). Gaines's island bank account number is 365-266-099002-002. Jamey is reading an agency report on one Brahim Mohammed, an unemployed computer analyst living at 452 Oakwood Avenue. Walsh was with the CTU for 16 years.

CRITIQUE 'Arriving awash in overpraise and hype, *24* certainly has more work cut out for it than the average new drama. But average it's definitely not,' noted the *Washington Post*'s Tom Shales. 'Cleverly constructed and invigoratingly ambitious, *24* endeavours to tell the story of a fateful day in the life of Los Angeles and our republic in minute-by-minute detail... Jack Bauer is in for a helluva day, you may want to be there with him for every agonising twist.'

CAST AND CREW COMMENTS 'I thought we were lucking out getting him because, in the programme, he's got an edgy, strong, tough, angry side to him, but he's a likeable guy in real life,' says Stephen Hopkins about Kiefer Sutherland. 'It's great that he dares to show all of that stuff. He became disenchanted by the Hollywood thing a little bit. *24* has revived his enthusiasm.'

'This is a guy who has some extraordinary gifts in his job,' notes Sutherland, concerning Jack Bauer. 'But he's given a task that seems impossible to accomplish. He approaches this in a very unorthodox way. He has flaws, I think people identify with that.'

DID YOU KNOW? In the days following the broadcast of this episode, Fox confirmed that it had ordered an additional 11 episodes of the series, bringing it to a total of 24. The series had been an immediate hit with critics but it took a while to get anywhere near the kind of viewing figures that Fox had anticipated. The network, however, was doing everything they could to make the series a hit, including re-airing the initial episodes on Friday during the first three weeks in December, replacing the cancelled soap opera *Pasadena*. Fox's FX cable network also reran *24* episodes weekly on both Sunday and Monday.

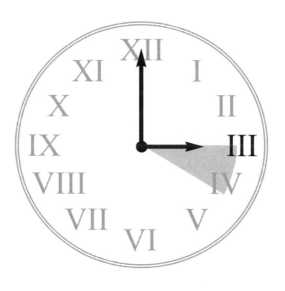

12:00 1:00 2:00 **3:00** 4:00 5:00 6:00 7:00 8:00 9:00 10:00 11:00 12:00 1:00 2:00 3:00 4:00 5:00 6:00 7:00 8:00 9:00 10:00 11:00 12:00

4 3:00 A.M. – 4:00 A.M.

3AM

US Transmission Date: 27 November 2001
UK Transmission Date: 24 March 2002
Writer: Robert Cochran
Director: Winrich Kolbe
Cast: Carlos Bernard (Tony Almeida), Penny Johnson Jerald (Sherry Palmer), Xander Berkeley (George Mason), Richard Burgi (Alan York), Daniel Bess (Rick), Matthew Carey (Dan), Jacqui Maxwell (Janet York), Karina Arroyave (Jamey Farrell), Michael Massee (Ira Gaines), Vicellous Reon Shannon (Keith Palmer), Glenn Morshower (Aaron Pierce), Zach Grenier (Carl Webb), John Hawkes (Greg Penticoff), Yolonda Ross (Jessie Hampton), James MacDonald (Officer #1), John Cothran jr (Officer #3), Wiley Pickett (Simms), Kathy Byron (Woman), Mike Siegal (Agent), Johnny Vasquez (Janitor)

3:02: Jack placates an angry Nina by telling her about Walsh's death. He says that they have to trust each other because they can't trust anyone else. Except Jamey. Tony tells Jack about a discrepancy in the passenger list on the downed airliner. Files suggest that first class was fully booked, yet the list shows one empty seat. Jamey extracts more information from the key-card: an address. Jack plans to check it himself. Before he can, a CTU 'lockdown' is initiated. Mason arrives and says that this is standard procedure following the deaths of agents. Jack attempts to leave the building. An agent tries to stop him so Jack uses force.

L.A. STORY The address that Jamey finds on the card is 18166 San Fernando Road. This runs from Glendale[24] through Silver Lake and ends behind Elysian Park near the Dodger's Stadium. Again, it is physically impossible to drive from CTU in, or very near, Santa Monica to this address in the time that it takes Jack to do so. Ditto the Fifth Street Bridge, in Downtown L.A. This is several miles the wrong side of the Hollywood Hills to be a mere 10 minutes drive from the location that Alan and Teri arrive at when searching for Janet and Kim.

3:13: Mason, discovering that Jack is on the loose, tries to coax information on his where-abouts from Nina. Pierce assures Palmer of the severity of this particular threat on his life and recommends changing the Senator's schedule. Palmer, however, is more concerned with winning the election.

QUESTION Given that it is Jamey and Nina who give Jack the address from the card, it's worth asking if this entire part of the plot could have been an elaborate trap for Jack? One in which it was hoped that he would either be killed or, at least, side-tracked for a while. Otherwise it would make little sense for either Jamey or Nina to actually give Jack the real location of a member of Gaines's team, no matter how insignificant he subsequently turns out to be.

• •

24 West of Pasadena, beyond the Verdugo Mountains, and stretching down to the northern tip of Griffith Park, Glendale is a rather nice middle-class suburb that completely gives the lie to the idea that every part of the Valley is an example of the land that taste forgot. Glendale features a particularly nice bunch of bookshops on the attractive Brand Boulevard, and the Art Deco-fronted Alex Theatre is certainly worth seeing.

3:19: Rick tells a distraught Kim that Janet is probably dead. Dan, however, realises that if Janet is still alive, she can identify them and turns the van around.

POINTS AT WHICH KIM NEEDS A SLAP Her baiting of Dan, by trying to get Rick to think and act independently, is both dramatically obvious and indescribably stupid given Dan's previous displays of violence with little or no provocation. Dan's order to Rick to put tape over Kim's mouth comes, frankly, not a moment too soon.

3:20: Teri and Alan are ordered to stop by a police officer because Alan was speeding. Whilst attempting to explain that they are searching for their missing daughters, Alan becomes angry at the delay and is placed under arrest.

CLUE It's great when viewers are able to say '*that* was the point at which I *knew* he/she was lying.' I'm sure most readers will be able to point to some specific moment from *24* at which they strongly suspected that one of the characters on the show was actually *not* who they seemed to be. For this author, it was Alan York's completely over-the-top reaction to an, admittedly officious, motorcycle cop. Getting oneself placed under arrest is, of course, a brilliant delaying tactic. 'I wonder if he's done that deliberately?' I asked myself. He had.

3:29: Jack arrives at the address. Within minutes he comes face-to-face with a gunman. A female police officer hears shooting and stumbles upon Jack, who displays his badge and asks for her assistance.

QUOTE/UNQUOTE Jack, held at gunpoint by the policewoman: 'This guy's not waiting around for me so you better shoot me or help me. But decide now.'

POINTS AT WHICH TERI NEEDS A SLAP Jack and the policewoman begin to stake out the building just as Teri picks the *single* most inopportune moment possible to call Jack. His ringing cellphone alerts the gunman to Jack's location.

LOGIC, LET ME INTRODUCE YOU TO THIS WINDOW Despite much temptation, it's not really fair to blame Teri for this. Jack, seemingly, doesn't think it necessary to switch off his cellphone whilst he's tracking a suspect at gunpoint? That's a somewhat elementary schoolboy-type error, one could suggest. Pierce mentions to Palmer that an airliner exploded outside L.A. an hour and a half ago. Actually, it was almost *two* and a half hours ago. The traffic cop's rather judgmental moral outrage at finding a man and a woman who aren't married in a speeding car seems a bit... well, old fashioned, to say the least. This is *L.A.*, not Mayberry. *Everybody* in Los Angeles has extramarital affairs. It's *the law*. 'You've committed a serious crime,' the cop subsequently tells a very pisscd-off Alan York. Not *that* serious, seemingly. Once it's established that a 911 call *was* placed earlier, as Teri had said, then Alan is released immediately.

The traffic cop gets confirmation that Teri's 911 call was received by the police approximately half an hour ago. It was, actually, over 50 minutes ago. So, *very* approximately, then? Teri, presumably, impressed upon the police the urgency of Kim and Janet's situation when she made that initial call. Yet, by the time that she and Alan arrive at the spot where Kim called from, by now almost an hour earlier, no police officers seem to have responded to it yet. Maybe they were all having a long coffee break? Jessie Hampton's ignorance concerning CTU ('what the hell is *that*?' she asks) suggests that the existence of this rather high-profile part agency isn't common knowledge amongst your average law enforcement officer. Note that, many episodes later, the narcotics cop Krugman doesn't know who or what CTU is either. A sort of *If I told you, I'd have to kill you afterwards*-type unit, presumably? Who was it that called the ambulance for Janet? There don't seem to be any working pay phones around and neither of the car drivers that we briefly see shows much interest in her condition.

3:30: Mason reminds Nina that Jack dumped her and now her reputation in the agency is simply as Jack's *bitch*. Dan pulls the van up to Janet's body, intending to shoot her. But, an ambulance arrives just at that moment and Dan is forced to speed away.

QUOTE/UNQUOTE Mason: 'True love is a beautiful thing. Why go to extremes?'

3:40: Nina warns Jamey not to be intimidated by Mason. Jack and the policewoman, Jessie Hampton, see the gunman running into the neighbouring building. Carl contacts Palmer with the source for Kingsley's story - George Ferragamo. The Senator finally tells his wife what Kingsley intends to reveal. Ferragamo was Keith's therapist and Keith has, seemingly, confessed to him that he killed Nicole's rapist. Sherry says that Ferragamo must be lying.

REFERENCES Mason's interrogation of Nina has a few, possibly unconscious, links to *Basic Instinct*. There are also visual allusions to *The X-Files* and *Go*.

3:44: Having confirmed that a 911 call was placed concerning two girls in North Hollywood, the traffic cop releases Alan. Jack tells Jessie that he needs to capture the gunman alive. Police backup arrives in the shape of a helicopter. The gunman uses the confusion to grab Jessie as a hostage. Jack rushes them and, in the ensuing melee, Jessie is shot dead. Teri and Alan see an ambulance drive past and ask a passing bag-woman what happened. They are told that a girl was hit by a car. Gaines meets Dan and Rick and asks where Janet is. Dan says that he killed Janet. Gaines tells Kim that if she co-operates, she'll be safe. Mason calls Jamey into Jack's office and suggests that she is involved in Jack and Nina's web of deceit. The interrogation is cut short, however. Jack has been found.

3:57: Jack tells one of the arresting officers that he wants to question the gunman. The gunman clearly knows who Jack is and says that Jack will never see Kim again if he doesn't let him go. Jack lunges for the gunman, is held back by the police, races to his car and drives off.

'YOU MAY REMEMBER ME FROM...' Yolonda Ross was in *The Taste of Dirt*. James MacDonald appeared in *Space Cowboys* and *Buffy the Vampire Slayer* (as Detective Stein). John Hawkes was Pete Bottoms in *From Dusk Till Dawn*, Bugsy in *The Perfect Storm*, Dave in *I Still Know What You Did Last Summer* and Phillip Padgett in *The X-Files*. He also appeared in *Blue Streak* and *Hardball*. John Cothran has been in *Star Trek: The Next*

Generation, ER, Felicity, Get Shorty, Spawn and *The Cell*. Wiley Pickett's CV includes *Mighty Joe Young, The X-Files* and *Walker, Texas Ranger*.

BEHIND THE CAMERA Winrich Kolbe has worked on *Angel, Millennium, JAG, Star Trek: Voyager, Tales of the Gold Monkey, Ice Planet, Star Trek: The Next Generation* (including the finale 'All Good Things'), *Enterprise, Dark Skies, Magnum PI, Battlestar Galactica, CHiPS, Lois & Clark: The New Adventures of Superman, T.J. Hooker, Battlestar Galactica* and *The Rockford Files*.

NOTES 'These are serious people and they want you dead today.' Yet another full-blooded episode containing the first proper indications that today will likely be a descent into hell for Jack as he is forced to withhold information from his own side. There are two standout set-pieces here; the gripping Mason/Nina interrogation and, even better, Jack's pursuit of the shadowy gunman through a dank and miserable warehouse to the roof. The gunshots are some of noisiest you'll ever have heard in a television series.

Nina has been with 'the agency' for seven years. (She doesn't specify whether this figure applies purely to CTU - see previous note about whether CTU is part of the CIA or not.) Mason tells Nina that Jack talks about his affair with her all the time. Lyle Gibson, the man who raped Nicole, was 19 when he died.

SOUNDTRACK The episode includes a fantastic percussion-heavy rhythm track.

CRITIQUE On the website *PopPolitics.com*, lecturer Douglas L Howard wrote an interesting piece on the initial impact of *24*: 'Critics agree that it is clever and innovative (which often is the kiss of death for a show); *Time* went so far as to call it "the most distinctive, addictive new TV series this season."' Yet, according to a *New York Times* article, *24* was, at one point, ranked behind both *Family Law* on CBS and *According to Jim* on ABC in the Nielsen ratings. If the network were attempting to cultivate a highbrow audience by rerunning *Masterpiece Theater* or *Upstairs, Downstairs*, Howard argued, then perhaps this disparity between critical acclaim and viewer disinterest would be more understandable. 'But, with *24*, Fox is clearly trying to appeal to popular tastes. So why has it failed to attract more of an audience?'

CAST AND CREW COMMENTS The creators of *24* were optimistic about introducing the show amid a real life atmosphere already full of suspense and surprises. 'I think just the opposite,' said Joel Surnow, when asked during a press interview if viewers would be likely to embrace such a hard-edged series in the middle of a national crisis. 'There's more of a desire on the part of the public to learn more, to process it. I think that's why we watch crime shows and shows about child molesters. It helps us understand the world we're in.'

'It's not like it's education, but it *is* emotional,' added Robert Cochran. 'You want to process these things emotionally. Storytelling is one of the ways people [do] and in which they try to come to terms with the world around them. During World War II, a lot of war movies were made.'

DID YOU KNOW? The 'events occur in real time' narration used at the beginning of the first three episodes subsequently disappeared. (Possibly the producers realised that having Jack get from anywhere to anywhere in five minutes through heavy Los Angeles traffic was stretching credulity somewhat.)

3AM

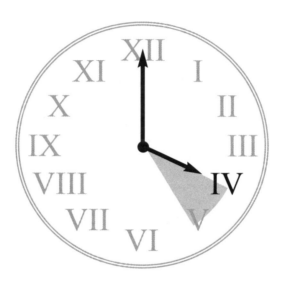

4:00 A.M. – 5:00 A.M.

12:00 1:00 2:00 3:00 4:00 5:00 6:00 7:00 8:00 9:00 10:00 11:00 12:00 1:00 2:00 3:00 4:00 5:00 6:00 7:00 8:00 9:00 10:00 11:00 12:00

5 4:00 A.M. – 5:00 A.M.

US Transmission Date: 11 December 2001
UK Transmission Date: 31 March 2002
Writer: Chip Johannessen
Director: Winrich Kolbe

Cast: Carlos Bernard (Tony Almeida), Penny Johnson Jerald (Sherry Palmer), Xander Berkeley (George Mason), Richard Burgi (Alan York), Daniel Bess (Rick), Matthew Carey (Dan), Jacqui Maxwell (Janet York), Karina Arroyave[25] (Jamey Farrell), Tanya Wright (Patty Brooks), Devika Parikh[26] (Maureen Kingsley), Michael Massee (Ira Gaines), Vicellous Reon Shannon (Keith Palmer), Megalyn Echikunwoke (Nicole Palmer), Glenn Morshower (Aaron Pierce), John Hawkes (Greg Penticoff), David Barrera (Phillips), Tony Perez (Sergeant Douglas Newmans), Sharon Madden (Receptionist), James Haley jr (Dr Kinnard), Ray Hale (Intern), Nynno Ahli (Policewoman Abbot)

4:02: At St. Mark's Hospital, Janet is prepared for surgery. Teri and Alan arrive at the hospital to inquire about the girl that was recently brought in. Teri calls Jack and reveals where she and Alan are. Jack promises to be at the hospital as soon as he can.

POINTS AT WHICH TERI NEEDS A SLAP Could Teri *be* any more rude and annoying? Bursting into a busy L.A. hospital full of people bleeding all over the floor and demanding that her case take absolute priority over everyone else. *What* a thoroughly selfish attitude. It's actually quite fun to watch when she's talking to Jack a few moments later and she loses it completely whilst telling him about all of the terrible things that have happened to her in the last few hours. The little whimper at the end is especially satisfying.

4:04: Rick dumps a gagged Kim in the back of Gaines' car. Gaines tells Rick and Dan that there has been a change of plan. They have to drive to the compound to get their money. Frightened, Rick wants to forget it, but Dan isn't about to forfeit $20,000.

LOGIC, LET ME INTRODUCE YOU TO THIS WINDOW Isn't Kim a bit conspicuous sitting on the back seat of Gaines's car with that strip of tape over her mouth? Jack says that the gun man was picked up in North Hollywood. As we've seen, the San Fernando Road address is actually in Glendale.

4:06: At Palmer Headquarters, Sherry pleads with David not to say anything to Keith or Nicole about Kingsley's allegations. Palmer disagrees, as he wants the pair to be prepared.

L.A. STORY Nicole says that even if traditionally conservative Orange County votes against Palmer, he should win the state comfortably. Palmer himself is less sure, arguing that he is only guaranteed this if he takes Ventura County by

25 Credited on-screen as appearing but, in fact, she doesn't.
26 Incorrectly credited as Davika Parikh.

a 10 percent margin.[27]

4:10: Tony suggests that Nina is mad at him for precipitating the lockdown. Nina agrees, but Tony is unapologetic, saying he believes Jack has been lying to them. Jack tells a desk sergeant that Jessie Hampton was helping him investigate a federal case. Just as the sergeant is about to open the cell for Jack to speak to the gunman, Mason arrives.

LOGIC, LET ME INTRODUCE YOU TO THIS WINDOW Mason gets from Santa Monica to Van Nuys Police Precinct in 12 minutes. Not quite as ludicrous as Janet's driving performance in the first episode, but pretty close. When Mason asks Davis for stills at 30 second intervals of the police station entrance, what he actually gets is nothing of the sort. Rather, he's provided with a series of real time moving images of Jack and Penticoff walking to Jack's car. Jack suggests that he can get from North Hollywood to Santa Monica in 10 minutes and then, from there back to St Mark's hospital in Sherman Oaks in another 10. Not without a helicopter, he can't. Oh, he's *got* a helicopter? Fair enough...

4:16: Dan says that if Rick has the hots for Kim, he should have done something. When Rick says he doesn't want Kim to get hurt, Dan is amazed at his naiveté. She has, after all, seen all of their faces. There isn't a remote chance that she will get out of the situation alive. Mason escorts Jack into a private room, refusing to let him go until he explains what he was doing at Dunlop Plaza.

QUOTE/UNQUOTE Mason: 'I was following orders. I know that's a concept you may be unfamiliar with, Jack.'

4:19: Jack says that Walsh and Baylor were killed because they obtained information about the Palmer hit. Mason tells Jack that the gunman, Penticoff, has refused to talk to anyone but him.

THE CONSPIRACY STARTS AT CLOSING TIME Jack interrogates Penticoff, but becomes aggressive, so Mason's men intervene. Penticoff yells that he wants to make a phone call. Outside, Jack receives a call on his cellphone - from Penticoff, who says that he will tell Jack where Kim is once Jack gets him out of custody. The people that Penticoff works for will call him in 20 minutes, and will know something's wrong if he doesn't answer the call.

4:29: Jack sees Officer Phillips, Jessie's partner, and persuades him to allow Jack to see Penticoff. Jack immediately attacks Penticoff again and Phillips breaks up the ensuing scuffle. Jack provokes Phillips by asking where *he* was when his partner needed him most. Phillips, enraged, wrestles Jack to the ground. Penticoff, however, has been able to steal Phillips' keycard to the cell.

• •

27 Orange County is one of America's most well-known suburbs. Not just for Anaheim, the home of Disneyland, but also as a bastion of traditional conservative values and right-wing politics. Formerly an agricultural zone, thick with citrus crops from which its name and wealth derives, it was during the mid-1950s that Orange County first became a housing area to aspire to for large chunks of LA.'s white middle-classes. The, not altogether inaccurate, stereotype of a *Leave it to Beaver*-style suburban wasteland of beautiful houses with massive lawns, and of Reagan and Nixon-loving, two cars in every drive and two shotguns in every cupboard families is, slowly, changing. Nevertheless, it is surely no coincidence that Orange County's airport is named after that noble symbol of right-wing Americana, John Wayne.

4:32: Maureen Kingsley meets Palmer and tells him that she wishes she hadn't received the information. She tells Palmer about hospital records she discovered relating to a teenage boy named Edward Johnson who was admitted shortly after Gibson's death with injuries consistent with a violent struggle. Kingsley has had Johnson's signature analysed and suggests that it is Keith's handwriting. Palmer tells Kingsley to do what she has to, but to be prepared to accept the consequences.

COOL GADGETS CTU has access to high quality infrared satellite images which can be zoomed-in so close that they identify Jack and Penticoff's location. Nosy neighbours everywhere will want one of *those* for Christmas.

4AM

4:40: Palmer wakes Keith up and asks him about the night that Gibson raped Nicole. Keith refuses to answer his father's questions. As Mason apologises to the desk sergeant for Jack's actions Phillips offers to start processing Penticoff. The desk sergeant asks what Phillips is doing there? His computer shows that Phillips left seven minutes ago.

FLUNKING MATH Teri tells Alan that she feels guilty over the things she said to Kim recently. She received a letter from Kim's school yesterday, saying that Kim was failing algebra. This was, she notes, the second such correspondence, Kim having intercepted an earlier one. Alan comforts Teri by promising to stay together until Kim is found. As we subsequently discover, adding up isn't all Kim is useless at.

4:47: Jack and Penticoff wait by a pay phone. Penticoff continues to claim that he doesn't know the name of the person he works for. The phone rings, but Nina is unable to trace it. Penticoff speaks to Gaines who tells him to collect a set of keys for a car which is parked nearby.

QUOTE/UNQUOTE Gaines, casually: 'There's a body in the trunk. Get rid of it.'

4:53: Jack and Penticoff locate the car. Mason arrives, and Jack allows him to take Penticoff back to jail. He shows Mason the body in the trunk, reveals everything that Walsh told him and apologises for having misjudged Mason. Jack prepares to take the body back to CTU for identification. Janet is in surgery as Jack calls Teri to say he'll be there in 20 minutes.

Gaines asks what really happened to Janet. Dan reiterates the lie he told earlier. But Gaines knows, from a source, that someone fitting Janet's description has turned up in hospital. Dan suggests that maybe Janet wasn't quite dead.

QUOTE/UNQUOTE Gaines: 'You're either dead or you're not dead. There's no such thing as sorta-dead. Here, let me show you...'

4:59: To emphasise his point, Gaines shoots Dan, killing him. Gaines then congratulates Rick on his promotion. At the hospital, Janet flatlines as Teri and Alan look on helplessly.

'YOU MAY REMEMBER ME FROM...' Tony Perez played Mike in *Hill Street Blues*, appeared in *MacGyver*, *Alien Nation*, *Blow* and *Gang Related* and was an assistant director on *Terminator 2: Judgment Day*. David Barrera was Victor Carreras in *NYPD Blue* and appeared in *Millennium, Space: Above and Beyond* and *Infinity*. Sharon Madden was in *Code Blue, Charmed, Jagged Edge and Two Moon Junction*. Ray Hale played Todd in *Flush*. James Haley appeared in *Ruby, Will & Grace* and *JAG*. Nynno Ahli was Gregory Charmain in *Days of Our Lives*.

BEHIND THE CAMERA Chip Johannessen previously wrote episodes of *Beverley Hills 90210, The X-Files, Millennium* and *Dark Angel*.

NOTES 'Forget Kimberly, man. She's history.' For the first time, chunks of this episode see the ongoing story-arc somewhat running on the spot. Teri becomes irredeemably annoying throughout. (Notably during the first scene in the hospital. A quick show of hands for everyone who would have just loved to see that harassed desk clerk give Teri a good chinning? See **Points at Which Teri Needs a Slap**.) The sudden change in character motivation in George Mason - which occurs within the space of about three lines of dialogue - is, likewise, far too throwaway. They could have got a whole episode out of that subplot, particularly as Xander Berkeley is always so watchable. And, little actually happens to any of the principals. Despite one truly great moment (the discovery of the mutilated corpse) this is one hour of Jack Bauer's life that's actually worth forgetting.

Something happened in Phoenix last month leaving Rick deeply in Dan's debt. Given subsequent information about the pair's activities, it was probably some sort of botched drug deal. Nicole Palmer went to high school with twins called Suzy and Rachel Brenner. CTU's liaison officer to the LAPD is called Ryan Sealey. The unit's top forensics man is Perry Tanaka. The night that Nicole was raped, Palmer was making a speech in Chicago or, possibly, accepting an award in New York. Keith can't remember which.

SOUNDTRACK 'New Noise' by Refused, plays as Dan and Rick discuss what Gaines is likely to do with Kimberly.

CRITIQUE 'An avant-garde experimental drama, representing events as filtered through the sleep-deprived mind of Jack Bauer,' wrote Charlie Brooker in *the Guardian*. 'It's random and disjointed, like a dream. There are even recurring events - such as Palmer's noble chinwags with his son Keith, a scene that replays itself every 25 minutes like something out of *Groundhog Day*.'

CAST AND CREW COMMENTS 'What defines the show is its style,' noted Leslie Hope. 'The split screens and the ticking clock were largely determined by Stephen Hopkins. It wasn't until we got on set where we started to see how Stephen was working. When we saw the pilot for the first time, that shit kicked ass.' In the same interview, Leslie added that she had particular admiration for the work done by the series' continuity department. 'Usually, as an actor they say "No, the coffee cup was in your right hand, not your left." So [their] job was not just that, it was also "Three minutes ago, that thing we shot a week ago, the gun was in the back of your head and you just turned like this."'

DID YOU KNOW? Joel Surnow, the man responsible for the format of *24*, was still insisting, when he spoke to the press around this time, that he had no idea how the series was going to end. 'It's impossible to come up with a 24-episode arc,' he noted. 'You can do about six or eight at a time. We have a rough idea of where we're going, but because it's so many episodes, you have to divert. That's a separate kind of storytelling and a separate discipline.'

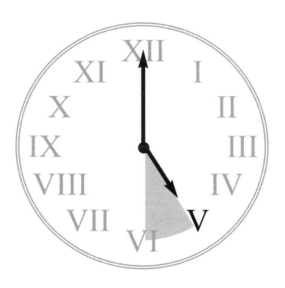

5:00 A.M. – 6:00 A.M.

12:00 1:00 2:00 3:00 4:00 **5:00** 6:00 7:00 8:00 9:00 10:00 11:00 12:00 1:00 2:00 3:00 4:00 5:00 6:00 7:00 8:00 9:00 10:00 11:00 12:00

6 5:00 A.M. – 6:00 A.M.

US Transmission Date: 18 December 2001
UK Transmission Date: 7 April 2002
Writer: Howard Gordon
Director: Brian Spicer
Cast: Carlos Bernard (Tony Almeida), Penny Johnson Jerald (Sherry Palmer), Richard Burgi (Alan York), Daniel Bess (Rick), Matthew Carey (Dan), Jacqui Maxwell (Janet York), Karina Arroyave (Jamey Farrell), Michael Massee (Ira Gaines), Zach Grenier (Carl Webb), Eric Balfour (Milo Pressman), Jude Ciccolella (Mike Novick), Suzan Brittan (Anchorwoman), Todd Jeffries (Claude Davenport), Norma Maldonado (Nurse), Kim Miyori (Dr Collier), Chuck Walczak (Ben), Ariel Felix (Anaesthesiologist), Linda Klein (Surgical Nurse)

5:02: Jack calls Teri and warns her not to let anyone suspicious see Janet as she may be in danger. Jack then arrives at CTU and asks Nina to identify the body in Penticoff's car.

EMERGENCY OVER Janet was flatlining at the end of the previous episode but her condition is stabilised remarkably quickly by the prompt actions of the crash team.

CAN HE DO THAT? Jack takes a CTU helicopter to St. Mark's in a clear example of the unauthorised use of a company vehicle.

QUOTE/UNQUOTE Gaines: 'Bury your friend.' Rick: 'Where?' Gaines: 'In the ground.'

5:05: Kim tells Rick that he will end up like his friend if they don't work together to escape. Palmer discovers that Carl covered-up Keith's crime. Carl admits that Keith came to him confessing to killing Gibson, but claimed that it was in self-defence. Palmer asks why didn't they go to the police. Carl believes if they had it would have ruined Palmer's career, reminding him that Gibson was white.

QUOTE/UNQUOTE Carl, to Palmer: 'Before you're finished crucifying me, save some nails for your wife.'

5:16: Jack arrives at the hospital and is reunited with Teri. Alan introduces himself and Teri is angry when Jack treats Alan like a suspect.

REFERENCES Carl watches a CNN newscast. There are dialogue allusions to *Aliens* ('look into my eye'), *1984* and *Sliver* ('I'm watching you'). Visual references include the video for Oasis's 'Live Forever' (the burial of Dan).

5:19: Sherry admits to Palmer that she, Keith and Nicole all hid the truth from him because they were protecting his career. Palmer thinks that, on the contrary, she was protecting herself.

Sherry asks if Palmer really wants to see Keith in jail.

SEX AND DRUGS AND ROCK 'N' ROLL The man that Jack stops from entering the hospital with a briefcase is called Ben. His brother, Virgil, is in detox and Ben is attempting to smuggle some pills in for him.

5:27: Kim and Rick remember how both Dan and Janet acted like they were invincible.

POINTS AT WHICH TERI NEEDS A SLAP When Jack tells her that Kim may have been kidnapped, she squeals in a very high-pitched voice: '*What do they want from you?*' *Top* bit of overacting there, love. Also, her subsequent, and very whiny, '[Jack] promised he wouldn't leave,' to Alan.

5:37: Nina takes Jamey off the keycard assignment and gives it to another operative, Milo. She reassigns Jamey to forensics on the dead man. Alan has good news for Jack and Teri, Janet is out of surgery. Nina calls Jack to say that they have found a surgical pin in the body's ankle which is one-of-a-kind and should make identification easy.

QUESTION Do Nina and Jamey know that they're both working for the away team? The implication of this scene is no. Of course, as we subsequently find out, Nina is working with (although not, specifically, *for*) the Drazen family. Jamey, on the other hand, is employed directly by another of the Drazens' hired-hands, Ira Gaines. This appears to put her several steps further down the conspiracy ladder than Nina.

5:39: Palmer's chief-of-staff, Mike Novick, agrees that as soon as Kingsley breaks the story, Palmer is guaranteed to lose the election. But Mike doesn't think that Palmer should drop out, saying that Palmer has responsibilities as the first African-American presidential candidate. Mike tries to reassure Palmer that he, himself, wasn't a part of the cover-up and tells the Senator that if he really wants the job of President, he needs to pre-empt Kingsley.

REAL WORLD JUNCTION Mike's assertion that voters are more forgiving than they're given credit for, depending on how an issue is 'sold' to them, is a probable allusion to Bill Clinton's reputation following the Monica Lewinsky scandal. Many political commentators feel that, although Clinton endured much sniggering over the more lurid aspects of the affair he was, ultimately, seen as the victim of an attempted right-wing conspiracy rather than as a philandering liar who thoroughly deserved his impeachment. His landslide victory over Bob Dole in the 1996 Presidential Election suggests that the American public, generally, agreed.

LOGIC, LET ME INTRODUCE YOU TO THIS WINDOW When Janet is flatlining there's a brief shot of a medical monitor which shows a strong heartbeat. Jack tells Teri that he's still on the West Side (presumably heading towards Santa Monica which is part of West L.A.). Yet he was deep in the Valley just five minutes previously. In the previous episode Gaines told Penticoff that the car containing the body that he wanted disposed of had the Nevada licence-plate 782 NOF. When Jack arrives at CTU driving it, we can see a Nevada plate reading 528 MDF.

What job, exactly, does Carl do for Palmer? Dialogue in previous episodes had suggested that Carl takes care of the more messy problems that your average politician wouldn't wish to dirty his hands on. A political fixer, basically. This episode confirms that, whatever it is, Carl has been doing it for *at least* seven years. Yet from this point onwards, Palmer suddenly acts like a man who has never needed such an employee as he is (politically) whiter-than-white. Indeed, one has to wonder how such an idealistic individual as Palmer has lasted more than five minutes in professional politics without someone with better spin-doctors walking all over him. Similarly, there has been not a single suggestion in the previous five episodes that David and Sherry don't have an absolutely perfect marriage (see, for instance, the very loving scenes between the two early in the first episode). Yet, suddenly, within the space of two lines of dialogue (Sherry telling David that she married him because he was as ambitious as she, David retorting that *he* married *her* because he loved her), this image is completely shattered. Given Nicole's and Keith's ages (early twenties, at least), and the subsequent revelation that David and Sherry have been married for 25 years, it's odd that it's taken this long for them to discover that they're mutually incompatible. Also, why is Palmer so angry *specifically* with Sherry for keeping secrets from him when both Nicole and Keith were, seemingly willing, partners in deception?

Dan's corpse changes position at least twice as Rick and Kim dig his grave. Later, the dead Dan moves his arm slightly when Rick is dragging him into the freshly dug hole. When Jack is in the elevator and Gaines gives him directions to the car through Jack's cellphone, there is one shot of Gaines drinking from the blue mug. Clearly, he's not wearing his communication earpiece and microphone. How did Gaines manage to gain access to the hospital's security system? Does he have a mole there, as with CTU? But why would he? He had no way of knowing that Janet would escape from Dan and Rick and then be hit by a car and taken to that particular hospital. Indeed, Gaines's entire plan, as we subsequently find out, revolves around Jack being used to aid in the assassination attempt. For this to work it is, seemingly, essential that Jack will be at this particular hospital at some point. That is, after all, where the car that Jack will drive is parked, filled with Gaines's surveillance equipment so that Jack's movements can be monitored. But, again, how did Gaines know that there would be any need for Jack to be at the hospital? Finally, how long has Gaines had Jack's cellphone number anyway?

5:42: Dr Collier tells Alan that she is optimistic Janet will pull through. Jack gets a call from Gaines, who tells him that Jack won't see Kim again unless he does exactly as he's told. Alan is left alone with Janet who, in a daze, says 'hi' to her father... Then her vision clears and she doesn't know who the man standing over her bed is. Alan interrupts the oxygen flow to Janet and smothers her.

5:51: Gaines orders Jack into a car and directs him to a transmitter which Jack is told to put in his ear. Alan says that Janet told him some boys got rough with Janet and Kim. He has an address in Bel Air.[28] Teri starts to panic again when she realises that Jack has disappeared.

28 One of the most fashionable and stylish areas of L.A. situated in a gap in the Santa Monica Mountains - the Sepulveda Pass - between the University of California campus and the Stone Canyon reservoir. Bel Air is an insular little community that defines its elite subdivision from the rest of the world, with imposing black

Alan offers to drive Teri to the address. An identification of the corpse has been made. Unable to contact Jack, Nina calls Teri and asks her to pass along the victim's name to Jack. It's Alan York.

QUESTION Why does Nina do this? Is this a part of the operation that she, herself, had no knowledge of? Would she know the details of every one of the, presumably dozens, of freelance contractors that Gaines has brought in to handle his end of the conspiracy? Having said that, she presumably knows that Jack is, by now, operating under Gaines's control. So she may consider that it's safe to tell Teri pretty much anything. But there still doesn't seem any reason, other than the purely sadistic, to let Teri know that she's sitting in a car with an impostor, who is possibly a murderer.

L.A. STORY The road on which Teri and Alan are travelling when Nina calls is one of the most famous in the world, Mulholland Drive, named after pioneering hydrologist William Mulholland.[29] From its starting point near the 101 Freeway to its terminus at L.A. County's Pacific boundary, the road twists for 21 miles through winding mountain passes and steep canyons and offers some quite extraordinary views of Los Angeles to the south and the Valley to the north. The stretch between the 101 and the 405 Freeway is particularly impressive, especially at night.[30] The road goes right through the Hollywood Hills and is famous for the numerous high-ranking celebrities who have had homes on or near it. (These include Elvis Presley who, in August 1965, had his only meeting with the Beatles there.) Mulholland has also been immortalised in songs (notably R.E.M's 'Electrolyte') and in movies (David Lynch's *Mulholland Drive*, for instance).

'YOU MAY REMEMBER ME FROM...' Eric Balfour played Jesse in *Buffy the Vampire Slayer* and was in *What Women Want, Six Feet Under, Can't Hardly Wait, The West Wing* and *Shattered Image*. Jude Ciccolella appeared in *The Shawshank Redemption, Insignificance* and *Law & Order*. Todd Jeffries was in *The Deep End of the Ocean, The Fabulous Baker Boys, Murder One, Dark Skies* and *L.A. Law*. Norma Maldonado appeared in *Erin Brokovich, Time of Fear* and *Mad About You*. Kim Miyori played Yoko Ono in *John and Yoko: A Love Story*, and was in *Body Shot, St Elsewhere, Babylon 5* and *Magnum P.I.* Chuck Walczak appeared in *Just Shoot Me*. Linda Klein acted in *Boston Public* and *Very Bad Things*, was an Associate Producer on *Chicago Hope* and Medical Technical Advisor on *Vanilla Sky, Nixon* and *Point of No Return*.

BEHIND THE CAMERA Bryan Spicer's impressive CV includes *Veritas, Wolf Lake, The Others, Night Visions, The Lone Gunmen, Strange Frequency, Harsh Realm, Third Watch, Mighty Morphin' Power Rangers: The Movie, SeaQuest DSV,*

gates fronting Sunset Boulevard and discouraging visitors. *Beware*, they seem to say, *rich people live here. Leave now unless you are loaded.*

29 William Mulholland (1855-1935). Civil engineer; born in Belfast. He came to the US around 1872 and settled in California. Between 1886 and 1928 he designed and built the water system that supplies Los Angeles, including the 500-mile long aqueduct from the Sierra Nevada and a series of 27 earth dams for storage.

30 With its striking panoramas of the illuminated city-grid below, Mulholland easily justifies film director Roman Polanski's famous comment that L.A. is one of the most beautiful cities in the world: 'Provided it's seen at night and from a distance!'

The X-Files, The Adventures of Brisco County Jr., Salute Your Shorts and the seminal *Parker Lewis Can't Lose*.

NOTES 'This is all happening because of me. I've tried to keep a wall between my work and my family.' A definite case of gears moving into place as the first of the series' great shocking, jaw-dropping revelations occurs. (That Alan York isn't, actually, Alan York.) Howard Gordon is one of this author's favourite writers, easily able to sample his gift for characterisation and his keen ear for clever and naturalistic dialogue into virtually every series he works on. This is a fine example.

The car that Gaines has prepared for Jack is a silver Taurus licence-plate 4IMV 486. The Lyle Gibson incident happened seven years ago. Rick didn't get on with his mom ('not all women are meant to be mothers'). Jack and Teri have often planned to take a holiday, with Kim, up the Pacific Coast Highway, through Oregon and Washington State and into Canada.

CRITIQUE 'I first met Sarah Clarke in seventh grade when she was a ponytailed student in St Louis with an infectious laugh,' wrote Mike Schneider. 'We went to junior high and high school together. On *24*, one of the most-hyped new shows of the season, she plays Nina, the sexy, computer-adept colleague of CIA counter-terrorism agent played by Kiefer Sutherland.' Schneider's piece also quoted Sarah as saying: 'I've had a dream situation. To come out here with a great show and a great role in it.'

DID YOU KNOW? Kiefer Sutherland appeared on *The Tonight Show* on 12 November 2001 and, during his interview with Jay Leno, unintentionally gave away the surprise ending to this episode.

5AM

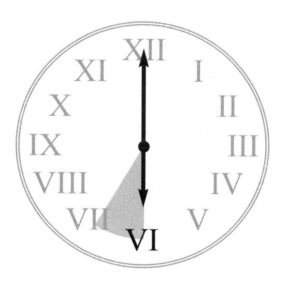

6:00 A.M. – 7:00 A.M.

12:00 1:00 2:00 3:00 4:00 5:00 **6:00** 7:00 8:00 9:00 10:00 11:00 12:00 1:00 2:00 3:00 4:00 5:00 6:00 7:00 8:00 9:00 10:00 11:00 12:00

7 6:00 A.M. – 7:00 A.M.

First US Transmission Date: 28 December 2001[31]
US Network Transmission Date: 8 January 2002
UK Transmission Date: 14 April 2002
Writer: Andrea Newman
Director: Brian Spicer
Cast: Carlos Bernard (Tony Almeida), Penny Johnson Jerald (Sherry Palmer), Rudolf Martin (Jonathan), Richard Burgi (Kevin Carroll), Daniel Bess (Rick), Karina Arroyave (Jamey Farrell), Michael Massee (Ira Gaines), Vicellous Reon Shannon (Keith Palmer), Megalyn Echikunwoke (Nicole Palmer), Glenn Morshower (Aaron Pierce), Eric Balfour (Milo Pressman), Suzan Brittan (Anchorwoman), Silas Weir Mitchell (Eli), Jesse Corti (Charles McLemore), Steve O'Connor (Phil)

6AM

6:02: Jonathan, the Martin Belkin lookalike, is due to meet Palmer in an hour. Gaines orders Jack to retrieve the keycard from CTU and replace it with a duplicate. Nina asks Milo if he has got any information from the card yet. Milo says that he has found a scrambled medical file.

REFERENCES There are visual links to *The Man Who Fell To Earth*, *The Terminator* (Jonathan putting in his contact lenses) and *Goodfellas* (see **The Bit That's...**). CNN and Sister Sledge's disco classic 'We Are Family' are mentioned.

6:05: Keith is jogging with his bodyguards as dawn breaks. Palmer arrives and explains that if *he* doesn't release the story, Maureen will. Keith angrily suggests that his father always puts his career before his family. Kim, again, tries to persuade Rick to escape with her, but Rick believes that Gaines will let him go now that he's buried Dan.

L.A. STORY Amongst the locations briefly glimpsed when Jack is driving around the Valley are Sepulveda Boulevard and Van Nuys Boulevard, both in Van Nuys, and Magnolia Boulevard in Sherman Oaks, the home of Allen's Wholesale Flower Market. Teri tells Jamey that she is on Mulholland, a mile east of Coldwater Canyon Drive. That places the location close to the gorgeous Laurel Canyon Park area. The lengthy Jefferson Boulevard is also mentioned. This runs right across Los Angeles, from Marina Del Rey in the west, through Culver City and ends at the University of Southern California just south of Downtown. Quite what Jack and Nina would be doing on Jefferson at this stage of proceedings is anyone's guess as it is not revealed exactly where the mining site is located. In the next episode, however, Nina tells Tony that she is 'just east of Downtown,' which does make vague geographical sense of Nina and Jack having been travelling on Jefferson.

---

31 This episode was previewed at 3:00 A.M. on 28 December 2001 on KTTV in Los Angeles and at 3:00 A.M. on 30 December 2001 on WNYW in New York. The reason for these broadcasts was to fulfil a Golden Globes requirement which states that, in order to be eligible for nomination, a series has to have aired at least seven original episodes in the previous calendar year. It was good enough for the Hollywood Press Association, who agreed to let *24*'s two nominations stand, but angered other commentators who felt that Fox were bending the rules. At the end of the day, of course, it proved to be worthwhile for Kiefer Sutherland who won the award for Best Performance by an Actor in Television Drama Series.

Further information is revealed regarding the location of Gaines's compound: it is said to be about a mile from Highway 14. That road ends when it meets Interstate Highway 5 (also known as the Golden State Freeway) south of the small town of Santa Clarita in the extreme north of the Valley. This does, indeed, tie in with some information revealed subsequently, but it makes a complete nonsense of Teri being delivered to the compound less than 10 minutes after she was picked up by the fake CTU agents over 15 miles away on Mulholland Drive. And, also, of Mandy's landing site in the Mojave being just 15 minutes drive away in episode two.

IDENTITY CRISIS Jack arrives at CTU and casually tells Nina that Kim was at a party. Discovering that the murder victim was Alan York, Jack angrily asks Gaines who is with Teri. Gaines fires a gun and says that this is the last sound Teri and Kim will hear unless Jack calms himself. Gaines calls the Alan York impersonator, Kevin, to say that Teri knows he's not York. His cellphone is out of range, so Gaines leaves a message. Teri tells Kevin that she's feeling sick and begs him to stop the car. When he does, she runs into some bushes. When Kevin follows, Teri hits him on the head with a rock.

QUOTE/UNQUOTE Jack: 'If Alan York is dead, who's the man with my wife?' Gaines: 'He's not an accountant from the Valley, that's for sure.'

6:17: Teri ties Kevin to a tree. She tries to call for help, but her phone is dead. Rick tells Gaines that Dan has been buried and requests his money. Gaines doesn't want to pay him now and won't allow Rick to leave as he has more jobs for him. Jack attempts to write a note for his co-workers, but Gaines sees it and makes Jack shred the evidence. The CTU security cameras have, apparently, been compromised. Nina tells Jack that Milo is close to finding a name on the keycard.

6:21: Jack goes to see Milo, causes a distraction, and switches the cards. Milo immediately realises that something is wrong. Kevin regains consciousness and warns Teri not to flag down a passing car, as Kim will be killed if he doesn't deliver Teri in half an hour.

6:31: Gaines has Jack get himself clearance to attend Palmer's breakfast. Rick tells Kim that she was right - Gaines isn't letting him go. Rick shows Kim an escape route, but one of Gaines's thugs interrupts. Rick makes it appear as though he is raping Kim. Milo tells Nina that he believes the keycard has been switched. When Nina confronts Jack with this, he says that Division have received information that they didn't trust Milo with. Then, Jack draws his gun and takes Nina hostage. He apologises, puts a jacket on her and escorts her to the exit. Tony asks where they're going. Jack says that Division[32] have called them to a meeting.

LOGIC, LET ME INTRODUCE YOU TO THIS WINDOW The keycard appears to contain a very odd assortment of information - an address where a minor member of the conspiracy is situated along with details of the plastic surgery performed on Jonathan to turn him into

---

32 There appear to be two local levels of command within CTU. These are Division, whom Jack answers to (Mason and, later, Alberta Green are based at Division) and, the more powerful, District (the representative of whom is Ryan Chappelle).

Martin's duplicate. Where did the camera footage of Nina's body at the base of the embankment come from for Gaines to view it? It seems to be a jerky, hand-held camera that sweeps from Jack down to Nina and then back up. But neither of the two men in the car following Jack are seen to be carrying a camera.

Why does Nina tell Jack that the body was Alan York? The only explanation here is that she really *is* unaware of this element of Gaines's activities and Nina is hoping that the information, even if it means something to Jack, will not be of any direct use to him. Where did the jump-leads that Teri uses to (rather ineffectually) attempt to tie Kevin to a tree come from? Remember that Kevin had thrown away the car keys so, presumably, Teri would have been unable to get into the trunk where they would most likely be kept. Does Gaines know who Nina really is? Seemingly not, otherwise why would he instruct Jack to kill her? The bullet holes on Nina's jacket don't correspond with where Jack actually shot her. Isn't Teri being dragged through the compound shouting 'Where is my daughter?' laughably ludicrous? One would have thought she'd be more likely to ask 'Can somebody please take this bag off my head, I must look ridiculous?' before worrying about Kim.

6:42: Teri finally gets her cellphone to work. She calls Jack, but Gaines made him leave his phone in the hospital garage, and it's answered by a startled doctor. Next, Teri calls CTU and speaks to Jamey. Teri explains her situation, Jamey gets her location and says that she will send someone immediately.

SEX AND DRUGS AND ROCK 'N' ROLL Rick brags to Gaines's thug, Eli, about how good a lay Kim was. Eli wants to go back and confirm this for himself. But Rick reminds him that they need to load a truck for Gaines. Unbelievably, this ruse works.

THE CONSPIRACY STARTS AT CLOSING TIME Two men arrive at Teri's location. One introduces himself as Agent McLemore as the other unties Kevin. Too late, Teri realises that she's a hostage once again.

6:50: Jamey, clearly a double agent, is asked by Tony if she has confirmation about the supposed meeting that Jack and Nina were attending. Jamey doesn't, but she says that the computer has been glitchy since the lockdown. Tony remains suspicious and asks Jamey to find the security footage from Jack's office. Reluctantly, she complies.

THE BIT THAT'S AN OVERT HOMAGE TO *GOODFELLAS* Nina is so angry with herself for trusting Jack that she almost rear-ends another vehicle. An almost shot-for-shot tribute to a famous sequence in the Scorsese classic.

6:54: Jack and Nina arrive at a deserted mining site. Jack asks Gaines what he wants done with Nina. Gaines tells Jack to shoot her. Jack orders Nina out of the car, apologising that he has no choice, *they* have Kim. Nina suggests that whoever they are will kill Kim anyway. Jack asks Nina to forgive him and tries to turn her around so that he can shoot her in the back. Nina demands that he face her when he kills her. Gaines shouts 'Shoot her!' Jack shoots and Nina falls down a steep embankment.

6:57: Kim and Rick dig their way under a perimeter fence but, just as they are about to escape, Kim hears screaming and sees her mother being bundled into the compound. Kim tells Rick to go without her, but he won't. Tony views security footage and sees Jack pull a gun on Nina. What he doesn't understand is why Jack also put a bullet-proof flak jacket on her. At the site of her *death*, a rather bewildered-looking Nina gets up and wanders away.

'YOU MAY REMEMBER ME FROM...' Silas Weir Mitchell appeared in *Rat Race*, *Private Parts*, *ER*, *Nash Bridges* and *The Practice*. Jesse Corti's movies include *Last Mistake*, *Gone in Sixty Seconds* and *High Stakes*. He was also in *The West Wing* and was the voice of LeFou in Disney's *Beauty and the Beast*. Steve O'Connor appeared in *The Sky's on Fire*, *Frasier* and *Sliders*.

NOTES 'You implicate yourself, you cease to be useful. And so does your family.' Well, *that* was completely unexpected. Jamey, the one person whom *everybody* had been assured that they could trust with their lives ... is, actually, the mole within CTU. That, actually, makes remarkably little sense given what's gone before. Never mind, this is still one of the best individual episodes of *24*. A frantic runaround through some of the more scenic locations on the show and with loads of visual treats. Gaines is at his most dryly sarcastic during his cat and mouse game with Jack. And the double cliff-hanger and revelation that the heroic Nina isn't dead, are amongst the series' finest moments.

Jack's clearance code for attending high security events is Q22Q17. Palmer's opponent, Hodges (see episode 3), is a governor. Teri uses an Ericsson cellphone. Kevin's is a Nokia.

SOUNDTRACK A turbo-charged 40-second trailer used by the BBC to advertise this episode, and the next, made fabulous use of Bernard Sumner's collaboration with The Chemical Brothers, the techno rave classic 'Out of Control'.

CRITIQUE 'Sitting through an entire episode of the unnervingly suspenseful *24* is a gleeful exercise in masochism, both thrilling and torturous,' noted *salon.com*'s Ian Rothkerch. 'With double-dealing moles, shady government bureaucrats, fancy techno gadgets and ice-cold assassins, *24* plays every element of the spook genre. Where the show distinguishes itself, however, is in its audacious episodic structure. What could have easily degenerated into a tiresome gimmick has actually turned out to be a taut, deftly rendered storytelling device.'

CAST AND CREW COMMENTS The drama of *24* is, according to Robert Cochran, not about the show touching too closely on any real life issues. Such concerns had, reportedly, prompted the producers of the hit series *Alias* to drop storylines focusing on Osama bin Laden-like characters, and an anthrax-type alert. 'Our show was never planned to be a terrorist-of-the-week show,' said Cochran. 'Everything takes place on one day revolving around the assassination attempt. We're following the exploits of our heroes and how they cope with this day.'

DID YOU KNOW? 'I came up with an idea of doing a show in real time and I pitched it to Bob [Cochran],' Joel Surnow noted. 'He thought it was a good idea, but impossible to do. And I agreed with him. But we decided it had such a great hook that we started to think of what kind of story you could tell that would keep people up for 24 hours, not sleeping or eating. It's got to be a very compelling story. We thought a presidential candidate's about to be assassinated. Then we had to do something that [made it] a more personal story. Bob and I both have teenage daughters, so we thought, "What if our daughter disappeared?"' So, how long did it take for Surnow and Cochran to come up with the series premise? 'Four hours and 17 minutes,' he continued. 'We knew it was a complicated concept. Fox liked the pilot that we wrote. Everyone at the studio, all the way up to Rupert Murdoch and Peter Chernin. Then there were meetings about how to mitigate the risk. We don't want to rely on everyone having to watch every episode, so could we come up with close-ended stories to make it palatable? I think, to their credit, Fox knew it was a risk, but they decided to go for it. One thing we learned from *Twin Peaks* is you can't string an audience along so much that they get frustrated with it.'

7:00 A.M. – 8:00 A.M.

12:00 1:00 2:00 3:00 4:00 5:00 6:00 **7:00** 8:00 9:00 10:00 11:00 12:00 1:00 2:00 3:00 4:00 5:00 6:00 7:00 8:00 9:00 10:00 11:00 12:00

8 7:00 A.M. – 8:00 A.M.

US Transmission Date: 15 January 2002
UK Transmission Date: 21 April 2002
Writers: Joel Surnow, Michael Loceff
Director: Stephen Hopkins
Cast: Carlos Bernard (Tony Almeida), Penny Johnson Jerald (Sherry Palmer), Rudolf Martin (Jonathan), Daniel Bess (Rick), Karina Arroyave (Jamey Farrell), Michael Massee (Ira Gaines), Vicellous Reon Shannon (Keith Palmer), Glenn Morshower (Aaron Pierce), Eric Balfour (Milo Pressman), Silas Weir Mitchell (Eli), Jesse D Goins (Alan Hayes), Jackie Debatin (Jessica Abrams), Rick Garcia (Fox Anchor), Mark Clayman (Man At Bus Stop), Ron Roggé (Jared), Al Leong (Neill)[33]

7:02: As Nina limps painfully back towards civilisation, the California primary election opens. Keith and his father have another argument, Keith saying that he expects he'll soon be going to prison for killing a white dude. Jonathan reaches a security checkpoint and Palmer's press assistant, Jessica Abrams, introduces herself, saying that she's a big fan of the photographer's work. Pierce gives Jonathan clearance. Gaines orders Jack to pull over at a bus stop. A waiting man gives Jack a briefcase. Jack won't carry on until he can speak to his family. Gaines allows his new arrival, Teri, to talk to Jack briefly, before instructing him to drive to the power plant where Palmer's breakfast is being held. Gaines tells Teri that she will be released within an hour if Jack does as ordered. She asks to see Kim.

7:08: Jamey leaves her work station and goes into the restroom, turns on a Personal Digital Assistant, and takes an incoming message from Gaines, who is watching her on the security monitor. Gaines tells Jamey that Nina is dead.

COOL GADGETS Jamey's Samsung Sprint, a hand-held Personal Digital Assistant (PDA) which uses PEN-based technology.[34] Gaines, seemingly, has a fancy gizmo that can instantly transcribe his speech into text which he then transmits to Jamey's PDA. Not only that, but it appears it can also amend contractions to more grammatically correct English. For example, Gaines asks: 'Does this kid Milo know he's working on the wrong keycard?' The machine transcribes this as: 'DOES THIS KID MILO KNOW *THAT HE IS* WORKING ON THE WRONG KEYCARD?' [my italics]. That's clever.

7:15: Reunited, Kim apologises to her mother for lots of things and explains the complicated situation *vis-à-vis* Rick, Dan and Janet.

● ●

33 Uncredited.

34 First pioneered as a portable alternative to a bulkier laptop by Apple Computers in the early 90s, PDAs use a hand-held pointer as a writing tool to input commands and data without the use of a keyboard. The model used in the series - the Samsung SPH-1330 - features 16MB of memory, direct web access, with 160x240 pixel display facility, a 256-colour touch screen that supports full HTML pages, a speakerphone, polyphonic ring tones and voice-activated dialling. And it weighs just 6 ounces. The model, which costs around £325, was one of *the* success stories of the *24* phenomena, selling hundred of thousands of units on the strength of its appearances in this, and future, episodes.

LOGIC, LET ME INTRODUCE YOU TO THIS WINDOW When Kim says that Janet was hit by a car, Teri simply replies 'I know'. Why doesn't she tell Kim that, as far as she is aware, Janet survived and is safe in hospital? Which is, fundamentally, true. She *may* have some dark suspicions about what Kevin could have done to Janet, but it's surprising that Teri doesn't at least *try* to comfort her daughter. Note also that, from this point onwards, Janet is never even mentioned by Kim again. Isn't it odd that, when she comes face-to-face with Gaines, Teri turns from a whimpering ornament into a calm, rational and rather scary Sigourney Weaver-clone? It's also noticeable that, as soon as their meeting is over, within seconds she's snivelling and whining again. Obviously stress brings out the best qualities in most of the Bauer family.

Nina finds a deserted building where, conveniently, there is a working telephone for her to use. When she's just about to pick up the phone for the second time, at the extreme right of shot somebody's arm (presumably one of the production team) is visible for about two seconds. Nina gets from 'just east of Downtown' to Santa Monica through what is, by now, heavy rush-hour L.A. traffic in approximately 25 minutes. That, in itself, is ridiculous enough. That she, seemingly, does this in *a taxi* is even more outrageous. As somebody who once paid $80 and spent almost an hour going a far shorter distance (LAX to North Hollywood) this author suggests that, of all the geographical nonsenses that occasionally pepper *24*, this is *easily* the worst.

When she's arrested, Jamey is still holding her PDA. Didn't Tony think it prudent to take this from her? Thankfully Nina, subsequently, *does* retrieve it. When we see the day's local breakfast news broadcast, wouldn't one expect the overnight downing of an airliner bound for L.A. and the loss of, presumably, hundreds of passengers to feature somewhat prominently? Seemingly not. The room that Nina hides in and where Jamey is subsequently held is, specifically, chosen because it has 'no active cameras'. Yet CCTV footage of Jamey's death will be shown in episode 24. This may seem a rather indelicate question but why are there security cameras in the CTU ladies *loo*? Do the girls working there know that someone has access to videos of them doing, you know, *stuff*?

THE CONSPIRACY STARTS AT CLOSING TIME Nina speaks to Tony. She won't explain the situation, except to say that no one else at CTU can know that she's alive. She asks him to get Jamey. Tony overhears Milo arguing with Jamey about when Nina will return. Jamey tells Tony that she has just talked to Nina and that Nina is unlikely to be back all day. Tony tells Nina that Jamey has just lied about Nina's whereabouts. Nina realises that they can't trust Jamey either. She tells Tony that Jack believed CTU had been infiltrated. Nina asks Tony to secretly bring her back in, as the surveillance system is probably bugged.

7:20: As Palmer and Sherry arrive at the power plant, Jack gets to a security checkpoint. Pierce asks him to open the briefcase he is carrying. Inside is a laptop. Pierce allows Jack to enter.

POINT AT WHICH JESSICA NEEDS A SLAP The *very annoying* Jessica recognises Jack and wants to engage in small talk. Jack excuses himself on Gaines's instructions. Jessica, meanwhile, introduces Palmer to the photographer, Martin Belkin. Jessica is the very epitome of a clingy wannabe High School girlfriend.

7:29: While Kim is sleeping, Teri looks for an escape route. She is interrupted by Rick, who has brought some food. Teri, not realising that Rick is a *nice* kidnapper, angrily berates him. Eli arrives to find Teri attacking Rick and warns Rick not to make friends with the hostages, as they won't be around for much longer. Gaines sees that Jack is trying to write a message to Jessica and has another of his men, Jared, distract Jessica.

Nina arrives back at CTU. She explains that terrorists have kidnapped Jack's wife and daughter. Tony wants to call the Secret Service and, after a moment's hesitation, Nina agrees.

CLUE Subsequently, when Nina's true role in the conspiracy became apparent, one of the main 'but, what about...?' moments highlight ed by fans was her willingness, here, to allow Tony to call the Secret Service. This could, and indeed does, directly lead to the hit on Palmer failing. However, as we also subsequently discover, there is a contingency plan already in motion. It *does*, actually, make sense for Nina to play along with Tony's suggestion so as not to raise his suspicions about her motives.

7 AM

COOL GADGETS Away from the crowds, Jonathan makes Jack assemble the rifle that he is going to shoot Palmer with from various parts of Jack's laptop. With Jack's fingerprints now on the weapon, Jonathan takes the rifle but Jack then pulls a gun on him.

QUOTE/UNQUOTE Jonathan, coolly, as Jack holds a gun to his head: 'Put that away. Somebody might get hurt.'

7:41: Tony tells Milo, with Jamey in earshot, that the keycard was a forgery. Whilst Nina monitors Jamey's subsequent panic attack, Tony calls Pierce and tells him that Jack may have been compromised. Jamey goes to the bathroom. Timing his entrance and exit as the cameras are on a 20-second loop, Tony storms in and orders Jamey out at gunpoint. Pierce tells Palmer that there is a problem with one of the CTU agents. Palmer refuses to leave.

L.A. STORY The San Clarita power station is at 417 Ridgeway Road. Ridgeway is actually in San Gabriel in the east of the Valley.

7:45: Jamey explains that *they* only asked her to tap into the security cameras, but later started sending her messages about Jack and the keycard. She refuses to say who she is working for unless she is given Agency Counsel.

REFERENCES The visual nods to *JFK*, *The Parallax View* and *The Manchurian Candidate*, during the assassination attempt, are all fairly obvious given the subject matter. The assembly of the gun is a probable tribute to a similar scene in *The Man With The Golden Gun*.

7:52: Gaines tells Jack that Jonathan will hand Jack the smoking gun after he has shot Palmer. Jack is warned not to interfere or his family will die and they will kill Palmer anyway. Palmer begins his speech, focusing on themes of integrity and honour. Agent Hayes spots Jack and, after a brief confrontation, Jack lunges for Hayes's gun. In the confusion, agents hustle Palmer out of the building as Gaines watches his plot fall to pieces on live TV. Jack's earpiece has fallen out and Jack reaches for it as agents struggle to restrain him. Jack begs Gaines not to hurt his family. Gaines orders the disposal of Teri and Kim. Then Gaines receives a message from Jamey. Nina and Tony have made her call to say that Division have picked up Jack. They've been looking for him all night for breaking protocol.

POINTS AT WHICH KIM AND TERI NEED A HUG The kidnappers drag Teri and Kim kicking and screaming into the yard. At the last moment, as they're on their knees and about to be executed, Gaines tells Eli that he still needs them alive. As she's being hauled back to the shed, Kim sees Rick and gives him a filthy look. She *doesn't* ask him if he has any clean underwear available, as most people who had just been seconds from death probably would.

7:59: The Secret Service place Jack under arrest.

'YOU MAY REMEMBER ME FROM...' Jackie Debatin played Cassie Ann in *Macon County Jail*, and appeared in *Friends, Caroline in the City, Dr Quinn Medicine Woman* and *I Love You, Don't Touch Me!* Rick Garcia was in *Collateral Damage, The American President, The A-Team* and *The Incredible Hulk*. His day job is the anchorman of Fox's sports show *Fox Overtime*. Jesse Goins has appeared in *Soldier, Malcolm in the Middle, Diff'rent Strokes, Ally McBeal, The Dukes of Hazzard, Patriot Games* and *Street Corner Justice*. Mark Clayman was in *Rush Week* and *Married... With Children*. The great Al Leong was Uri in *Die Hard* and 'Bob' Genghis Khan in *Bill and Ted's Excellent Adventure* and appeared in *Hart to Hart, Godzilla, Escape From L.A.* and *Joshua Tree*. Ron Roggé was in *Buffy the Vampire Slayer, Letters from a Killer* and *Ticker* and played Captain Mitchell in *Lightspeed Rescue*.

NOTES 'Are you saying Jamey's a spy?' A pocket action movie and 42 minutes of breathless excitement, this powerful episode keeps the motor running on all of the necessary subplots. It also successfully draws several key elements together. Palmer and Jack are in one room for most of the episode, and Teri and Kim find themselves in another location for the *whole* time. Meanwhile, at CTU things take a dramatic twist with the revelation that monosyllabic Tony *can* be trusted whilst Jamey *can't*. Highlight of the episode, out of many: Jack's ingenious prevention of the assassination attempt on Palmer. For all the thanks that the poor sod gets.

Pierce says that Jack is 160 pounds and 5'11". Jessica notes that Jack used to be a motorbike racer before his daughter was born. Jessica reminisces about a girl called Tracy Zigler whom she and Jack went to high school with. Tracy Zigler is the name of the series' script supervisor whilst Jessica Abrams, herself, is the script co-ordinator. On a similar theme, Gaines's contact list on his telephone dialler shows Michael Loceff (producer), Virgil Williams (writer), Nicole Burke (assistant director) and Tony Pacheco (production accountant) as well as names like Todd Wasserman, Doug Miller, Manny Hernandez, Jason Savage and Randy Engle. Jamey's remote IP address is 485.698.176.64.

CRITIQUE 'Even before the war made heroes out of CIA agents, this thriller was the talk of TV,' noted *Time* magazine in its *Best of 2001* issue. 'Deservedly so: its pulse-pounding premise, gimmick and look made its pilot the most exciting of the year. Some later episodes had a draggy, shaggy-dog quality, but at its best, *24* had us counting the seconds.'

DID YOU KNOW? According to eagle-eyed viewer and web-designer Dean Browell, there's an easy way to spot who the good guys are in *24*. As he told computer webzine *wired.com*, all of the heroes seem to use Macintosh PCs whilst the villains all have IBM-compatible units. For instance, Tony, whom many fans initially assumed was the mole within CTU, has an Apple Mac. Yet Jamey, the one person whom Walsh told Jack he *could* trust was using a Dell. 'I thought my theory had been blown,' Browell noted, until this episode's revelation that Jamey was a spy. 'It almost seems like a visual clue that was there from the beginning. It would be a big coincidence if they didn't [include it] intentionally.' Producer Michael Loceff subsequently wrote to *wired* and parodied the notion, claiming that it was also true that, in *24*, the good guys use Ericsson phones and eat popcorn and soy protein, whilst the baddies use Nokia and eat red meat.

This is the first episode to feature Keifer Sutherland's by now legendary and much quoted opening monologue, which begins: 'Right now terrorists are planning to assassinate a Presidential candidate...' Or the first version of it, anyway. It changes at least three times before the season concludes.

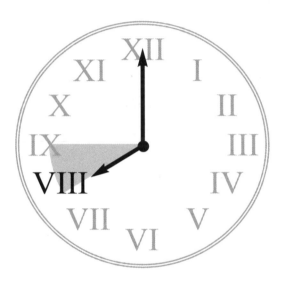

12:00 1:00 2:00 3:00 4:00 5:00 6:00 7:00 **8:00** 9:00 10:00 11:00 12:00 1:00 2:00 3:00 4:00 5:00 6:00 7:00 8:00 9:00 10:00 11:00 12:00

9 8:00 A.M. – 9:00 A.M.

US Transmission Date: 22 January 2002
UK Transmission Date: 21 April 2002 (BBC Choice) [35]
Terrestrial UK Transmission Date: 28 April 2002 (BBC2)
Writer: Virgil Williams
Director: Stephen Hopkins
Cast: Carlos Bernard (Tony Almeida), Penny Johnson Jerald (Sherry Palmer), Karina Arroyave (Jamey Farrell), Devika Parikh (Maureen Kingsley), Michael Massee (Ira Gaines), Vicellous Reon Shannon (Keith Palmer), Glenn Morshower (Aaron Pierce), Eric Balfour (Milo Pressman), Jude Ciccolella (Mike Novick), Silas Weir Mitchell (Eli), Jesse D Goins (Alan Hayes), Michael Bryan French (Frank Simes), Kathleen Wilhoite (Lauren Proctor), Talitha Peters (Anna), Al Leong (Neill)[36]

8:02: Hayes turns a handcuffed Jack over to his boss, Frank Simes. Jack tells Simes that Palmer's life is still in danger. Jack says that the terrorists used the threat of killing his family to get him to smuggle the weapon through security. Jack notes that it was his tussle with Hayes that actually saved the Senator's life. Simes seems to believe Jack but says that he doesn't have the authority to free him. Only District can do that. Jack knows that District won't. Simes says that he is sorry. Jack replies that he *will be* when Palmer dies.

8AM

THE CONSPIRACY STARTS AT CLOSING TIME Jamey divulges Gaines's identity to Tony and Nina. Both know that they need to stop his access to their cameras, but realise they can't simply cut the feed as that will look suspicious. So Jamey is instructed to call Gaines and tell him that she has had to shut off his visual access because Milo was becoming suspicious.

8:09: As he's being led through the power plant, Jack ingeniously opens a valve with his elbow which blows steam in the agents' faces giving him the chance to obtain a gun and make his escape. A chase ensues, during which Jack jumps a chain-link fence, slides down an embankment leading to the highway, runs into the street and with stolen pistol in hand, hijacks the oncoming car of a startled waitress.

8:16: At gunpoint, Jack forces the waitress, Lauren, to drive him into a deserted parking lot on a construction site. With Lauren unwillingly in tow, Jack smashes his way into a, seemingly, disused office.

REFERENCES This aspect of the plot seems inspired by *The Thirty Nine Steps* (an innocent, handcuffed, man escaping from the authorities with the reluctant help of a female hostage).

8:18: Tony expresses his disgust with Jamey for betraying her country. He asks how much she is being paid, and is even more disgusted to learn that it's a mere $300,000. Jamey says she

---

35 From this point, until episode 23, the BBC previewed each episode a week prior to terrestrial BBC2 broadcast on their BBC Choice digital/cable channel on Sundays at 22:45.
36 Uncredited.

has to support her son since her husband left. Nina asks Jamey to call Gaines and tell him that Jack is on his way back to CTU, but Jamey refuses to comply until she is given written immunity. Jack rings Nina and explains that he put the flak jacket on her because he suspected that he would be ordered to kill her. Jack finds it difficult to believe that Jamey is the mole, as Walsh specifically cleared her. Jack tells Jamey, over the phone, that he doesn't care about protocol and that he'll protect her if she helps them. Jamey again demands immunity. Jack tells Nina to bring in Jamey's son so that he can see his mother in handcuffs. Jack requests that a car be dropped off near his location. With his call concluded, Lauren says that she isn't afraid of Jack.

QUOTE/UNQUOTE Jack: 'Lauren, I have killed two people since midnight. I haven't slept in 24 hours. So maybe you should be a little more afraid of me than you are right now.'

CIGARETTES AND ALCOHOL Lauren, the frumpy and rather skanky waitress, says that Jack isn't the only one with problems. She is due in court in 45 minutes on a charge of Driving Under the Influence. She admits to Jack that she's guilty and that this isn't her first offence. He asks if she has a drink problem. She says, no, she just has bad luck.

Palmer is having a whisky at his hotel room. Mike notes that it's not even nine o'clock. *This* is the man, seemingly, whom the American public are soon to elect as the person with his finger on The Button.

8:29: Returning to his hotel, Palmer finds that Keith stormed out half an hour earlier. Palmer tells Sherry that Keith just needs some time alone. Since Palmer didn't break the story himself, Sherry wonders if there is anything they can do to stop Kingsley.

TORN AND FRAYED Whilst Tony is interrogating Jamey, Nina takes the opportunity to check out the bruises left on her torso when Jack shot her. And, coincidentally, to give the audience a glimpse of her black underwear.

8:31: Tony tells Jack that Nina has arranged to have Jamey's son, Kyle, brought in. Jack says he knows that Tony was the one who turned him in. Tony explains that he had no choice, but Jack reassures him that he made the right decision given the circumstances. The news that Jack has escaped from custody makes Palmer uneasy. Mike asks if Palmer knows who Jack is. Palmer says that the name is familiar.

RAPE At the compound, Eli intends to rape Kim. Teri intervenes and suggests that Eli take her instead, noting that she won't protest. He accepts, leaving Kim alone. Listening at the door, she hears the clink of a belt-buckle and the sound of a pair of trousers being lowered.

L.A. STORY Lauren says that she works at Cable's Coffee Shop on Ventura Boulevard ('Home of the $3.99 All Day Breakfast', apparently).

37 Sandwiched between North Hollywood, Burbank and the huge Universal Studio site, Studio City was built in the 1920s when producer Mack Sennett found that he had outgrown his own studio facilities in what would later become the area of Silver Lake. He built a new facility near Ventura Boulevard and Laurel Canyon. Today,

Ventura runs from Sherman Oaks, through North Hollywood and Studio City,[37] and ends close to Universal Studios. The construction site in which Jack hides is said to be near the junction of Temple and Mercer. This appears to be a fictitious location as there is no street named Mercer listed in the entire Los Angeles area. There *is* a Temple Street which goes from Downtown to Echo Park but that's nowhere near where the power plant is said to be.

8:40: Sherry speaks to Maureen Kingsley and strongly suggests that Kingsley should not air the story. Sherry says that she can give the reporter an even bigger exclusive. That an assassination attempt on Palmer this morning was part of a government conspiracy. Maureen won't kill the story entirely, but this alternative exclusive interests her. Eli has finished with Teri and she's now back with her daughter. To Kim's surprise, Teri pulls a cellphone out of her trousers which she stole from Eli whilst he was busy raping her.

LOGIC, LET ME INTRODUCE YOU TO THIS WINDOW What is a large mural of a palm tree-covered beach doing in a portakabin office on a construction site? Seems a bit ostentatious, doesn't it? In the office, Lauren is seen holding an *I ♥ NY* coffee mug at one point. Presumably she found it lying in the office. But why is she holding it? She can't, surely, be drinking anything out of it (there's no kettle visible, for instance). Sherry tells Kingsley about what she describes as a government conspiracy to kill her husband. Given that Mike had only just revealed Jack's identity to Palmer a moment before, where did Sherry get this information from?

8:44: Keith returns, relieved that his father didn't tell the press. Palmer warns that it's going to come out soon anyway. He thinks that his lawyers will have Keith cleared, but Keith believes otherwise. Mike tells Palmer that Maureen is sitting on the story for now. This infuriates Palmer, who knows exactly why this has happened. After Sherry feigns surprise, Palmer says that he will call Maureen to discover her true motives.

A DREAM WITHIN A DREAM? Jack apologises to Lauren for dragging her into this mess. Then, exhausted, he begins to drift off to sleep. As Lauren decides to make a dash for the door, Jack suddenly wakes up, startled, and scowls at her. Some critics have spuriously suggested that Jack actually does fall asleep at this point, and that everything that subsequently happens in *24* is down his fevered imaginings.

8:53: Tony and Nina tell Jamey that they're bringing Kyle in. Tony reminds her that as soon as Gaines discovers that she's in custody, he will grab her son to prevent her from testifying against him. Jamey asks for time to think. At the construction site, police are combing the area. Jack asks Lauren to get the parked car for him. Jack watches her from the window, but as soon as she gets to the street, Lauren turns and runs towards the police and Secret Service agents. Jack opens the back window and escapes. He gets to his new car, with surprising ease, and drives off.

8:58: Nina and Tony return to the room where Jamey is being held. There, they find that Jamey

the site is home to the CBS Studio, where such TV shows as *Hill Street Blues*, *Roseanne* and *Seinfeld* were filmed, and also a thriving residential community.

has, apparently, broken a mug and slashed her own wrist. The pair desperately attempt to revive Jamey. They are interrupted by the ringing of Jamey's palm pilot. Gaines is trying to contact her.

'YOU MAY REMEMBER ME FROM...' Michael Bryan French appeared in *How to Get Laid at the End of the World*, *I Still Know What You Did Last Summer* (as Doctor Smith), *Big Fat Liar*, *Independence Day*, *Judging Amy*, *The West Wing* and *The Drew Carey Show*. Talitha Peters was Fancy in *Planet of the Pitts*. Kathleen Wilhoite played Betsy in *Private School*, Patricia in *Cop Rock*, Chloe in *ER* and Rosalie in *L.A. Law* and appeared in *Angel Heart*, *Girl*, *Nurse Betty* and *Pay it Forward*. She's also a singer/songwriter, her ballad 'Wish We Never Met' featuring prominently in an episode of *Buffy the Vampire Slayer*.

NOTES 'If I can get back out there I can be the main conduit to these people. I can bring them down.' Again, the action never lets up for a single second, with Jack taking an interesting detour, spending the episode in the company of the cynical Lauren. Here, we see some social comment to go with the *realipolitik* that the series was, already, developing a reputation for. Plus, an implied rape, just in case anyone was in danger of forgetting how genuinely disturbing *24* can be. Only the rather laboured Maureen Kingsley subplot in any way disappoints, and *that's* almost over.

Jack says that he used to be in the military and did field work for the CIA. Palmer once had a similar security alert at a rally in Annapolis. It turned out to be a false alarm. The silver Sedan left for Jack has the number G11 28159. Lauren's Chevrolet licence-plate is 4IEH 672.

CAST AND CREW COMMENTS 'We exist, like most TV shows, in a parallel universe; and we're not directly referencing current events because it takes so long to make an episode,' says Robert Cochran, noting that it can take two months or more for a completed script to air. 'God forbid it should get to the point where there are things you just can't bring yourself to watch because the real world is so awful.'

'In a lot of ways, we make an incredible effort to create a sense of realism in an incredibly implausible situation,' Kiefer Sutherland adds. 'Yes, there are huge soap operatic qualities to the show. But it's counterbalanced with a real effort on everybody's part to make it as realistic in that vein as possible.'

GIRL POWER CRITIQUE One aspect of *24* that drew occasional comment from the media, was the perceived toughness, bravery and ruthlessness of many of the series' female characters. As Matt Zoller-Seitz noted: 'Emotionally, the kidnap plot is a two-way street; as hard as Jack fights to save his wife and daughter, they fight just as hard to be reunited with him. When a wrongly-framed Jack eludes law enforcement by carjacking a waitress and briefly holding her hostage, we're asked to understand (if not condone) his actions. The programme asks that we cut a similar amount of slack when Teri has sex with a captor in order to pilfer his cell phone. [The series is] the most sexually egalitarian on television. No matter what side of the moral spectrum they inhabit, the show's women, like its men, are under too much pressure to worry about fulfilling or resisting gender stereotypes.'

Elisha Cuthbert thinks that there may be a horrible shock in store for the person who, reportedly, paid $5,000 on *eBay* for the bracelet that she wore during the first season. 'It's a cheap $2 bracelet,' she noted sadly. 'I don't know if the person who bought it knew that before. But they will do now.'

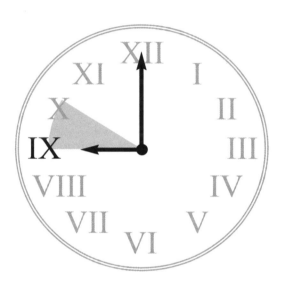

9:00 A.M. – 10:00 A.M.

12:00 1:00 2:00 3:00 4:00 5:00 6:00 7:00 8:00 9:00 10:00 11:00 12:00 1:00 2:00 3:00 4:00 5:00 6:00 7:00 8:00 9:00 10:00 11:00 12:00

10   9:00 A.M. – 10:00 A.M.

US Transmission Date: 5 February 2002
UK Transmission Date: 5 May 2002
Terrestrial UK Transmission Date: 12 May 2002
Writer: Larry Hertzog
Director: Davis Guggenheim
Cast: Carlos Bernard (Tony Almeida), Penny Johnson Jerald (Sherry Palmer), Daniel Bess (Rick), Karina Arroyave (Jamey Farrell), Michael Massee (Ira Gaines), Zach Grenier (Carl Webb), Eric Balfour (Milo Pressman), Jude Ciccolella (Mike Novick), Silas Weir Mitchell (Eli), Tamara Tunie (Alberta Green), Željko Ivanek (Andre Drazen), Currie Graham (Ted Cofell), Ivar Brogger (Frank Ames), Tracy E Wilson (Cofell's Assistant), Desmond Bull (Kid), Martin Morales (Attendant), Manny Perry (Cop), Maurice Dunster (Security Guard), Burke Stuart (Chauffeur), Jenny Gago (Principal)[38]

9:02: Paramedics attempt to resuscitate Jamey. Jack rings Nina needing directions, as the police have set up roadblocks. Nina recommends that Jack turn himself in, but he refuses, knowing that Gaines won't keep Teri and Kim alive if he's in custody. Teri calls Nina, with Kim acting as lookout. Teri has no idea where she is, so Nina asks her to leave the line open for them to set up a trace. Teri hides the phone on a wooden beam as Eli and Rick arrive. Jack and Nina listen to Eli threatening the women concerning his missing cellphone.

9AM

L.A. STORY   Dave Thompson, the 'Arnie Pye in the Sky'-clone, in *Jetcopter 3* tells listeners to an L.A. radio station that delays on the 405 Freeway are affecting the Sepulveda Pass southbound, but that traffic loosens up at Culver Drive. He does this whilst a gorgeous tracking shot shows the helicopter flying *not* over the 405, but rather the 101. Still, it's lovely to look at, so why quibble over details? Also known as the Hollywood Freeway, the 101 is the main connecting route between East L.A. and the Valley. A further report on the Valley itself indicates that there is congestion in North Hollywood at Ferduso, site of the Grant Street Elementary School.

Nina tells Jack that his best way to avoid police roadblocks is to stay on Thurston. So now, seemingly, Jack is in Bel Air, since that's where Thurston Drive is located. Confusingly, a Montana is also mentioned. The only such street name anywhere in L.A. (Montana Drive) is in Silver Lake, a *third* possible location for the area of the power plant and the construction site that Jack has been driving around for the last couple of episodes.

Yet more information is given about the geographical location of Gaines's compound. It is north of Highway 10 and east of the 405. Teri mentions the presence of eucalyptus trees in the area and speculates that it is somewhere in the north Valley and inland.

9:09: The Palmers, en route to the elementary school, have another argument over Kingsley. Nina tells Jack that they have a preliminary trace for the location of Gaines's compound, but that it covers a wide area. Tony, meanwhile, is sifting through Jamey's e-mail. Jamey deleted all of her messages bar one, sent this morning and concerning a Ted Cofell. Tony learns that

---

38 Both *TV Guide* and Fox listings credit Jenny Gago as appearing in this episode, but her character's lines were cut before transmission. She also appears, uncredited, in the following episode.

Jamey has died on her way to hospital.

Logic, Let Me Introduce You to This Window Jamey's e-mail address (*jamey@ctu...* is how it appears on screen), isn't a valid one. When Jack is stopped by the two police officers and then races off, he drives into a car park followed by the same chasing police car. Yet the officer from whom Jack hides under a car is not one of the two seen following him earlier. Teri says that it took half an hour to get from Mulholland Drive to the compound. It actually took less than 10 minutes. Even if it *had* taken half an hour, that still wouldn't be anywhere near enough time to get from Mulholland to somewhere in the north Valley which is where she speculates the compound is located.

9:18: After Eli and Rick leave, Teri retrieves the phone and Nina puts her through to Jack. Milo tells them that the trace will take approximately 20 minutes. Jack is ordered to pull over by two police officers. He waits until the men walk to his car, then speeds away. The police follow in hot pursuit. A lengthy chase follows, during which Jack hides in a parking lot. He also spends time whilst hiding from the police asking Teri to give more details about her location. Teri says that the kidnappers are coming back and she hides the phone again. When Eli furiously knocks Teri to the ground, Rick attempts to stop him. Eli is about to punch Rick when the phone starts bleeping. Finding the hidden phone, Eli asks to whom he's speaking. Jack tells him.

Quote/Unquote Eli: 'Who is this?' Jack: 'I am the last thing you will ever see if anything happens to my wife or my daughter.'

9:32: Eli intends telling Gaines what has happened. Rick reminds Eli that Gaines will not be happy when he finds out whose phone was used to call for help, and how it was acquired. The police finally locate Jack's deserted vehicle. Jack, meanwhile, is breaking into another car. After hotwiring it, he drives off without being seen, then calls Nina to find how close to a trace Milo got. Nina says within a 25-mile radius.

L.A. Story Cofell is said to be the CEO of an investment bank based at 21500 Riverside Drive, Burbank.[39] This is situated just behind Griffith Park. The largest municipal park in North America, Griffith is a sprawling combination of gentle greenery and steep, rugged mountain slopes. It was named after the land's original owner, mining millionaire Griffith J Griffith (1850-1919). In 1896, he deeded the area to the city for the sole purpose of public recreation. The park contains approximately 53 miles of trails and numerous tourist attractions including the L.A. Zoo, the Gene Autry Western Heritage Museum, the Griffith Observatory and the Greek Theatre.

9:35: Gaines gets a call from a man named Andre Drazen, who is on a Lear jet bound for L.A and is clearly giving Gaines his orders. Drazen asks why Palmer is still alive. Gaines reassures

---

39 Although Hollywood remains the name most synonymous with the movie industry to the world at large, most of the studios actually relocated from Tinseltown many years ago. The new locale for most was on the other side of the Hollywood Hills in 'beautiful downtown Burbank', the subsequent butt of weekly jokes on *The Johnny Carson Show* and *Rowan and Martin's Laugh-In*. Hot, very smoggy and home to some of the ugliest architecture in the Western Hemisphere, Burbank is still the location of Disney Studios, NBC and Warner Brothers, all of which are based close to the junction of Ventura and Riverside Drive.

Drazen that Palmer will be dead by the day's end and that Jack Bauer will return, to rescue his family. Drazen says that he will be at the compound in an hour and warns that if things aren't back under control soon, he will have Cofell empty the account. Drazen threatens Gaines that he will lose something more than money if Palmer survives.

THE CONSPIRACY STARTS AT CLOSING TIME This conversation acknowledges that Gaines is simply a hired mercenary, something alluded to in previous episodes with Gaines seen calling an unseen someone to explain various bits of the plot. It also confirms that Drazen has a personal agenda against both Senator Palmer and Jack.

QUOTE/UNQUOTE Andre, to Gaines: 'If Plan A doesn't work, you should have a Plan B. Not Plan A-recycled.'

9:36: Sherry calls Carl and asks him to stop Kingsley. He says that he is already taking care of the evidence against Keith. This shocks both Sherry and one of three men who are in a meeting with Carl. Milo finally decodes Jamey's e-mail. It's a wire transfer for one million dollars to Gaines's Swiss bank account. Jack calls Cofell's office pretending to be an old friend. He is told that Cofell is going out of town in a few moments.

9:43: Tony gives Nina more bad news. Division have notified him that Jack's temporary replacement is to be Alberta Green. This annoys Nina whom Green used to work for.

BACK STORY Kim asks Teri why her father moved out. Teri doesn't want to talk about that now, but Kim persists. Teri tells Kim how Jack once went on what he said was a training exercise, but Teri suspected strongly to be a mission. When Jack came back, Teri notes, he was another person, distant, preoccupied and angry. He hid this change of personality from Kim, but it put a severe strain on his relationship with Teri. They decided to separate in an attempt to patch things up.

9:46: Alberta Green arrives at CTU and tells the assembled staff that protecting Palmer is their primary objective. She notes that Jack was implicated in the assassination attempt. Palmer is chatting with a classroom of children when Mike receives a call from Frank Ames, the man in Carl's meeting. Ames is Palmer's biggest contributor and tells Palmer that he knows about Ferragamo and Keith. He fears that Carl and Palmer's other financial backers are planning something illegal. He intends to wash his hands of the campaign.

SEXUAL OFFICE POLITICS Nina assures Green that she hasn't talked to Jack since earlier in the morning. Green doesn't believe her, and promises immunity in exchange for the truth about Jack. Green further suggests that Jack trusts no one. The meeting ends angrily with Green advising Nina to 'let him screw you, don't let him screw you over.'

9:57: Jack arrives at Cofell's office but discovers that Cofell has just taken the elevator to the parking garage. Jack activates a fire alarm and runs down the stairs. In the elevator, Cofell calmly tells those trapped with him that after a 30-second reset, the elevator will descend automatically. Jack finds Cofell's driver and takes the man aside. Cofell arrives and his limo is summoned. He asks Mark, the driver, to turn on the air conditioning. Mark, however, isn't driving, Jack is.

COMPLETELY POINTLESS CLIFFHANGER #1 Teri suddenly has a terrible pain in her stomach.

'YOU MAY REMEMBER ME FROM...' Slovenian-born actor Željko Ivanek won a Tony award in 1983 for his stage performance in *Brighton Beach*. He subsequently featured in *Black Hawk Down*, *Hannibal*, *A Civil Action*, *The Rat Pack* (as Bobby Kennedy), *From the Earth to the Moon*, *Donnie Brasco*, *School Ties*, *Courage Under Fire*, *Ally McBeal*, *Homicide: Life on the Street* (as Ed Danvers), *Oz* (as Governor Devlin), *The Sun Also Rises* and *Murder, She Wrote*. Tamara Tunie appeared in *Law & Order: Special Victims Unit*, *As the World Turns*, *Rising Sun*, *The Devil's Advocate* and *Wall Street*. Ivar Broggar was in *For Richer, For Poorer*, *Academy for Boyz*, *Mom's on Strike*, *Star Trek: Voyager* and *The West Wing*. Desmond Bull appeared in *Just for Kicks*. Currie Graham played Nate in *Suddenly Susan* and was in *Judging Amy* and *Portraits of a Killer*. Martin Moralez appeared in *Double Take*. Manny Perry acted in *Rush Hour*, but he's better known as a stunt-man on movies like *Sunset Strip*, *Stigmata*, *The Mod Squad*, *Armageddon*, *Star Trek: First Contact*, *Kuffs* and *The Last Action Hero*. Jenny Gago appeared in *The Cross*, *The Prodigal Daughter*, *Innerspace* and played Beatrice Zapeda in *Alien Nation*.

BEHIND THE CAMERA Larry Hertzog wrote episodes of *Nowhere Man*, *La Femme Nikita*, *Hart to Hart* and *Walker, Texas Ranger*. Davis Guggenheim directed the movies *Teach* and *Gossip* and episodes of *Alias*, *ER*, *Party of Five* and *NYPD Blue*. He was also associate producer on *Don't Tell Mom the Babysitter's Dead*, music supervisor on *The Opposite Sex and How to Live with Them* and Los Angeles production co-ordinator on *sex, lies, and videotape*.

NOTES 'Carl has taken care of everything.' There's a sense of lots of coins dropping into lots of slots in this episode. The complex, labyrinthine nature of the fiendishly-linked plot against both Palmer and Jack becomes more focused. The internal power struggle at CTU takes a new twist with the arrival of a new character, the power-dressing *über-bitch*, Alberta Green, who initially promised much. Best bit of the episode, however, is Jack's stalking of Cofell at the climax.

The car that Jack avoids the police in is a battered cream Pontiac with the licence plate 2RHI384. In addition to his previously mentioned baseball prowess, David Palmer also played basketball for Georgetown University in Washington D.C. Tony has a USA logo coffee mug on his desk. Ted Cofell was born in Philadelphia and gained an MBA from UCLA in 1988. He's run his own finance company for five years. The two other men in the meeting with Carl and Frank Ames were called Phil Tuttle and Bob Jorgenson. Ted Cofell is named after Production Assistant Anne Cofell.

CRITIQUE Writer and broadcaster Andrew Collins describes Jack as 'like a tough office worker. He can handle a gun, *and* he can handle a mouse. He's the perfect hero for the world we live in.' Jeremy Clarkson, on the other hand, in a typically forthright piece for *24 Heaven* considered that 'Jack Bauer is *God*!

[He's] what all men would like to be. Brave, clever, somebody who picks up the phone and says "Get me chopper command!"'

CAST AND CREW COMMENTS Kiefer Sutherland says he still cannot understand why some TV shows click with audiences and others don't. 'I go into rehearsals with the best of intentions,' he notes, 'but I can never figure it out... I would never allow myself to believe from the beginning that this show would work out as well as it has. If I started out thinking it would get this kind of critical praise, I would be disappointed no matter what happened.'

DID YOU KNOW? 'The impetus for me to do television solely derived from the fact that I thought the idea of *24* was incredibly innovative,' notes Kiefer Sutherland. Over the past few years, Sutherland has floated in and out of Hollywood, doing occasional acting jobs. In 1998, he abandoned L.A., for a second time, to raise cattle on his 2,000 acre ranch in Santa Ynez, near Santa Barbara. Considering that he is best known for his film roles, television hardly seemed to be the ideal vehicle to put him back into the spotlight. But he simply couldn't resist *24*, even if it meant giving up the farm. 'There's a lot [about farming] that I miss,' he says. 'But I'm an actor. That's what I do.'

9AM

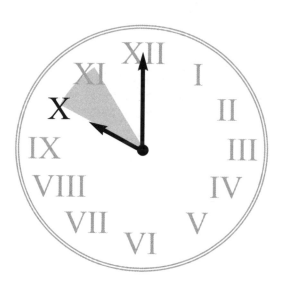

10:00 A.M. – 11:00 A.M.

12:00 1:00 2:00 3:00 4:00 5:00 6:00 7:00 8:00 9:00 **10:00** 11:00 12:00 1:00 2:00 3:00 4:00 5:00 6:00 7:00 8:00 9:00 10:00 11:00 12:00

11 10:00 A.M. – 11:00 A.M.

US Transmission Date: 12 February 2002
UK Transmission Date: 12 May 2002
Terrestrial UK Transmission Date: 19 May 2002
Writer: Robert Cochran
Director: Davis Guggenheim
Cast: Carlos Bernard (Tony Almeida)[40], Penny Johnson Jerald (Sherry Palmer), Richard Burgi (Kevin Carroll), Daniel Bess (Rick), Michael Massee (Ira Gaines), Zach Grenier (Carl Webb), Jude Ciccolella (Mike Novick), Silas Weir Mitchell (Eli), Tamara Tunie (Alberta Green), Željko Ivanek (Andre Drazen), Currie Graham (Ted Cofell), Jenny Gago (Principal)[41]

10:02: Green announces that the Secret Service believe Martin Belkin may have been part of the assassination attempt. Kevin, who's been lying low for a couple of hours since delivering Teri to Gaines, calls Cofell, arranging a meeting. Cofell tells his driver about this change of plans, but Mark doesn't acknowledge him. Cofell guesses that he isn't talking to Mark and asks his, apparent, kidnapper to stop the car. Jack does and forces Cofell to hand over his cellphone. The financier tells Jack that he doesn't know anyone called Gaines. Jack doesn't believe him and calls Nina to tell her that he has got Cofell. He asks Nina to put together an interrogation profile on Cofell in five minutes.

10AM

LOGIC, LET ME INTRODUCE YOU TO THIS WINDOW Jack tells Cofell that his wife and daughter have been 'missing since midnight'. That's certainly true of Kim, though Teri has only been missing *per se* since around 6AM. However, it's probably fair to say that Jack is just simplifying matters. Eli pushes Rick face-first against a pane of glass; note Rick's subsequent bruised face for the rest of the day. The pane shatters, yet Rick, seemingly, suffers no cuts whatsoever. Why, once Cofell makes an attempt on Jack's life, does he suddenly lapse into a Central European accent? Is it for any reason other than the purely dramatic?

10:07: Rick apologises to Teri for what happened. Teri tries to thank him but he asks that, since Eli sent him to interrogate them, it's better that they don't say anything. Kim then sees Eli give Rick a good kicking when the latter claims that the women refused to talk to him. Nina quickly halts work on the profile that she is preparing when Green comes to see her. Green says that she has been reviewing the passenger list of the 747 and it doesn't add up. Nina explains that records were altered to make it look as though there was an empty seat. Nina explains that Belkin was in that seat and died in the explosion and a lookalike assassin took his place at the breakfast. What Nina can't, as yet, explain is how this lookalike got a legitimate ID. Jack calls Nina. Nina tells Green that she has Bill Warner at the Bureau on the phone. Green says that she needs to talk to Warner, but Tony distracts Green's attention whilst Nina handles the call. She guesses that Cofell is a passive-aggressive personality. Her parting words to Jack are that the threat of pain can be more effective than actual pain for the kind of person that she perceives Cofell to be.

40 Uncredited.
41 Uncredited.

The scenes in the underground car park are reminiscent of *All the President's Men*. 'Things fall apart' is an allusion to *The Second Coming* by Irish existentialist poet W.B. Yeats (1865-1939).

10:17: Cofell says that he was due to meet a man named Kevin Carroll, who sells machinery. Jack calls Nina to run a background check on Carroll which, he guesses, is probably an alias.

SINISTER TORTURE TECHNIQUES Jack drenches a towel in water, and tells Cofell how the Soviet secret police used to torture political prisoners in the Gulags with makeshift devices like this. They would shove a towel down a man's throat, hold onto one end, and wait until the prisoner's stomach started to digest the towel. Then, they would pull the towel - and their victim's stomach lining - out. This is a particularly painful, and slow, way to die, Jack notes. It seems a rather unlikely and elaborate method of dispatch but, remarkably, it *is* true. During the early 1990s, former members of the Soviet *Spetznaznacheniya*, the KGB's Special Forces bully-boys, have confirmed that this, and other even more puke-inducing, practices were regularly used on both suspected spies and dissidents.[42]

10:20: Drazen arrives, and tells Gaines that it appears Drazen's people have made a big mistake in bringing Americans into this operation. He summarily pulls the plug on Gaines's involvement. Gaines doesn't understand how Drazen could close down something that's been so important to him for over a year, but Drazen says that he is not quitting.

QUOTE/UNQUOTE Drazen: 'We have a contingency plan. Bauer and Palmer will be dead by the end of the day.' Gaines: 'You never said anything about a contingency plan.' Drazen: 'It does not involve you.'

10:21: Gaines begs for two more hours to find Jack. Drazen gives him 30 minutes. If Gaines does not apprehend Jack by then, he will be required to kill Teri and Kim. Rick, standing nearby, overhears this. Speaking on his cellphone, Carl is not happy to hear his *former* boss. Palmer says that he has received a suggestion that Ferragamo's life may be in danger. Carl believes that Ames told Palmer this, and brushes off the allegation, but Palmer threatens to blackmail Carl if he does not agree to meet.

10:30: Teri's stomach pain returns. Cofell secretly acquires a hidden weapon in the back of the car, a Microtech HALO (a combined knife and taser). Palmer asks Sherry if she has spoken to Carl and she admits that she did. Palmer asks Mike if he has found out anything further about Bauer. Mike replies that Jack has a standard, gap-ridden, agency file and is surprised when Palmer asks if one of those gaps was during the summer two years ago.

10:34: Cofell attacks Jack but Jack easily disarms him. Cofell, in agony with a broken wrist, curses in Serbian. Jack spent time in Belgrade and recognises the language. Cofell bitterly taunts Jack, saying that he deserves what is happening to him. Jack hits Cofell in the chest and

----

42 One particularly uninviting technique for extracting information used by the notorious East German state police, the *Staasi*, has recently come to light. This involved the unfortunate victim being threatened with submersion in a bath full of human excrement.

Cofell has a heart attack. Jack holds Cofell's heart pills, claiming he will hand them over once he is told where his family are being held. But Cofell would, seemingly, rather die. Cofell spits out a pill that Jack forces into his mouth, and dies, much to Jack's distress.

LOGIC, LET ME INTRODUCE YOU TO THIS WINDOW Actually, come to think of it, what *is* Cofell's story? Unless Nina is spinning another elaborate web of deceit - and *that*'s perfectly possible given what we subsequently discover - then Cofell is a real, American, businessman. Certainly, the scenes in the previous episode with his secretary, suggest that Cofell is exactly who he claims to be, an L.A.-based financier with a heart-condition. It is possible that *this* Cofell, like Jonathan, is an impostor replacing a real person. But, if so, he's good enough to fool Cofell's personal staff. If this *is* the case, then the conspiracy has also, seemingly, made a monumental error of judgment in replacing a financier with a heart-condition with a *terrorist* with a heart condition. Speaking of which, Jack *knows* that Cofell (or whoever the man is) *has* a heart condition. Yet Jack still hits Cofell, very hard, in the chest, thus causing him to have a heart attack. Come on, that's *basic* 'How not to kill your only lead' technique, surely?

L.A. STORY The garage in which Cofell is due to meet Kevin is on the corner of Nordorff Street and Willingham Street in Northridge.

10:41: Nina consoles Jack who now knows that the terrorists have a personal agenda against him. He asks Nina to check a two-year-old assignment in Belgrade and Kosovo called Operation Nightfall which Jack led. Tony suggests to Nina that since Green knows that they are both lying, they may as well come clean and, hopefully, help Jack. Nina sternly refuses.

10:44: Rick apologetically gives Teri a handgun. Jack watches as another car pulls into the garage. Kevin enters the back seat of Cofell's limo and apologises for being late, just as all the doors lock. Kevin is surprised when Jack greets him by his real name, then asks where his wife is. Jack drives recklessly around the garage and, in the back, Kevin is thrown violently, face-first, against the divider.

10:51: Jack binds Kevin, who suggests that Jack's family are safe. Gaines's half hour is up, and he orders Eli to kill the women. Carl meets Palmer who puts him on the spot about his promise to murder Ferragamo. Carl denies that is what he meant. Instead, he warns Palmer how powerful *they* are, whilst reminding the Senator that Carl does not work for him. Rather both Palmer and Carl work for *them*. Palmer says that may apply to Carl but it certainly doesn't apply to himself.

QUOTE/UNQUOTE Carl: 'Power has a price, and that price has to be paid. Always.'

LOGIC, LET ME INTRODUCE YOU TO THIS WINDOW Convenient, isn't it, that there is a roll of grey duct tape in the trunk of Cofell's car for Jack to bind Kevin with? Why does Kevin, like an idiot who has watched too many Westerns, empty all six bullets from his gun into the car's safety glass divider when attempting to kill Jack? Surely, after the first couple of shots, he could see that the glass was bullet-proof and, therefore, perhaps save some bul-

10AM

lets for later when Jack would eventually have to open the doors?

Further to the fine upstanding and clean as a whistle politician that Palmer has been presenting himself as since around 4AM. He says that he knows some things about Carl's background that his former employee would not want to be made public. What could these possibly be? And, more importantly, what does the fact that Palmer *knows* about them and yet has still employed this man for seven years tell us about Palmer's supposed integrity? Ferragamo is a Los Angeles-based psychiatrist. Why, therefore, would he have Keith Palmer as a patient when evidence here, and elsewhere, suggests that the Palmer family live in Washington?

> **10:53:** Eli comes into the shed to kill Teri and Kim. Teri draws the gun that Rick gave her, but it jams. Eli pushes the gun away from Teri, grabs her throat and begins strangling her. Kim struggles with Eli and he turns his attentions to her, his own gun falling to the floor in the process. Eli pins Kim to the ground and pulls out a knife. Then he's shot dead by Teri. Teri shoots again, explaining to Kim that whoever sent Eli would be expecting two shots.

COMPLETELY POINTLESS CLIFFHANGER #2 Jack and Kevin drive towards the compound.

NOTES 'I don't want to hurt you. But I will do everything I have to do to protect my family.' Sudden changes of character motivation are something of a stock in trade in *24*. We've already seen this type of thing happen with both Mason and Tony before, but this episode suffers more than most. Teri has been such a pain in the ass for most of the early episodes. Yet, when faced with *real* trauma, suddenly she becomes a much more sympathetic and likeable character. And, a hardened killer to boot. Several of the characters do incredibly dumb things in this episode - Jack and Kevin, in particular. The ending is a bit inconsequential too, second time in two episodes that a brilliant penultimate scene has been spoiled by a weak climax. Best bit: Jack's description of some particularly nasty torture techniques to Cofell.

David and Sherry first met in elementary school. Cofell, Nina notes, is the oldest of three children. His father died when he was young and he went to college at 16. He was first in his class and became the Vice President of a company three years later. He has a heart condition and is not generous with money. Tony notes that the assassins' connection to Germany may lead, ultimately, to the Balkans but he doesn't elaborate. Drazen's car is a green Mercedes. Jack has considerable knowledge of the torture techniques used in the Russian Gulag, a string of prisons in Northern Siberia.

CRITIQUE 'You have missed a lot since the November premiere, which started at midnight,' noted the *Cincinnati Enquirer*'s John Kiesewetter. 'But it's not impossible to catch up. Just remember: Jack is trying to foil the assassination, which may involve the CIA, and he's trying to find his wife and daughter. "That's all you need to know for any episode," says executive producer Joel Surnow. "If you get that, you get the show." You'll get a *terrific* show, continued Kiesewetter. 'Each hour has more twists and turns than most theatrical action movies... This is the most addictive, riveting TV drama series I've ever seen. It's not yet noon, we've got practically a whole day to go.'

CAST AND CREW COMMENTS What was the worst thing that Penny Johnson faced on her time on *24*? According to the actress, it was realising that whatever clothes her character wore in the pilot episode, she'd be stuck wearing for, more or less, the entire season. 'You have to look the same over eight months,' she says. 'You don't gain weight, you don't change your hair. In nine months you can make a baby, but not on this series.'

DID YOU KNOW? Kiefer Sutherland splits most of his time between his main residence, in his native Toronto, and an L.A. apartment. He was delighted to win the Golden Globe for best dramatic actor, over such luminaries as *The West Wing*'s Martin Sheen and *The Sopranos*' James Gandolfini. 'It's been a long time since I've been invited to an evening like that,' says Kiefer. 'I was shocked.' In 2000, Sutherland had shot an unsold TV pilot for a series based on the movie *L.A. Confidential*, in which he assumed Kevin Spacey's role of policeman Jack Vincennes. He had better luck with *24*.

10AM

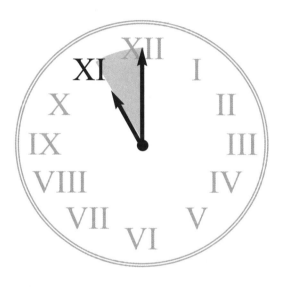

11:00 A.M. – 12:00 NOON

12:00 1:00 2:00 3:00 4:00 5:00 6:00 7:00 8:00 9:00 10:00 **11:00** 12:00 1:00 2:00 3:00 4:00 5:00 6:00 7:00 8:00 9:00 10:00 11:00 12:00

12 11:00 A.M. – 12:00 NOON

US Transmission Date: 19 February 2002
UK Transmission Date: 19 May 2002
Terrestrial UK Transmission Date: 26 May 2002
Writer: Howard Gordon
Director: Stephen Hopkins
Cast: Carlos Bernard (Tony Almeida), Richard Burgi (Kevin Carroll), Daniel Bess (Rick), Michael Massee (Ira Gaines), Jude Ciccolella (Mike Novick), Al Leong (Neill), Tamara Tunie (Alberta Green), Željko Ivanek (Andre Drazen)[43], Jon E Epstein (Assistant)[44], John Prosky (George Ferragamo)

11:02: Jack warns Kevin that if Teri and Kim have been harmed, someone will pay. And, Kevin is looking a likely candidate.

COOL GADGETS Jack asks Nina to open the Global Positioning System function on his palm pilot so that he can get a visual layout of the compound.

11:05: Teri and Kim cover Eli's body beneath a metal tub. Nina sends photographs of the compound to Jack's palm pilot. Jack drags Kevin from the car and wipes the blood from his face. He uncuffs Kevin, hands him the car keys, and tells him to drive into the compound.

11 AM

REFERENCES The subplot concerning Teri and Kim killing the abusive rapist Eli and hiding his body seems to have two direct sources, Henri-Georges Clouzot's *Les Diaboliques* (1955) and its 1969 British remake, *The Corpse* (also known as *Crucible of Horror*). Jack warns Nina that the situation could develop 'into another Waco'. This refers to the controversial armed conclusion to a 51-day stand-off between law-enforcement officials and members of David Koresh's fundamentalist Branch Davidians cult at Waco, Texas, in February 1993, which resulted in over 80 deaths.

11:09: Palmer tells Mike what he believes that Carl intends to do. Mike promises to call Ferragamo himself. Palmer says that he has already done so, but only got through to Ferragamo's voicemail. Jack hides under a blanket on the back seat of Kevin's car as he and Kevin approach the security gate. Jack warns Kevin that if anything goes wrong, he will start shooting. Neill greets Kevin, telling him that Gaines is waiting for him.

LOGIC, LET ME INTRODUCE YOU TO THIS WINDOW Eli audibly grunts as Teri and Kim hide his body. He also, clearly, moves fractionally a moment later then Teri removes his beeper from his pants pocket. Kevin arrives at the gate looking like he's just gone 10 rounds with Lennox Lewis. Though Neill *does* inquire about the cause, shouldn't Kevin's angry and sarcastic reply tell Neill that *something* is wrong? See the **L.A. Story** section for

• •

43 Uncredited, voice only.
44 Character named Al in dialogue.

another couple of whopping great geographical boobs. Jack tells Rick that he has five minutes to get the truck. After this, presumably, Jack will put Plan B into operation and go for the abandoned car himself. Yet when Rick finally returns, over *20 minutes* later, Jack is only just about to initiate Plan B. All he seems to have done in the meantime is to have a (quite short) telephone conversation with Alberta Green. Tony refers to Jack as Jake at one point. Kevin mispronounces Cofell's name. Gaines's men (including Ira himself) seem to be thoroughly rotten shots considering that they're supposed to be a crack gang of international terrorists. When Jack and co. are escaping in the van, bullets fly through the vehicle from every angle possible, but all of them conspire to miss their intended targets.

11:16: Jack asks Kevin where Teri and Kim are being held. Irritated by Kevin's vague response, Jack hits him. Kevin points out the shed where, he believes, Kim and Teri are likely to be. Jack then viciously pummels Kevin into unconsciousness.

QUOTE/UNQUOTE Kevin: 'This whole rescue act. You really think it's gonna make up for how you screwed up your marriage, Jack?!'

11:20: Rick, and others, are moving equipment into numerous red vans. Gaines sends Rick to find out what's delaying Eli. Ferragamo returns Palmer's call. When Palmer says that he called to talk about Keith, Ferragamo reminds the Senator that this would be a violation of doctor/patient privileges. Palmer notes that Ferragamo, seemingly, had no problems in violating such privileges when he talked to Kingsley.

THE CONSPIRACY STARTS AT CLOSING TIME Ferragamo mistakenly believes that Palmer is threatening him. Palmer attempts to tell Ferragamo that his life may be in danger. But Ferragamo is under the impression that it was Palmer, himself, who covered up Gibson's murder, and he hangs up.

11:22: Palmer wants to go and see Ferragamo in person. Mike reminds Palmer that he has to give a speech in an hour, but Palmer remains defiant. Teri and Kim are preparing to make their escape when the door opens. A figure leaps out of the doorway, knocks the gun from Teri's hand and pulls her to the ground. Luckily, it's Jack, and he doesn't kill her. The three Bauers are reunited.

L.A. STORY Palmer's motorcade is seen driving along Ventura Boulevard. Yet more information on Gaines's compound is given: The location is now confirmed as being in the north Valley, east of Highway 5. The compound is also said to be between Tampa and Reseda and to be close to Placerita Canyon Road in an area of orange groves. However, both Tampa Avenue (which is in Tarzana) and Reseda Boulevard (which is located in Reseda itself), which run parallel to each other, are situated *west* of Highway 5. Quite considerably in the case of the former.

11:28: Green suggests that Nina and Tony are conspiring to harbour Jack. Nina tells her that Jack is not a threat to Palmer. Green wonders how Nina could possibly know this if she hasn't talked to him. Since neither Tony or Nina will co-operate, Green orders them to go into separate holding rooms, saying that they are both suspended. Nina does not believe that Green has the authority to do this. Green says that whichever of them tells her where Jack is will have a career with CTU. The other will be sacked and prosecuted.

11:30: Rick knocks on the door. Kim tells Jack that Rick is the one who gave them the gun. Rick enters and Jack grabs him by the throat. Teri and Kim both plead with Jack to let Rick go as he has demonstrated that he has no wish to harm them. Jack asks Rick why he is helping them. Rick admits that it was he who got Kim into the situation and that he feels responsible. Green interrogates Tony. She says that they both know that Nina is covering for Jack. Green believes that Tony's motivation is to cover for Nina who, she suggests, is using Tony.

POINTS AT WHICH TERI NEEDS A SLAP Jack says that he's going to get the car, but Teri begs him not to leave her again as terrible things have happened to her whenever they have been separated. One has to wonder, if she is seriously suggesting that Jack never venture more than 12 inches from her side for the rest of his life, because that's what it sounds like.

11:32: Rick suggests that *he* could steal one of the vans. Gaines, he notes, still believes that Rick is working for him. Even if this doesn't work, at least he may be able to create a diversion so that Jack *can* make it to the car. Jack tells Rick that he has five minutes.

THIS IS WHAT SHE'S LIKE? Some pretty bad messages are sent out from this episode concerning female empowerment. It has been noticeable over the last couple of hours that Kim and, especially, Teri are getting stronger and more confident in how they handle themselves, culminating in Teri shooting Eli to stop him from killing her daughter. Yet, the second that Jack turns up again, both Teri and Kim appear to allow the trauma of their life and death struggle to overcome them once again. This, inevitably, leads to yet more of the kind of pathetic blubbering that we thought we had seen the back of a couple of episodes ago. Teri, without Jack, seems to be a capable woman with a strong independent streak. *With* her husband, sadly, she appears to meekly surrender all of this.

11:39: Neill finds the unconscious Kevin. Just as Rick gets into one of the vans, Gaines asks Rick what he's doing. Neill calls Gaines to tell him about Kevin. Gaines tells Rick to drive him. Mike warns Palmer to be careful what he says to Ferragamo. When they get to the doctor's office, however, they find the building on fire. A policeman tells Mike that there has been a gas explosion. Palmer angrily speculates that Carl's men must have torched the office. Green returns to Tony's holding room to see what choice he has made. Before Tony can speak, an assistant tells Green that she has a call from Jack Bauer. Jack tells her that he has located the people behind the conspiracy and has found his family, whom they had kidnapped. He says that he has not spoken to anyone at CTU because he couldn't risk putting his family in jeopardy. Jack gives Green his location. He tells her to bring in air support. Green calls Central Dispatch and requests that they find out where Teri and Kim Bauer have been for the last six hours.

11:52: As Tony and Nina are released, Tony asks Green which one of them she intends to suspend. She says neither, as she does not have actionable evidence. Nina plans to monitor the

11AM

commando units that Dispatch sends.

POOR TONY

Tony says that Green worked him pretty hard, and that if Jack hadn't called when he did he might have turned into a nark. Nina thanks Tony for putting himself on the line for her, and promises that she won't forget what he did. Don't trust her, mate, she's a spy.

11:54: Gaines wakes Kevin up. As Kevin announces that Jack is here, Rick slips into the van and speeds off. Gaines orders that the compound gates be sealed. Rick arrives at the shed. The Bauers rush into the van, where they are warned that Gaines knows about Jack's presence. Jack orders everyone to get down as Gaines's men open fire on the van. Gaines punctures one of the tyres, leaving Rick and the Bauers no choice but to abandon the vehicle. Jack makes everyone hide behind the van, as the terrorists continue to spray bullets at the van. Jack returns fire, then throws the palm pilot to Teri and tells her and Kim to go to an abandoned water tower. He will make sure that CTU picks them up there. Teri doesn't want to split up again but, eventually, does as she's told. Jack uses his knife to puncture holes in the van's petrol tank. He orders Rick to run towards the trees, but Rick is shot in the arm as he does so. As a number of terrorists surround the van, Jack shoots at petrol until a spark ignites it and it explodes. Jack helps Rick into the woods.

'YOU MAY REMEMBER ME FROM...'

John Prosky appeared in *Stargate SG-1*, *Artificial Intelligence: A.I.* and *Bowfinger* and played Bart Simon in *Chicago Hope*. Jon H Epstein was David Duchovny's stunt double for several years on *The X-Files*.

BEHIND THE CAMERA

Set Designer Cloudia Rebar worked on *Vanilla Sky*, *Good Burger* and *Who's That Girl?*. Gaffer David St Onge's movies include *Brink!*, *Bad Girls* and *The Karate Kid III*. Second Assistant Director Rebecca Levinson previously worked on *Where Truth Lies*, *Red Shoe Diaries* and *Kiss of a Stranger*. Assistant Director Michael Klick's CV includes *The X-Files*, *Profiler* and *She Spies: Bad Girls Gone Good*.

NOTES

'Our most promising lead continues to be Jack Bauer.' For the second episode running, we see a thoroughly bizarre change in the characters of Kim and, especially, Teri midway through the episode. (See **This is What She's Like?**.) Despite that, here is another episode packed with a lot of really good ideas and action. Seeing Jack charging around the compound like a one-man army on a mission to shoot everything that moves or thinks about moving is exciting enough in its own right, but there's also good work on display in other areas, notably the still-ambiguous nature of Tony's allegiances.

The getaway truck is a Ford Econoline 250 with the licence plate 4NT1848.

CRITIQUE

'24 has been acclaimed as one of the best shows of this season, but the acclaim, while ecstatic, sometimes seems a bit condescending,' noted *All TV*'s Matt Zollar-Seitz. 'The show's concept and format are fresh, with a preposterously tangled narrative, blunt violence and dazzling split-screen imagery. But *24* is much more than a technical stunt. I love *24* for its characterization and performances. Its battered, harried people don't just roam a vast, surprising fictional space. They also illustrate different aspects of a bona fide moral vision - something few TV series, few pop culture works, period, even bother developing.'

CAST AND CREW COMMENTS On the BBC's *24 Heaven* documentary, Howard Gordon confirmed that comparisons between Hillary Clinton[45] and Sherry Palmer *were* brought up on more than one occasion in the writers' room.

DID YOU KNOW? With its big-name star, huge explosions, helicopters and generous location filming *24* is, in comparative terms, an expensive show to produce. Certainly considering the ratings that it initially received. The cost of each episode to Fox is something in the region of $2 million.

11AM

45 Hillary Rodham Clinton: Lawyer, former First Lady and current US Senator. Born 26 October 1947, in Park Ridge, Illinois. The daughter of a prosperous store owner, she graduated from Wellesley College and Yale Law School. In 1975 she married Bill Clinton and practised law whilst her husband became Governor of Arkansas. During this time Hillary gained a reputation for her contributions to issues of women's and children's rights and public education. In the 1992 presidential campaign, she emerged as the dynamic partner of her husband. During the President's impeachment trial in 1998, Hillary earned widespread praise for 'standing by her man.' Preparing for a Senate bid in 2000, representing New York, in order to counter attacks by her opponent, Mayor Rudolph Giuliani, Clinton spent time on listening tours of New York. She subsequently won the Democratic nomination and, on 7 November 2000, became the first sitting First Lady to win elected office. The Clintons have one daughter, Chelsea, who graduated from Stanford University in 2001.

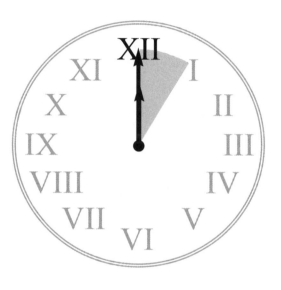

12:00 NOON – 1:00 P.M.

12:00 1:00 2:00 3:00 4:00 5:00 6:00 7:00 8:00 9:00 10:00 11:00 **12:00** 1:00 2:00 3:00 4:00 5:00 6:00 7:00 8:00 9:00 10:00 11:00 12:00

13 12:00 NOON – 1:00 P.M.

US Transmission Date: 19 February 2002
UK Transmission Date: 26 May 2002
Terrestrial UK Transmission Date: 2 June 2002
Writer: Howard Gordon
Director: Stephen Hopkins
Cast: Carlos Bernard (Tony Almeida), Penny Johnson Jerald (Sherry Palmer), Richard Burgi (Kevin Carroll), Daniel Bess (Rick), Devika Parikh (Maureen Kingsley), Michael Massee (Ira Gaines), Zach Grenier (Carl Webb), Jude Ciccolella (Mike Novick), Al Leong (Neill), Tamara Tunie (Alberta Green), Željko Ivanek (Andre Drazen), Christine Avila (Erica Farrell)[46], Ricardo Antonio Chavira (Bundy), Pete Antico (Commando), Misha Collins (Alexis Drazen)[47]

12:02: Gaines orders Neill to cut Jack off at the service road. Teri tries to follow Jack's route, but is forced into a detour.

THE CONSPIRACY STARTS AT CLOSING TIME Tony discovers that Gaines's compound was leased six months ago by a company that, seemingly, does not exist.

12:05: Green notes that she has just found out that Tony and Nina are bringing in Jamey's mother. She suggests that they may wish to question the woman about the $300,000 recently deposited in her bank account. Palmer says that he intends to talk to Kingsley and then go to the district attorney with the evidence that he has, despite Mike's protests. Gaines is on his cell-phone with Drazen, noting that, as he predicted earlier, Jack is at the compound and that Gaines expects to have him captured soon. Gaines wants to complete his contract to kill Palmer. Drazen says that they will talk about that after he sees Jack's body. Gaines tells Kevin that if they don't kill Jack, Drazen will certainly kill them. Kevin suggests that, as he expects CTU backup to arrive at any moment, perhaps they should cut their losses. Gaines responds that no matter where you go, *they* will find you. If they want to live, Jack Bauer must die.

12:10: Jack leads Rick to the water tower, and wonders why Teri and Kim aren't there already. He assesses Rick's wound, telling him that the bullet has passed through his arm without hitting any bones or major arteries.

POINTS AT WHICH TERI NEEDS A SLAP Teri makes Kim stop for a moment whilst checking where they are. But even with the palm pilot, she simply has no idea.

12:16: Palmer tells Sherry about Ferragamo's death. Sherry says that she does not want him to turn his career into a media circus, which is what will happen when Carl and his people have finished twisting the truth. Sherry reminds Palmer that he needs power to fight Carl - the kind of power that he will have once he becomes the President. Jack calls Green and requests that the rescue team pick up Rick even if Jack is not there when they arrive. Rick is apologetic over

----

46 Credited, on-screen, as Erica Farrell but the character's surname is given in dialogue as Vasquez.
47 Uncredited.

what has happened, and blames Dan for getting him into this chaos. This doesn't satisfy Jack, who feels that Rick should have done something when he saw the situation spiralling out of control.

SANCTIMONIOUS GIT Before leaving to kill some more terrorists, Jack gives Rick a little speech about accepting responsibility when presented with a second chance. That's rather hypocritical coming from somebody who has broken as many laws and internal rules as Jack since midnight.

12:20: Teri and Kim hide in an abandoned cabin and narrowly avoid a confrontation with Neill. As he is leaving, Teri has another attack of stomach pain, and cries out, alerting Neill to their location. Jack comes to their rescue, and shoots Neill. After checking to make sure that the coast is clear, Jack leads them back into the woods.

POINTS AT WHICH TERI NEEDS A SLAP Watch out for her flapping-of-hands panic when she realises that she has managed to get herself and Kim lost in the woods. It's *so* far removed from the angry, capable mother who shot the man who raped her, and threatened to kill her daughter, just over an hour earlier that it's scarcely credible.

LIVING BY NUMBERS At this point, the clock stopped at 12:24:48 - all multiples. It's unknown as to whether there was any intended significance in this or if it was merely a coincidence.

12:29: Jamey's mother arrives at CTU. Mrs Vasquez is angry that her daughter was allowed to bleed to death. Tony notes that Jamey was a self-confessed traitor. He warns Vasquez that she could be tried as an accomplice. Nina produces Mrs Vasquez's tax records which indicate that her salary is $45,000 a year. Yet Vasquez has a bank account in her name with over $400,000 in it. Vasquez says that this money was from Jamey for Kyle. Tony wonders where Jamey got the money, but Vasquez argues that she never asked.

KIM'S SHOES Many eagle-eyed *24* fans had spotted, by this stage, the huge discontinuity in Ms Bauer's footwear. Originally, Kim was wearing a pair of brown high-heeled sandals in the early episodes. 'There was so much running involved,' noted Elisha Cuthbert, 'that I got to the point where I had sprained my ankle and I couldn't run in them anymore. I said, if you want me to run fast, you've got to change them.' Costume designer James Lapidus came up with an ingenious solution, a pair of Nike running shoes painted brown and flesh-coloured to look like the sandals. This was a comfortable alternative for Elisha but, sadly, the shoes look so odd that numerous viewers spotted them whenever they were briefly glimpsed on screen. Indeed, word reaches this author of a drinking game played by regular viewers involving Kim's shoes.

12:31: Jack listens to conversations between Gaines and his men on Neill's radio. Palmer finds Maureen packing. The Senator asks why she is leaving, before realising that the reporter already knew about Ferragamo's death. Her announcement that she is quitting the network shocks Palmer. He initially believes that Carl's people have bought her silence, then guesses that they have threatened her. Palmer promises Maureen protection, but she considers that her resignation will protect her. When Palmer berates her for aiding in a cover-up, she suggests that *these people* are too powerful to fight.

Palmer: 'How can I do the job when my own house isn't in order?'

12:35: Gaines and Kevin find Neill's body, with his radio missing. After Vasquez leaves, Tony and Nina discover that the money was transferred from a company called Luca Univox in Belgrade. Nina remembers that Jack once had an assignment in Belgrade. Jack leads Teri and Kim to the creek, but the rescue team have not yet arrived. Kim asks about Rick. Jack says that he was wounded and was told to wait in the tower until the chopper arrives.

POINTS AT WHICH KIM NEEDS A SLAP Kim, with no warning, decides to pick this tense moment to throw her rattle out of her pram and have a *really pointless* tantrum. More significantly, she disobeys Jack by standing up and revealing their location. Gaines, hiding in the trees with a rifle, shoots at them. Luckily, as we've seen before, he's a rotten shot.

12:40: Jack rushes Teri and Kim to a new hiding place. Teri asks Jack where he's going. Jack replies: 'He wants me.' A lengthy game of cat and mouse through the woods between Gaines and Kevin, and Jack, follows. Gaines uses the radio to taunt Jack. Whilst the two indulge in trading insults, Kevin fires a couple of shots, watches the chopper arrive, and flees.

REFERENCES The subplot of Jack getting a radio, discovering the terrorists movements from it, and the subsequent conversations between Jack and Gaines appears to have all been inspired by John McClane's and Hans Gruber's interaction in *Die Hard*.

12PM

12:43: Palmer still intends to tell his story to the D.A. Mike and his men escort the Senator to Carl's room. Carl hints that he has planted evidence which would frame Keith for Ferragamo's murder. The people that they both work for, continues Carl, know how to get what they want. Palmer asks Mike to tell the D.A. that he has made a mistake. Palmer continues that he intends to win the presidency.

12:51: Teri and Kim attract the attention of the CTU helicopter. One of the commandos orders Teri to drop her weapon and asks if she is Mrs Bauer? Teri replies that she is and that Jack needs help.

POINTS AT WHICH KIM NEEDS A SLAP Kim defies direct orders yet again to run into the water tower in search of her beloved kidnapper, Rick. Teri chases her daughter and tries to calm her down when Kim worriedly wonders why Rick isn't where he was supposed to be.

12:53: Jack and Gaines continue their badinage. Jack attempts to appeal to Gaines by suggesting that neither of them has to die. He mentions Cofell and Belgrade in the hope of learning their connection but Gaines claims that he doesn't know any more than Jack does. Jack asks why his family were brought into it. Gaines replies that *they* wanted to make it personal.

With his gun pointed squarely at Gaines's back, Jack again promises Gaines protection. Gaines knows that CTU can't protect him from Drazen. He wishes Jack good luck as he turns and opens fire. Jack shoots first, and kills Gaines. A very bloody Rick waits at a bus stop.

12:57: Teri and Kim wait at the water tower. Jack returns and the three rush to the chopper. As it takes off, Rick is heading to his own destination and Mike escorts Palmer back to his room. At CTU, Green tells Nina that Jack and his family have been rescued. Nina, however, says that the threat on Palmer should be upgraded. After backtracking Jamey's payments to Belgrade, she and Tony have discovered that the same account shows a transfer to a known assassin. There's a second hitter, and he's in Los Angeles now.

LOGIC, LET ME INTRODUCE YOU TO THIS WINDOW Given that it is approximately a 14 hour flight from any part of Central Europe to the West Coast of America, it would be impossible for the second shooter to have left Yugoslavia 'this morning' (i.e. since midnight L.A.-time) and be there by 1:00 PM. Also, of course, this suggests the even bigger question of why he was flying out *at all*, unless Drazen had expected Gaines's operation to fail. If Drazen *did*, then why was Gaines hired in the first place? Mrs Vasquez was originally called Erica Farrell in the script. The name was changed in dialogue, but her on-screen credit remained as Farrell. She is said to earn $45,000 a year. That's a pretty good wage by most standards. But, of course, some people are just greedy. Green notes that $300,000 have been placed in her bank account recently. When we see the transactions, we discover that it's actually $345,000.

Jack's Palm Pilot seems to do additional things each time someone uses it. Specifically, in this case, it appears to give Teri up-to-date positions for the terrorists. This, despite, as Nina noted in the previous episode, the satellite information she sent to the Palm Pilot being several hours old even at that stage. When Gaines shoots at Kim and Jack pulls her to safety, watch closely. Kiefer Sutherland grabs Elisha Cuthbert by the top of her jeans and comes very close to yanking them down completely. Rick pushes past a couple of people to board a bus whilst covered in blood and yet nobody bats an eyelid. Well, this *is* L.A.

'YOU MAY REMEMBER ME FROM...' Misha Collins played Derrick in *Between Us* and Tony in *Girl, Interrupted*. Christine Avila appeared in *Sliver*, *NYPD Blue*, *Dangerous Minds*, *Wonder Woman* and *The Rockford Files*. Ricardo Chavira was in *The Grubbs*, *Six Feet Under* and *JAG*. Pete Antico's stunt-work can be seen in *Pearl Harbor*, *The Rock*, *Crimson Tide*, *F/X: Murder By Illusion* and *Die Hard 2*.

BEHIND THE CAMERA Stunt Co-ordinator Eddy Donno previously worked on *Godzilla*, *Con Air*, *Grosse Pointe Blank*, *Star Trek: First Contact*, *Shattered*, *Die Hard 2*, *Point Break* and *The Hitcher*. Production Assistant Kenneth M Twohy's movies include *Spider-Man*, *Pitch Black*, *Jade* and *Soldier*. Key Grip Mike Reyes worked on *Foolish*.

NOTES 'Congratulations. You may have bought yourself a second chance.' Andrea Newman's action-packed script could have been the final episode of *24*. It does, indeed, manage to tie up many of the series' dangling threads in a mostly satisfying way. If it had ended here, there would still have been lots of questions (notably concerning Palmer's campaign), but at least Teri and Kim would have been safely back with Jack. The final two scenes, however, subtly move the series off in an entirely new direction. The end of the beginning in one way, and the beginning of the end in another.

The man leading the CTU rescue operation is called Bundy. Tony considers him very good at his job. The surnames of other members of Gaines's team include Maxton and Pearson. From Mrs Vasquez's file, her date of birth is given as 10 June 1954. Her social security number is 155-01-6629 and her bank account is 3125784-78850.

CAST AND CREW COMMENTS In an era when television networks are being criticised for a lack of racial and ethnic diversity, Dennis Haysbert is a one-man wrecking crew of stereotypes. 'That's kind of the way I'm built. I lend myself to characters that can't be stereotyped,' he says. 'I don't like stereotypical characters. I always want to be challenged. I want to have something that's out of the ordinary and something that people can look at and say, "Oh, that's interesting." That's why he so loves playing David Palmer, a complex, thoughtful man who is anything but a clichéd, superficial saint. He has issues. But he has so much more.'

'I love that Palmer is a straightforward guy,' he told another interview. 'And that he has a love of his country firmly grasped... And that he's honest.'

DID YOU KNOW? Had a decision been taken not to commission a full series, *24* would have ended at this point with Jack, Teri and Kim together again in the chopper as the final scene of the episode, and the series.

12PM

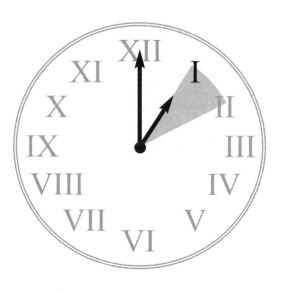

12:00 1:00 2:00 3:00 4:00 5:00 6:00 7:00 8:00 9:00 10:00 11:00 12:00 **1:00** 2:00 3:00 4:00 5:00 6:00 7:00 8:00 9:00 10:00 11:00 12:00

14 1:00 P.M. – 2:00 P.M.

US Transmission Date: 5 March 2002
UK Transmission Date: 2 June 2002
Terrestrial UK Transmission Date: 9 June 2002
Writers: Joel Surnow, Michael Loceff
Director: Jon Cassar
Cast: Carlos Bernard (Tony Almeida), Penny Johnson Jerald (Sherry Palmer), Richard Burgi (Kevin Carroll), Tanya Wright (Patty Brooks), Vicellous Reon Shannon (Keith Palmer), Eric Balfour (Milo Pressman), Jude Ciccolella (Mike Novick), Tamara Tunie (Alberta Green), Željko Ivanek (Andre Drazen), Jon E Epstein (Al), Misha Collins (Alexis Drazen), Paul Schulze (Ryan Chappelle), Kara Zediker (Elizabeth Nash), Judith Scott (Dr Kent), Mina Badie (Agent Holmes), Angelo Pagan (Agent), Henri Lubatti (Jovan Myovic)[48]

1:02: The helicopter delivers the Bauers to CTU. Jack tells Teri that arrangements have been made for her and Kim to see a doctor. Teri wants to stay with Jack, but he has to be debriefed. Green tells Jack that she is placing him under arrest. Jack asks Nina if she will make sure that Teri and Kim are taken care of. Nina subsequently asks Green for an hour to go home and freshen up. Green knows that she is lying and, when Nina tells her the true reason, Green notes that it's ironic that Jack asked Nina to look after Teri, the woman she and Jack hid their torrid affair from. Green then gives Nina the hour that she requested.

LOGIC, LET ME INTRODUCE YOU TO THIS WINDOW In the previous episode the rescue helicopters took over 50 minutes to get from CTU to Gaines's compound. Here, the return trip is made in a little over 10 minutes. How does Nina fail to recognise Jovan, the fake FBI agent, as part of Drazen's team? Come to that, Nina's entire actions at the hospital, and her conversations with the FBI agents, and with Jack, simply do not make sense in light of subsequent revelations. Unless, of course, it was all part of an elaborate and complex plan to get Teri and Kim to the safehouse sooner rather than later. But, if that is the case, and it seems to be the only explanation, then there are some severe dramatic issues to be answered with regard to the narrative point of view that is used in the scenes featuring just Nina and Jovan.

1:07: Sherry warns Palmer that he can't talk publicly about Keith or Ferragamo. Palmer says that he is being blackmailed not to and that his financiers *really* want to see him in the White House. This is what happens when you cover things up, he notes. At the clinic, Dr Kent tells Teri that she has been alerted to Teri's abdominal pain. Teri tells the doctor that she was raped and says that she wishes to keep this knowledge from Jack.

1:15: Mike advises Palmer to meet some important Senators to boost his profile. Keith hears Mike mention Ferragamo and asks how they know him. Palmer tells Keith that Ferragamo died in a fire. Keith, a smart lad, guesses what really occurred and begs his father to go to the police with the truth. Palmer reminds his son that *he* didn't go the police with regard to Gibson.

QUOTE/UNQUOTE Milo: 'What do you think they're gonna do with Jack?' Tony: 'They're not gonna name a street after him!'

1:18: Regional Director Ryan Chappelle arrives at CTU. He meets Jack, and begins recording their conversation. Nina arrives at the clinic, but instead of finding Teri and Kim in their room, she meets an FBI agent who says that his team are there to interrogate the injured prisoners. Nina introduces herself to Teri and Kim and tells them that Jack has asked her to make sure they're taken care of. Teri inquires about Jack, and Nina tells her that he's being questioned. Because this was a terrorist plot, Division, Secret Service and CTU will all want to question him. Nina returns to the room where she met the agent, but he is gone. Speaking to another FBI agent, Nina discovers that the first man appears to be an impostor.

1:29: Jack tells Chappelle that he didn't call CTU earlier because he was worried that things could get out of control. Even though he did *eventually* call, Chappelle says that he can't reinstate Jack because he broke protocol. Jack says that Palmer is still in danger and that he can help. He has, Jack says proudly, never deviated from his original goal of protecting Palmer. Chappelle says that he knows this, and thinks that fact may ultimately save Jack his job, but he still plans to leave it up to the justice system to decide.

LOGIC, LET ME INTRODUCE YOU TO THIS WINDOW When Nina asks if Jack thinks that there is a second mole in CTU, Jack replies that someone had to recruit Jamey. However, as previously discussed, it seems highly unlikely that Jamey knew of Nina's true allegiances, even if Nina *did* know about Jamey's. It's surely more likely that Nina merely suggested Jamey as a possible recruit to the terrorists who, then, passed on her details to Gaines for him to do the actual hiring, rather than have Nina risk exposing herself by approaching Jamey directly. It also, of course, gives Nina a convenient scapegoat to have in case of accidents.

1:31: Green asks Tony if he has found out anything new regarding the backup assassination plan. Tony says that CTU have uncovered three additional shooters, who all entered the country during the past few days. But they can only find the names of two of them. Meanwhile, a mystery gunman is in the desert, spying on passing cars with a set of binoculars.

1:33: Kevin's car and one of the red vans pull up at a shack in the desert. As the terrorists unload the vans Kevin calls Drazen and tells him that they have arrived at the transfer point and that Gaines is dead. He says that he tried to tell Gaines there were gaping holes in his plan. Drazen notes that 'Plan B is already in effect.' The watching gunman detonates a bomb, which blows most of the terrorists to smithereens. Kevin is knocked off his feet and rises to find the gunman standing over him. The man asks if there's anything left in the van. Kevin tells him to go to hell. The gunman shoots Kevin.

LOGIC, LET ME INTRODUCE YOU TO THIS WINDOW It seems, despite Jack's suspicions, that Kevin Carroll was not an alias after all. When Alexis detonates the bomb in the shack, Kevin is holding his gun in his right hand. He is thrown to the ground by the explosion but is still holding the gun. When Alexis reaches him, however, the gun is lying on the ground, some feet away from Kevin's *left* hand. The CTU fingerprint expert that Nina asks Tony to send to the clinic arrives and does his (presumably quite detailed) examination within a ridiculously short space of time. Jack says that Cofell had family connections in the Balkans. Did he? That's never been mentioned before. Jack *fails* to mention Cofell's sudden and implausible acquisition of a Serbian accent, however.

1:41: Tony tells Green that it is important to get Palmer out of L.A. Green bluntly asks if Tony is satisfied with his current position at CTU, noting that she has always believed he was too talented to be third in command. Green says that Chappelle will wish to talk to Tony before making his final evaluation of Jack, as Tony called for the initial lockdown.

SEXUAL POLITICS Green tells Jack that Chappelle has asked her to debrief him. After admitting that she is uncomfortable doing what used to be Jack's job, she asks Jack to tell her what he thinks she should know. Jack wants to call Teri and Kim first. When Green says that she can't allow this, Jack tells her to cut the crap.

1:43: Jack says that they need to search the Balkan terrorist database. When Jack refers to Ted Cofell in the past tense, Green demands an explanation. Jack notes that Cofell is dead.

REFERENCES *Time* magazine is mentioned. Copies of *Forbes* and *USA News* are on the table in Teri's hospital room. There are allusions to the CIA headquarters at Langley, Virginia, and to the Nellis Air Force Base.[49]

1:44: Keith asks his mother to find out why his father has suddenly stopped being interested in exposing the truth. Believing that there is a fine line between covering up an accidental death and covering up what may have been a murder, Keith announces that he is going to the police himself. Sherry orders him not to. Palmer announces that they have to leave the state immediately. Sherry asks why the threat on Palmer has been upgraded if Jack is in custody. Palmer notes that Jack may not have been working alone.

1PM

L.A. STORY Again, the Palmer motorcade is seen on the lengthy Sepulveda Boulevard heading, roughly, in the direction of Los Angeles International Airport.

1:51: Tony is interviewed by Chappelle. Since Tony appears to be the most impartial observer, Jack's fate may rest on his testimony. Tony admits that whilst he is not Jack Bauer's biggest fan, given the circumstances regarding his family, Tony doesn't disagree with a single thing that Jack has done since midnight. Chappelle thanks him, though it's clear this wasn't the answer that he wanted to hear.

BACK STORY Mike gets off the phone with the Pentagon,

49 Nellis is the central part of the Groom Lake facility, a slightly-less-secret-than-it-used-to-be USAF base near Las Vegas, built in the 1950s as a home for America's U-2 spy planes. Also known as Area 51 (or 'Dreamland'), it is home for numerous 'black ops' experimental aircraft programmes (including the revolutionary F-117 stealth fighter). The site, and its surrounding area in the Nevada desert, are also associated - to varying levels of credibility - with numerous UFO sightings and conspiracy theories. The location, and its associated mythology is a key-element in the backstory of TV series like *The X-Files*, *Dark Skies*, *Stargate SG-1* and *Roswell*.

and tells Palmer that Jack Bauer used to be in Special Forces and led a six-man team into Kosovo a couple of years ago. Everything suddenly falls into place for Palmer. He mentions 'the Drazen operation' and notes that, since Jack was the only one from his team who survived, Jack must blame Palmer for the loss of his men.

1:55: Patty asks another of Palmer's aides, Elizabeth, why she is not coming with them to the airport. Elizabeth says that she intends to take a later flight as she is visiting a sick relative.

SEX AND DRUGS AND ROCK 'N' ROLL Elizabeth knocks on a door whilst looking around furtively. The room's occupant is the gunman who earlier killed Kevin. Elizabeth says that she can't stay very long. They then begin to tear each other's clothes off, and passionately kiss.

1:57: Nina calls Green to request permission to move Teri and Kim to a safehouse now. Green grants this. Dr Kent tells Teri that her pain was caused by a burst follicular ovarian cyst. Kent notes that it could have resulted from the assault, or from an enlargement of her womb and she would like Teri to take a pregnancy test. Nina says that Teri and Kim are to be moved to the safehouse. The fake FBI agent watches Nina, Teri and Kim leave the hospital. Palmer arrives at CTU. Tony asks if he can help. Palmer replies that he's come to see Jack Bauer.

'YOU MAY REMEMBER ME FROM...' Kara Zediker played Maria in *Rock Star*, Ellen in *The Sex Monster* and Missy Scroach in *Action*. Mina Badie (Jennifer Jason Leigh's half-sister) was in *Cookies* and *Star Trek: Deep Space Nine*. Henry Lubatti played David Sherman in *Felicity* and appeared in *Angel*. Angelo Pagan was in *Almost a Woman* and *Virus*. Paul Schulze was Father Phil in *The Sopranos*, and appeared in *Flirt* and *Panic Room*. Judith Scott was in *CSI: Crime Scene Investigation*, *Forever Knight*, *Virtual Sexuality* and *L.A. Doctors*.

BEHIND THE CAMERA Jon Cassar previously worked on *Danger Beneath the Sea*, *Mutant X*, *Queen of Swords*, *CHiPs '99*, *La Femme Nikita*, *Psi Factor: Chronicles of the Paranormal*, *Profiler*, *Due South*, *Forever Knight*, *Ghost Mom*, *Hurt Penguins*, *Popcorn* and *The Cutting Edge*.

NOTES 'I've been through hell today.' After the frantic pace of the previous two or three episodes, this one actually feels like something of a comedown. The chill-out after the rave, if you like. This is mainly because Jack is confined to an interrogation room for virtually the entire episode. Conceptually, of course, this is very much a pilot script for 'season one, part two' and it very much feels like that with a lot of stray plots being dropped and some new ones initiated. There are a few very nice scenes, the episode never gets boring, despite being rather talky, and the ending is a corker. But the logic is really starting to get stretched in places.

Kevin boasts to Drazen that he used to work for the Drug Enforcement Agency in Florida and that he once managed to assassinate a witness that no-one else could find. Chappelle says that he has five priority cases on his desk and that Jack's name is on all of them. Mike mentions two Senators whom, he feels, David needs to be seen cultivating the support of; Blalock and Gleeson. Two of the three suspected shooters are Jovan

Myovic who entered the US two days ago and Mishko Suba, who came in the day before that through Florida.

CRITIQUE

'Both Fox's *24* and ABC's *Alias* seek to make action-packed suspense as entertaining as, say, a hospital drama or some courtroom caper,' wrote Tim Goodman. '*24* became the buzz show early on with critics. In poll after poll they've called it the best show on TV - even beating *The West Wing* and *The Sopranos*.' Calling *24* 'required viewing,' Goodman also noted that: 'To miss an episode of *24* and its heart-pounding background music is to feel as if you've put down a great book to do the dishes.'

CAST AND CREW COMMENTS

'For me,' Dennis Haysbert told the BBC, 'the motivating factor in playing Senator Palmer is not so much the power. [It's] having integrity, knowing that I represent so many people.'

Kiefer Sutherland is not surprised to hear Haysbert espouse these sentiments: 'There is a period quality to Dennis; he's not very cynical. When people play kings for a long period of time, they start to become quite regal. Dennis has embraced that character and given it a kind of dignity. He takes the role on with [a] huge level of awareness of responsibility of that character. I keep waiting for Dennis to walk in one day and have his own Secret Service. When he starts work, his voice drops a notch. He gets very deep.'

DID YOU KNOW?

This episode was originally broadcast in the US on the day of the *real* 2002 California Primary.

1PM

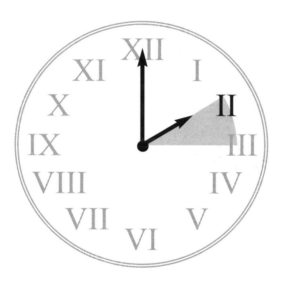

2:00 P.M. – 3:00 P.M.

12:00 1:00 2:00 3:00 4:00 5:00 6:00 7:00 8:00 9:00 10:00 11:00 12:00 1:00 2:00 3:00 4:00 5:00 6:00 7:00 8:00 9:00 10:00 11:00 12:00

15 2:00 P.M. – 3:00 P.M.

US Transmission Date: 12 March 2002
UK Transmission Date: 9 June 2002
Terrestrial UK Transmission Date: 16 June 2002
Writer: Michael Chernuchin
Director: Jon Cassar
Cast: Carlos Bernard (Tony Almeida), Penny Johnson Jerald (Sherry Palmer), Daniel Bess (Rick), Eric Balfour (Milo Pressman), Tamara Tunie (Alberta Green), Željko Ivanek (Andre Drazen), Misha Collins (Alexis Drazen), Paul Schulze (Ryan Chappelle), Kara Zediker (Elizabeth Nash), Kevin Ramsey (Agent Ted Paulson), Sam Ayres (Agent Breeher), Wade Andrew Williams (Robert Ellis), Logan Alexander (Lenny), Nina Landey (Amanda).

SEX AND DRUGS AND ROCK 'N' ROLL Elizabeth and the gunman, Alexis, have what appears to be rather splendid sex in his hotel room.

> **2:02:** Tony realises that he cannot stall Palmer for much longer. He calls Chappelle who tells Tony not to give Palmer clearance until he assesses the situation himself. Tony asks Milo if he has any new information on the backup shooters. Milo says that one is likely to be Alexis Drazen who arrived in the US on Saturday, stopped in D.C. and is now thought to be in Los Angeles.

LOGIC, LET ME INTRODUCE YOU TO THIS WINDOW Two episodes ago, Nina said that CTU had sources claiming that an assassin had left Yugoslavia *that morning*. Now, we find that there are actually *three* shooters, and that they have all been in the US for at least a couple of days. Of course, this could be another example of Nina's nefarious skulduggery, of her trying to get CTU looking in the wrong direction, perhaps. One can perfectly understand how Palmer may not have realised until this moment that today is the second anniversary of Operation Nightfall, after all he's got a lot on his mind today what with the election and so on. But what about Jack?

> **2:04:** Jack requests a break from Green, so that he can speak to Teri and Kim. He's angry when Green tells him that they are on their way to a safehouse with Nina. Elizabeth says that she didn't think she would see Alexis again after D.C. She notes that Palmer has to go to Nevada.

> **2:07:** Palmer calls a friend in the Defense Department to get clearance to see Jack and soon Chappelle receives a call from Alan Optican at the Pentagon. Chappelle, with no other choice, says that Palmer can see Jack. Tony enters the holding room to tell Jack that Nina has called; Teri and Kim are fine, and are being guarded by Paulson and Breeher.

BACK STORY Jack greets Palmer in the conference room with surprise. Palmer says that he knows why Jack wants him dead. Jack doesn't know what Palmer is talking about, so Palmer reminds him about events in the Balkans two years previously. Jack is confused as to how Palmer knows about Operation Nightfall.

2PM

Palmer says that *he* authorised the mission. He is well aware that Jack terminated Victor Drazen with extreme prejudice. He also knows that six of Jack's men died in the battle. Angry that Palmer is insinuating he is seeking revenge, Jack sarcastically notes that he, apparently, wants revenge on the Senator so badly that he has almost died today trying to protect him. Jack says that if he blames anyone for the loss of his men, he blames himself. Palmer asks what Jack was doing at the power plant. Jack explains that he went for Hayes's gun to create a diversion and to get Palmer out of the room. He continues that the people who want Palmer dead had kidnapped his wife and daughter. Jack guesses that no one bothered to inform Palmer. He says that Chappelle can verify the bulk of his story. At least, the parts about Teri and Kim having been kidnapped. A formerly apoplectic Palmer is left speechless and, seemingly, chastened.

REFERENCES There's a dialogue allusion to Fatboy Slim's 'Right Here, Right Now'. Teri uses the True Blue 'Easy, Three Minute' pregnancy test. The *Los Angeles Times* is mentioned. Also, Exodus 21:23 ('An eye for an eye').

> **2:16:** Nina, Teri and Kim arrive at the leafy, suburban safehouse. Agents Ted Paulson and Jeff Breeher are waiting to meet them. Teri goes to the bathroom and uses the opportunity to take the pregnancy test.

REAL WORLD JUNCTION Victor Drazen's activities in Kosovo are a chilling reminder of the real world horrors of the recent series of civil wars in the Balkans. These raged throughout the 1990s and saw some of history's most dreadful acts of mass murder.

Yugoslavia was, frankly, an accident waiting to happen. Created in the inter-war years from a number of independent states, the country was, for many decades, wracked with nationalist and separatist tensions. Declarations of independence by the former Yugoslav Republics of Slovenia, Macedonia and Croatia in July 1991, led to heavy fighting between the Croatian militia and Serbian insurgents (*Chetniks*) backed by the mainly-Serb Yugoslav Federal Army. Yugoslavia officially ceased to exist in January 1992. A few months later, Muslim leaders in Bosnia-Herzegovina also declared their independence. Bosnian Serbs and the Serbian leadership in Belgrade rejected this and a horrific war began with the siege of the Bosnian capital, Sarajevo. Bosnian Serbs were subsequently accused of a programme of ethnic cleansing (which basically amounted to racial genocide) to secure territorial domination. Some of the worst atrocities happened in Srebenica and Gorazde. The war seemed to have ended with the Dayton Peace Agreement, brokered by Bill Clinton in 1995, which recognised Bosnian independence. However, the new Yugoslavia (comprising Serbia and Montenegro), under the leadership of Slobodan Milosevic continued to use Serbian nationalism as a weapon of total war.[50]

• •

50 Born on 29 August 1941, in Pozarevac, Serbia, tragedy marked Slobodan Milosevic's family life, with both of his parents committing suicide. Milosevic met his wife, Mirjana Markovic, during high school, when they were members of the same Communist youth committee. After graduating from the University of Belgrade in 1964 with a law degree, Milosevic gained a series of positions within the Communist party apparatus. In 1984, when his friend Ivan Stambolic became the leader of Serbia's Communist party, Milosevic became chief of the party organisation in Belgrade. The turning point in Milosevic's transformation from an obscure regional

BACK STORY Palmer explains to Jack his position on the senate three years ago, when the CIA notified him of numerous massacres carried out by Serbian warlord Victor Drazen in Kosovo. When the usual channels were of no help in ending Drazen's reign of terror, Palmer turned to the one person whom he knew could get results, Robert Ellis. Palmer says that his senate committee funded Ellis, a wetworks expert, whose job was to implement the mission whilst maintaining plausible deniability. Ellis appears not to have done a very good job, since both Jack and Palmer have ended up on someone's hitlist, notes Jack. He understands that if *they*, meaning presumably, the remnants of Drazen's private army, could track down both himself and Palmer, then they could certainly do likewise with Ellis. Meanwhile, in a dark New Orleans nightclub Ellis, a well built, sombre man, is playing dice.

QUOTE/UNQUOTE Ellis, when his opponent says that he could tell Ellis was bluffing by reading his eyes: 'If you could read what's in my eyes, you'd crawl under a rock, and cry!'

2:19: Ellis is neither happy to hear the Senator's voice, nor to learn that Jack Bauer is in the same room. Ellis says that he went to a lot of trouble to make sure that they would never meet. Palmer replies that someone close to Victor Drazen has connected them and now, apparently, they want revenge. Ellis tells Jack that if they want to crack this case, he and Palmer will need

Communist official to the volatile leader of Yugoslavia was his appearance, in April 1987, before a riotous crowd of Serbs in Pristina, the capital of Kosovo, Serbia's dominant province. When Milosevic told the Serbs, who were upset about their treatment at the hands of Kosovo's Albanian majority, 'No one will ever beat you again!' he established his reputation as a champion of Serbian nationalism. His growing powerbase among dissatisfied Serbs allowed Milosevic to wrestle control of the party and he become President in September 1987. His goal as party leader was the annexation of Kosovo, which had been granted autonomous status by General Tito. In March 1989, rioting by Milosevic's supporters led to the sweeping replacement of the provincial leaderships of Vojvodina and Kosovo, most of the control over these provinces was ceded to Belgrade. Faced with Serbia's growing power, the other Yugoslav republics began to break away, beginning with Slovenia in 1991. Only Montenegro was to remain with Serbia as part of an increasingly isolated Yugoslavia. The disintegration was marked by a series of civil wars pitting Serbs against Slovenes, Croats, and Bosnians. As the decade continued, Milosevic intensified the struggle to advance Serbian interests in Kosovo. He used a powerful police force and an obedient media to silence any opposition. Exact numbers vary, but by 1999 hundreds of thousands of Albanian Kosovans were believed to have either been executed or forced to live in refugee camps. Milosevic's ruthless attitude towards negotiations with NATO led to the commencement, in March 1999, of air strikes, spearheaded by the US and Britain. Despite the devastation that ensued, Milosevic - whom President Bill Clinton called 'Europe's last dictator' - managed to remain in power. In the fall of 2000, Milosevic called a general election, hoping to capitalise on the Serbian people's resentment towards the West's economic sanctions and the NATO bombing campaign. In an unexpected turn of events, the democratic opposition mustered its strength behind Vojislav Kostunica, a hitherto obscure lawyer, propelling him to victory. When Milosovic refused to accept the result, Kostunica alleged widespread electoral fraud and his supporters organising a national strike in protest. On 5 October 2000, several hundred thousand Serbs stormed and burned the federal Parliament building in Belgrade which signalled the collapse of Milosevic's reign of terror. For the next six months, however, Milosevic continued to live in the official Presidential residence. Early in the morning of 1 April 2001, police arrested Milosevic after an all-night siege, during which Milosovic brandished a gun and threatened to kill himself, his wife, and their daughter. He eventually surrendered and in June was transferred to the International War Crimes Tribunal in the Hague, where he remains, having been indicted over his actions in Kosovo.

to work closely with each other. Jack says that he's currently under investigation and that his hands are tied. Ellis recommends that Jack get himself reinstated with CTU somewhat quickly and suggests that Palmer may be able to help.

LOGIC, LET ME INTRODUCE YOU TO THIS WINDOW When did Rick write down his cellphone number for Kim? Ellis mentions that Milo has been in touch with MI5. Why would he be talking to them? That's the British *internal* security service. The *external* one is MI6. How does Palmer still have Ellis's cellphone number to hand after two years? Surely a man as security conscious as Ellis would have changed it by now? Kim's hairstyle changes radically between two relatively short scenes. She can't have washed and styled it *that* quickly. Not an error, *per se*, just an observation: Could the miniskirts of those two café waitresses *be* any shorter?

2:21: Teri's test has produced a positive result. A surprised Elizabeth meets Sherry in the hotel hallway. Afterwards she calls Alexis, who is having lunch with Andre. Elizabeth notes that Palmer may not be going to Nevada. The sound of a woman laughing causes Andre to muse that she looks like Martina. Alexis notes that their sister is dead. Andre changes the subject, asking if Alexis has spoken to Jovan and Mishko. Alexis replies that the pair have been given their targets.

2:24: Kim sees the pregnancy test box. Teri says that Kent wanted her to take it as a precaution. She admits to Kim that she is pregnant and explains that this has nothing to do with the rape, the father is most definitely Jack.

POINTS AT WHICH KIM NEEDS A SLAP As it's only been two hours since her last tantrum, Kim gets quite a lip-on, storming out of the room in high dudgeon that her parents had not consulted her in their family planning decisions. Teri yells that *she* wasn't expecting the baby either and informs Kim that birth control isn't always 100% effective. Teri reminds her daughter that once in a while Kim might like to think about what others are going through rather than always concentrating on herself.

2:31: Jack and Palmer continue their three-way conference call with Ellis regarding potential suspects. Teri and Kim share a meal in the kitchen. Kim asks Teri when she is planning to tell Jack about their forthcoming addition to the family. Teri decides to tell him immediately, so she calls CTU. Tony answers, but says that now is a bad time to speak to Jack. Teri asks Tony to have Jack call her back at the first opportunity he gets. Nina announces that she needs to start debriefing them, beginning with Teri. When she's alone, Kim calls Rick whilst he's in the process of dressing his wound. Kim suggests that Rick turn himself in and says that she will tell the police he helped them to escape. Rick suggests that she try not to tell them anything. Kim notes that they are about to begin interrogating her. Rick reminds Kim that bringing her to Gaines was kidnapping, a fairly serious crime.

EVEN MEN SOMETIMES CRY Palmer and Jack share some amused comments on how the day's events have nothing to do with Palmer running for President, the primary or him being black, all of the suspected reasons. Palmer uses Jack's shoulder to cry on regarding his not being there for Keith. Palmer says that it's not easy being the son of a politician. Jack suggests that, in fact, it's not easy being a son or a daughter. Or a father. Palmer asks if Teri and Kim are okay. Jack wishes that he knew.

2:43: Milo gives Jack and Palmer various Operation Nightfall information that Ellis has sent. Palmer alerts Jack to a key piece of evidence that was omitted from the initial reports. Victor Drazen's wife and daughter were, it seems, in a bunker that Jack's team blew up. They are reported to have died in the explosion.

MOTIVE Suddenly the entire day's events become clear. Revenge is the motive. Palmer asks who has the authority to add additional security to Teri and Kim. Jack notes that Chappelle does.

2:45: Nina asks Teri about Rick. Teri says that he gave them a gun and helped them escape. She doesn't, however, know anything else about him. Teri notes that Kim hasn't grown out of her problems like friends said she would once she became a teenager. She is surprised when Nina seems sure that Kim will be all right based on what Jack told her. Jack's job seemed so secretive to Teri that she can't picture him talking to anyone about his family.

THE OTHER WOMAN Teri wonders if Jack ever talked about her whilst they were separated. Nina says that he never discussed his marriage. Teri says that after they got back together, Jack told her that he had been with someone else during the separation. From looks exchanged when they got off the chopper, Teri guesses that it was Nina with whom Jack had an affair. Nina admits that she did sleep with Jack but that he soon realised that it was a mistake. Teri asks if Nina thought it was a mistake as well.

QUOTE/UNQUOTE Nina: 'I realise this is a terrible time for you to discover all this.' Teri: 'When do you think a *good* time would be?'

2:53: Palmer tells Jack to continue with the investigation and to keep him informed of developments. Jack notes that he is still under arrest. Palmer goes to Chappelle and demands that Jack be given his old privileges back. Chappelle claims that the agency would be held in contempt if Jack were reinstated without a hearing. Jack says that he doesn't have to be reinstated permanently; just give him provisional status until the end of the day. Chappelle submits, giving Jack what he asks for. Palmer tells Jack that the Secret Service want him to leave the state immediately. Jack agrees with this. Palmer tells Jack that he has no intention of leaving. The alternative is that they, and their families, will live in fear for the rest of their lives. Palmer apologises for misjudging Jack.

2:55: Nina asks Kim whether Rick was one of the kidnappers. Kim says that Rick was just as surprised as she was when the kidnapping began. Nina thinks that Kim is lying. Nina speaks to Jack on the phone who says that additional teams are being sent to the safehouse as he believes that Teri and Kim are terrorist targets too. He subsequently speaks to Teri.

POINTS AT WHICH TERI NEEDS A SLAP Given her discovery of Jack's affair with Nina, Teri has changed her mind about telling Jack about her pregnancy.

2:58: Ellis returns Jack's call and says that he hasn't located an important missing file. Hopefully, with what he has sent, Milo will be able to retrieve it. Ellis enters the men's room whilst still talking to Jack. As Ellis is about to answer one of Jack's questions, he is choked to death. Jack calls out Ellis's name as the sounds of strangulation continue.

'YOU MAY REMEMBER ME FROM...' Wade Williams played Ted Daniels in *Erin Brokovich* and was in *Terror Tract, Ali, Enterprise, Buffy the Vampire Slayer, The X-Files, Route 9* and *Star Trek: Voyager*. Sam Ayers was Sam the Sweeper in *The Pretender*. Kevin Ramsey appeared in *Play On!*

NOTES 'If this is about revenge, it has to be some-body either connected to you or your team.' At last, David Palmer and Jack Bauer come together and the sparks fly. In terms of *24* being, essentially, an 'action series', with its thrills largely coming from major set-pieces rather than atmosphere, this is something of a letdown. The Palmer/Jack scenes wildly fluctuate between sinister interrogation to bluster and posturing then on to mutual respect *far* too quickly. However, there's a much bigger problem with this particular episode: having, mostly, taken the audience with them during their kidnapping ordeal, Teri and Kim are, sadly, starting to get *really* annoying again.

Palmer was head of a Special Defense Appropriations Committee in the Senate. This was, he says, basically a euphemism for covert operations. Milo's log-in code for the CTU computer system is LFN. His password is 'foothill94022'. Ellis suggests that the conspiracy may be funded through fronted accounts in Belgium. Jack mentions a North African man named Rene Bonniere whom CTU suspected of trying to set up terrorist cells in the US. The Libyan Ambassador, notes Palmer, probably helped to keep Drazen's money hidden.

SOUNDTRACK 'I'm On the Wonder', 'Barely Available' and 'Louisiana Two-Step' by Clifton Chenier (the latter accompanies Ellis's death), Marvin Pontiac's 'I'm a Doggy' and 'Clocks Grow Old' by I Am Spoonbender.

CRITIQUE 'The series is a running battle between good and evil played out at fever pitch. Episode by episode and scene by scene, *24* insists that human lives are defined by actions, not words, and that the decisions we make under pressure reveal who we truly are,' wrote the doyen of *24* critics, Matt Zoller-Seitz. 'It all sounds simplistic when you read it on the page. But *24* is the most morally sophisticat-ed series on TV. Good guys pretend to be bad guys; bad guys pretend to be good guys; good guys pretend to be bad guys pretending to be good guys. They're all under pres-sure; they do what they have to do to survive and win. With its emphasis on tactical lies, hastily improvised cover-ups and sustained, secretive role-playing, it shows how it's pos-sible to be an immoral person in a moral enterprise (like the moles and betrayers work-ing inside the hero's counter-terrorist office), or a moral person in immoral circumstances.'

CAST AND CREW COMMENTS Penny Johnson Jerald notes that 'The writers took an opportunity to show a real person. You can't forget that [Sherry] can be quite sweet and loveable, and she's still a mother and a wife. Yet because of circumstances, she's torn between saving the day for her husband, so to speak, and making a mess of her marriage. Saving her husband, I guess, was more important to her.' The Palmer family's *Macbeth*-like struggle promises to continue in the second season of *24*. 'I have some idea of what's going on with Sherry,' says Jerald though she adds that she would rather not know the entire story. 'Then you find yourself anticipating [what's next], and that doesn't equal honesty on the screen. You want some kind of spontaneity. People tell me that they love to hate me, but they're excited about [the character] coming back.'

DID YOU KNOW? The harsh minimalist design of the CTU offices - excessive use of blue light and chrome surfaces - drew much comment and praise from both fans and critics. Interestingly, the set is actually a real office in the Fox Television production building.

Once notorious for being a hard-partying dude, with a healthy taste for the babes and the booze, Kiefer Sutherland readily admits that he wasn't exactly a paragon of virtue in his 20s. 'There were times when I'd go out and have a few drinks. Often too many,' he confesses. 'But if I did half the things I've heard that I've done, I'd be dead by now.' Still, a questionable personal reputation, coupled with a number of box-office bombs, had convinced Sutherland that it was time for a break. As noted, he joined the rodeo circuit in the early 90s, where he quickly excelled, winning prize belts for roping. What was supposed to have been a brief hiatus - 'seven or eight months, at the most' - however, ended up lasting nearly two years. 'Hollywood's a very fast merry-go-round. If you hop off you're going to need a running start to get back on again,' Kiefer admits. This may have temporarily hurt his career, but Sutherland says that the extended vacation actually did him the world of good. Though he has managed to earn back a wealth of industry respect, Sutherland has not been as lucky when it comes to his personal life. 'My [second] wife and I separated a year and half ago,' he says, adding that, whilst he has gone on 'a few dates' recently, these days he doesn't have too much leisure time. 'The hour-long drama is a time-consuming machine. It's the one thing everybody warned me about,' he adds. 'I'm just trying to figure out how to maintain that schedule.'

2PM

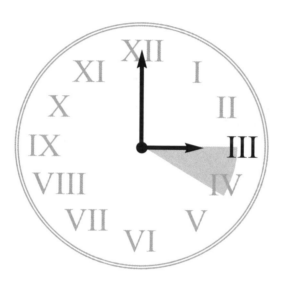

3:00 P.M. – 4:00 P.M.

12:00 1:00 2:00 3:00 4:00 5:00 6:00 7:00 8:00 9:00 10:00 11:00 12:00 1:00 2:00 **3:00** 4:00 5:00 6:00 7:00 8:00 9:00 10:00 11:00 12:00

16   3:00 P.M. – 4:00 P.M.

US Transmission Date: 19 March 2002
UK Transmission Date: 16 June 2002
Terrestrial UK Transmission Date: 23 June 2002
Writers: Robert Cochran, Howard Gordon
Director: Stephen Hopkins
Cast: Penny Johnson Jerald (Sherry Palmer), Xander Berkeley (George Mason), Daniel Bess (Rick), Vicellous Reon Shannon (Keith Palmer), Megalyn Echikunwoke (Nicole Palmer), Glenn Morshower (Aaron Pierce), Zach Grenier (Carl Webb), Eric Balfour (Milo Pressman), Željko Ivanek (Andre Drazen), Misha Collins (Alexis Drazen), Kara Zediker (Elizabeth Nash), Henri Lubatti (Jovan Myovic), Kevin Ramsey (Agent Ted Paulson), Sam Ayres (Agent Breeher), Pauley Perrette (Tanya), Navi Rawat (Melanie), Wade Andrew Williams (Robert Ellis)[51]

3:02: As Ellis lies dead on the men's room floor, Jack rings Agent Watson in CTU's New Orleans office. Jack tells Watson that he fears Ellis may have been murdered. Milo has received case files on all three assassins. One is Victor Drazen's son. Elizabeth tells Alexis that Palmer has changed his plans. Alexis says that he will be back at the hotel by 4:30.

LOGIC, LET ME INTRODUCE YOU TO THIS WINDOW Why does Jack continue shouting Bob Ellis's name? It's blatantly apparent to anybody who's ever watched a movie that a telephone line suddenly going quiet, except for the sounds of strangulation, usually means that the person you were talking to is now dead. When Andre's and Alexis's CTU files are visible on Jack's computer, the keen-eyed viewer can spot some brilliant mistakes. The two Drazen brothers' birth dates are, it seems, just three months apart. (Alexis was born on 24 January 1957; Andre, who most of the dialogue, here and elsewhere, suggests is the older brother, on 10 April 1957.) Impossible, of course. But, hang on; that makes gorgeous, hunky Alexis 45 years old?![52] Victor Drazen's date of birth is given in Andre's file as 28 February 1947. Thus making him aged 10 when his sons were born. Victor's wife, Elena, was seemingly *six* when she gave birth to Alexis and Andre. (Her birth date is in 1951.) We've all heard *rumours* about child brides in Central Europe, but that's *ridiculous*. Alexis told Elizabeth that his business was running an export company in Berlin. Doesn't she know the difference between a German accent and a Balkans one? Come to that, Alexis isn't a very Germanic-sounding name, is it? The Drazen brothers are shown as having both attended Zagreb University. Given that this is in the Croatian part of the former Yugoslavia, one suspects that *their* presence gave rise to some fun and games during their time on campus.

3PM

3:06: At Palmer's headquarters, CTU have sent photos of the three suspected assassins which Pierce shows to the staff. Seeing Alexis shocks Elizabeth and Palmer notices her distress.

POINTS AT WHICH TERI NEEDS A SLAP Resuming her debriefing, Teri tells Nina that

. . . .

51 Uncredited. The character of Ellis appears only as a corpse in this episode.
52 Another computer file gives Alexis's age as 35, indicating that the year of his birth should be *1967*.

she won't hold Nina's illicit affair with her husband against Nina personally. That's big of her, isn't it? Nina says that she believes Kim is withholding information about Rick. Teri, rudely, replies that Kim is her daughter, and Teri believes she knows her much better than Nina does.

3:08: Palmer calls Jack, and tells him that Elizabeth has identified Drazen's son. Jack asks what sort of contact she has had with Drazen. 'Intimate,' whispers Palmer. The Senator tells Jack that Elizabeth wants to help so Jack sends a helicopter to bring her to CTU for questioning. Jack also notes that they have to assume that Ellis is dead.

3:15: Kim rings Rick again and, again, suggests that Rick turn himself in, noting that she is not sure how much longer she can cover for him. His conversation is observed by his girlfriend, the surly looking Melanie.

'NICE PAD, MAN' Rick's horribly dated 1970s *Get Carter*-style pad contains a pinball machine, a purple lava lamp, two bead curtains, a glitter ball, various neon bar signs, dozens of unwashed shirts and, less surprisingly, a *very* skanky girlfriend.

3:17: Teri tells Nina that things tend to get complicated when you screw your boss. Nina suggests that her presence during the debrief is clearly counterproductive. She says that it will be for the best if she leaves the safehouse and lets Paulson finish the questioning.

POINTS AT WHICH TERI NEEDS A SLAP She really is *the* most unsympathetic and annoying woman when she puts her mind to it. Her baiting of Nina who, as she freely admitted herself less than an hour ago, is one of the main reasons why she and Kim are still alive, would be insulting if it wasn't so comically misjudged. We get regular appearances, too, of her 'victim face' (it's more or less the same one she uses when crying on Jack's shoulder as when she's pointing barbed, nasty comments in Nina's general direction). Still, at least she's stopped wincing with pain twice per episode by now. What a pity *that* turned out to be something trivial.

3:19: George Mason returns to CTU, having been sent in by Chappelle to replace Alberta Green. Mason asks about Victor Drazen's sons. He says that he knows why they are after Jack but is unsure about their motives in targeting Palmer. Jack mentions the developments with Elizabeth. Mason wants to have Alexis arrested immediately, but Jack suggests that if Elizabeth stages her date, this could give CTU a golden opportunity.
    Palmer tells Keith that he knows he cannot earn his son's trust overnight, but from now if Keith has any problems then he knows that he can come to his father. Jovan sits in a parked car, telling Andre Drazen by telephone, that he has found Bauer's wife and daughter.

3:28: Jack asks Milo if he has noticed anyone unusual accessing these files. Milo says no, but then he hasn't been looking for this. Keith calls Carl and suggests that they should meet. Keith needs Nicole's help to slip past the Secret Service. Reluctantly, Nicole agrees.

QUOTE/UNQUOTE Nicole, when Keith argues that he's trying to protect her: 'The last time you tired to protect me, somebody died!'

3:31: With Nicole's assistance, Keith slips out unnoticed. Mason and Jack greet the newly arrived, and rather bitter, Elizabeth. Jack asks if Elizabeth would be willing to keep her appointment with Alexis and plant a tracking device on him. Elizabeth is initially reluctant to see Alexis again, but then agrees. Breeher senses that something is wrong just as Jovan slips into the safehouse with a dart gun and shoots him in the neck.

REFERENCES Parts of this episode (the location, the car accidentally rolling down the hill, the amnesia subplot) are very reminiscent of aspects of David Lynch's *Mulholland Drive*. There's a reference to Spike Lee's *Do The Right Thing*. Nina alludes to 'Stockholm Syndrome', the psychological state in which kidnap victims can come to empathise and become emotionally bonded with their abductors, named after a famous hostage situation in Sweden, in 1973.

3:41: Paulson looks out a safehouse window and notices the unattended lawn mower. He moves Kim and Teri into a bedroom and gets them to lock the door. During a confrontation with Jovan, Paulson is stabbed in the back by Suba. Teri and Kim escape into the garage and find a parked car. A dying Paulson shoots Suba in the back as Jovan gets into his car and speeds off after Teri and Kim. Jack is on his way to join Elizabeth in the helicopter when he sees Nina returning to CTU. Nina tells Jack that she left Kim and Teri in Paulson's and Breeher's hands.

Teri tries to lose Jovan by taking a detour onto a dirt track next to a steep cliff. Teri tells Kim to wait in the car and gets out to make sure that they have lost their pursuer. The car slips over the cliff, crashes and bursts into flames. Teri faints.

L.A. STORY The Griffith Observatory has been a major Los Angeles landmark since 1935. A domed Art Deco monument on the southern slope of Mount Hollywood, it commands a stunning view of the Los Angeles basin below and of the famous Hollywood sign to the right. A gift to the city by philanthropist Griffith J Griffith, the Observatory's purpose is to provide information on astronomy to the general public. It is also a perennial favourite of generations of Hollywood filmmakers, probably best known as the location for the climax of Nicholas Ray's *Rebel Without a Cause*. (A bronze bust of that film's tragic star, James Dean, is one of the site's many icons.) The observatory, and its beautiful towering hexagonal monument,[53] have also memorably featured in dozens of TV series[54] and in numerous movies like *The Terminator*[55] and *Bowfinger*.

3PM

The location of the car chase and, specifically, the spot where Teri and Kim park their car, is yet another part of Mulholland Drive, this one close to the intersection with Laurel Canyon Boulevard and commanding a quite spectacular view of the Valley.

• •

53 The monument celebrates the work of several of history's greatest astronomers. These include: Sir Isaac Newton (1642-1727), Johan Kepler (1571-1630), Christiaan Huygens (1629-95), Galileo Galilei (1564-1642) and William Herschel (1732-1822).

54 An excellent recent example of its use was in the *Angel* episode 'Are You Now, Or Have You Ever Been?'

55 Readers may recognise the observatory best from the memorable opening sequence of *The Terminator* in which Arnie arrives from the future, stark naked, and asks a group of young men, nicely, for their clothes.

3:52: A belligerent Keith meets Carl who says that passing off Gibson's death as an accident will be a hard sell. Keith replies that Carl is now involved in two cover-ups. The people who fund Palmer's campaign aren't going to be happy and will probably see to it that Carl is the fall guy. Carl tells Keith that evidence was left in Ferragamo's office that would lead directly to Keith. The fire marshals didn't find it, but it would be easy for someone to point them in the right direction. Carl says that this is why Keith's father backed off. Carl leaves. Keith, however, has taped the conversation. Teri regains consciousness. In a daze, she wanders back towards the main road.

3:55: A car pulls over, and the woman driver asks if Teri is okay. Teri doesn't reply. The driver asks what her name is. Teri says she doesn't remember. The concerned driver tells Teri to get in. Kim, meanwhile, climbs back to the road, calling out for her mother.

LOGIC, LET ME INTRODUCE YOU TO THIS WINDOW Jovan can take out at least four well-armed and experienced CTU agents, but he can't, seemingly, catch two untrained women? Even given the hair-raising nature of Teri and Kim's escape from Jovan, what kind of idiot parks a car *that* close to the edge of a whopping great drop? Rather asking for trouble, isn't it? And just how did Kim manage to extract herself from her seat-belt and throw herself clear of the car in the, approximately, two seconds that it takes to roll down the hill, crash, and become a molten fireball? Finally, a brief word about the (audience's intelligence insulting) amnesia storyline. As Carl says: 'Oh brother...'

WHOSE IDEA WAS IT? I FORGET... It's interesting that, post-season, nobody seemed willing to take the blame for what is, unquestionably, the worst single plot idea in a popular TV show since *Dallas* thought it could get away with Bobby's resurrection in the shower. 'I always thought [the amnesia storyline] was a bit dodgy,' says Stephen Hopkins. 'And I was right.' Interestingly, Hopkins himself once reportedly suffered from amnesia for five hours whilst he was filming *Lost in Space*. So, *that*'s his excuse...?

Leslie Hope noted: 'I was certainly the butt of all the jokes for the three or four episodes, or however long it was. I'd say "Morning, Kiefer, how are you?" He'd say "I don't remember"!'

'[Teri] was a problem,' noted Virgil Williams. 'She'd been raped, kidnapped twice, shot at, didn't know where her husband was. We wanted Teri to just collapse in a ditch for two or three hours. Acceptable, believable, sellable. But the networks said we couldn't *not* use her, we can't have her just sleeping.' The writers thus came up with the amnesia storyline, rationalising it as something that *could* happen. 'But it doesn't play that way,' admitted Joel Surnow post-season. 'It's a case of where realism comes off as cheese.'

'YOU MAY REMEMBER ME FROM...' Performance poet Pauley Perrette was memorable as one of the groupies in *Almost Famous*. She played Alice Kramer in *Special Unit 2* and Gwen in *Murder One* and appeared in *The Drew Carey Show* and *Ring*. Navi Rawat was in *Jack the Dog* and *Roswell*.

BEHIND THE CAMERA Costume Supervisor Jean Rosone worked on *Shanghai Noon*, *Turner & Hooch*, *Equalibrium* and *Scorpion King* and won an Emmy for her costumes on *The Christmas Box*. Casting Associate Mindy Bazar's movies include *Very Bad Things* and *The Wedding Singer*. Script Researcher Ray Felipe also worked on

Spin City, *Evolution* and *The Powerpuff Girls*. Aerial Director of Photography Kurt E Soderling's impressive CV includes *Pearl Harbor*, *Armageddon*, *Titanic*, *Conspiracy Theory*, *Mars Attacks!* and *Men in Black*. Visual Effects Producer Charles L Finance's movies include *Bill & Ted's Excellent Adventure* and *Dune*.

NOTES 'I've got a very bad feeling about this.' This is the point at which *24* almost falls to pieces in the viewer's hands. The production had done *so* well up to this point, filling 15 hours with hardly a dull moment, or a wasted scene, or a plotline that doesn't, eventually, lead somewhere important. Even the slow-moving or poorly executed bits had, generally, *something* interesting about them. Then, horribly, in the space of one show, we see three of the worst subplots of the entire season initiated. This is especially applicable to Teri's amnesia *nonsense* - an idea which was, rightly, ridiculed by both fans and critics alike. There *is* some good stuff on display here, Keith's triumphant dirty trick on Carl being a particularly impressive touch. And, there's some gorgeous camerawork (the sinister scenes on Mulholland are, once again, staggeringly beautiful). But this is *24*, literally, pausing for breath. The seconds inch by in the slow, languid afternoon sunshine of a long, long day. Author's advice: Use your remote control judicially at this point.

Jack describes Ellis as 'a floating NSA operative.' He has a bottle of Pepto Bismol in his office locker at CTU. This is very good for settling acid stomach attacks, apparently. In his line of work, and given the fact that he's never once seen to eat during the entire 24 hours, it's probably essential. Eli, the kidnapper who raped Teri, is identified as Elija Stram from his record with the Compton Police Department. Teri says that another of Gaines's men was called Jensen. Alexis Drazen was born, like his brother, in Kragujevac, a large mining town in Southern Serbia. Both brothers studied at Zagreb University, with Alexis spending two years on a fellowship in the US. Alexis joined the Serb Democracy party in 1990, and served in the Serbian army from 1993-1999. He was, notes Milo, Special Forces trained in Belgrade. Andre initially trained as an engineer and worked on various construction projects before he, also, joined the army. One of the CTU agents that Jovan killed was called Daniels. Jovan Myovic is aged 31 and comes from Sombor in Vojvodina (Northern Serbia). Ironically, during the Yugoslav civil war Sombor was regarded as a mainly Croatian enclave. Myovic often uses the alias Joe Rigby and he has a very passable American accent. Mishko Suba is 32 and hails from Smederevo in Serbia.

SOUNDTRACK 'Who's That Kat?' by The Salads is heard coming from the next room as Rick talks to Kim on the phone.

CRITIQUE 'Last fall I raved about Fox's innovative thriller, which follows a convoluted assassination plot through 24 hours in second-to-second real time,' noted *The Oregonian*'s Peter Carlin. '"*24* would be a standout show in any season,"' I wrote. "It just may be the show of the era." That may have been a bit much. Which isn't to say that *24* isn't an intricately plotted thriller with crackerjack performances and a groovy directorial conceit holding it together. But while the multilayered tale of terrorists, political conspiracy and a high-tech, highly compromised intelligence community might seem to be emblematic of a larger issue, or paranoia, in the real world, *24* doesn't play on that level. Beneath its split screens, ticking clocks and omnipresent technology, the show is a very traditional thriller, complete with cliff-hangers, red herrings and characters struck suddenly with amnesia.'

CAST AND CREW COMMENTS 'What's remarkable to me is how well the whole thing has come together,' says Howard Gordon. 'The show really is about its relentlessness. [It] proceeds at such a breakneck pace that if there are holes, we're sort of skipping over them before we get there.'

DID YOU KNOW? According to Dennis Haysbert, *24* is known in Hollywood as: 'The most taped show in the industry.' He notes that the series' celebrity fans include people like Jack Nicholson and Steven Spielberg, who are amongst many industry insiders to have requested taped copies of episodes that they missed from the production office.

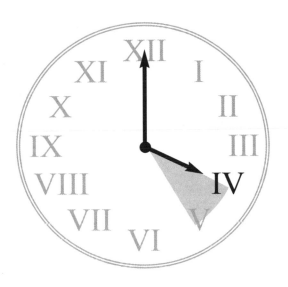

SEASON 1

12:00 1:00 2:00 3:00 4:00 5:00 6:00 7:00 8:00 9:00 10:00 11:00 12:00 1:00 2:00 3:00 **4:00** 5:00 6:00 7:00 8:00 9:00 10:00 11:00 12:00

I7 4:00 P.M. – 5:00 P.M.

US Transmission Date: 26 March 2002
UK Transmission Date: 23 June 2002
Terrestrial UK Transmission Date: 30 June 2002
Writer: Michael Chernuchin
Director: Stephen Hopkins
Cast: Carlos Bernard (Tony Almeida), Xander Berkeley (George Mason), Daniel Bess (Rick), Vicellous Reon Shannon (Keith Palmer), Glenn Morshower (Aaron Pierce), Željko Ivanek (Andre Drazen), Misha Collins (Alexis Drazen), Kara Zediker (Elizabeth Nash), Pauley Perrette (Tanya), Navi Rawat (Melanie), Vincent Angell (Dr Phil Parslow), David Franco (Man), Andre Canty (Henry Martin), John Tague (First Waiter)

4:02: A bewildered Teri is being driven to hospital by her rescuer, Tanya, who notices Teri's wedding ring. Teri says that she has no memory of her husband. Jack and Nina arrive at Palmer's hotel.

L.A. STORY The sweeping opening shot, from Mulholland facing north, is of the San Gabriel Mountains with the eastern and central Valley (specifically Burbank and Universal City) in the foreground. Tanya then turns her car onto Coldwater Canyon Drive, saying that there's a hospital at the bottom of the canyon. However, Teri is distracted when she sees the Tuptas Restaurant, which seems familiar to her.

Rick lives at 1804 Glade in Echo Park, a 26-acre area in Westlake just south of West Sunset Boulevard. It was used heavily as a location in Roman Polanski's *Chinatown*. Taking its name from an area that features a tranquil collection of lotuses and palm trees set around the idyllic eponymous lake, it's actually a very nice district indeed and the housing is probably far too expensive for scummy drug-peddling low-lives, like Rick and his girlfriend, to be living in.

The safehouse to which Teri and Kim were taken was, according to Mason, on Pine Canyon. No such address appears to exist (well, it *is* a *secret* safehouse after all) but, the location seems to be relatively close to both Mulholland Drive and Griffith Park from the respective directions in which Teri and Kim went subsequent to their getting separated.

4:05: Teri decides to wait for the restaurant manager, hoping that he will be able to help her regain her memory. Tanya leaves her a phone number and ten dollars for cab fare. Palmer is concerned for Elizabeth's safety. Jack assures the Senator that he will protect Elizabeth. Kim makes her way to a pay phone and calls CTU to tell them about the attack on the safehouse. Tony takes the call but Kim, not knowing who to trust at CTU, hangs up. Tony reports the loss of the agents. Mason orders him not to tell Jack what has happened, saying that the emotional response to this may cloud Jack's judgment.

4:19: Keith gives his father the tape he made of Carl explaining the plot to kill Farragamo. Andre is suspicious of Palmer's sudden change of plans and orders Alexis to kill Elizabeth. Jack briefs Elizabeth on how to plant the tracking device on Alexis. Teri meets the restaurant manager who has met her before. He tells her that she used to come regularly with a friend, Dr Parslow.

4:32: Nina admits to Jack that Teri had worked out that Nina was the woman with whom Jack had an affair. Alexis arrives at the hotel. A, by now very nervous, Elizabeth tries to place the tracking device in Alexis's wallet, and she does, eventually, succeed.

CIGARETTES AND ALCOHOL Elizabeth asks Alexis for some vodka as the pair contemplate another hot and steamy sexual liaison. Alexis returns with the drink, announcing that he loves Elizabeth.

QUOTE/UNQUOTE Elizabeth, to Alexis: 'How do you know how smart I am? We've spent, what, maybe 15 hours together? And most of *that* has been in bed.'

4:48: Jack calls Elizabeth on her cellphone to give her the exit message, but she doesn't answer the phone. She tells Alexis that she loves him too. When she enters the bathroom, she picks up a letter opener and stabs Alexis.

LOGIC, LET ME INTRODUCE YOU TO THIS WINDOW The 'safeword' phrase that Jack asks Elizabeth to say if she feels in danger is 'I hope I'm not getting a cold'. That's a rather long-winded and odd one for her to casually slip into the conversation with Alexis if she *is* feeling uncomfortable. Teri's amnesia storyline just gets more convoluted and ludicrous the longer it goes on. Teri remembers Parslow's first name (Phil), but not Jack's? Well, that's convenient, not to say a little Freudian.

That's got to be the sharpest letter opener in the world, surely? And how can a svelte little thing like Elizabeth manage to plunge it *that far* into Alexis's stomach? City cabs, the taxi company used by Kim, *are* a real firm. However, notice the 555-0127 number on the side of the cab? That *isn't* their real phone number.

4:54: Kim turns up at Rick's house and is met by a very unimpressed Melanie. Parslow arrives at the restaurant. Teri seems to recognise him. Palmer is incandescent with rage at Jack whom he blames for the stabbing. As Jack tries to defend himself, Alexis's cellphone rings. Jack answers it. The man on the other end arranges a meeting, Downtown. Jack takes a chance and asks how he, that is Alexis, will recognise the man. Luckily, they don't appear to have previously met as the man says he will be wearing a red cap.

4PM

'YOU MAY REMEMBER ME FROM...' Vincent Angell appeared in *We Were Soldiers*, *Looking for Richard*, *Search and Destroy* and *Charmed*. David Franco was in *Holy Smoke* and *ER*.

NOTES 'I hope you're not letting a desire for payback cloud your judgment.' Sadly, this is doesn't improve matters. Episode 17 is, probably, the single worst chunk of *24*. It's a little like having got a jigsaw puzzle three quarters completed then, overnight, some git sneaks into your house and steals half the pieces. Worse, they leave behind a bunch of completely random and arbitrary segments from something else entirely, just to confuse you. What on earth is this amnesia storyline trying to say? It's *so* unconvincing, dramatically obvious and not even particularly well acted. (Leslie Hope looks, frankly, embarrassed by the whole thing. She's not the only one.) One gets the feeling that the writers, apparently, didn't have a clue what to do with Teri by this stage, and that making her someone else for a couple of episodes was the best idea that they could come up with. The Elizabeth/Alexis plot is marginally better, and the tension is highly effective, but *that*, also, goes on *far* too long. And the climax to it, whilst dramatically satisfying on one level, doesn't really make an awful lot of sense. The hole where the rain got in, clearly.

Elizabeth's father is said to be one of Palmer's oldest friends. Palmer has known Elizabeth since she was born.

SOUNDTRACK 'Saturday' by Yo La Tengo, 'Cataract' by the Trephines, both playing at Rick's place.

CAST AND CREW COMMENTS 'You can't rely on everything being happy and great,' Stephen Hopkins noted as an ominous foreshadowing of things to come. 'In *24*, anyone can die.'

DID YOU KNOW? During an appearance on the BBC's *Breakfast* in 2002, Dennis Haysbert noted that when researching the role of David Palmer, amongst the individuals he studied closely was current US Defense Secretary, and former Head of the Joint Chiefs, Colin Powell. Not politically, Haysbert added, as Powell is a Republican, but in terms of Powell being a black man in, effectively, a white man's world.

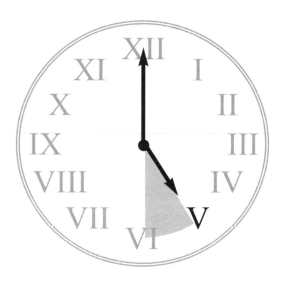

SEASON 1

12:00 1:00 2:00 3:00 4:00 5:00 6:00 7:00 8:00 9:00 10:00 11:00 12:00 1:00 2:00 3:00 4:00 **5:00** 6:00 7:00 8:00 9:00 10:00 11:00 12:00

18   5:00 P.M. – 6:00 P.M.

US Transmission Date: 2 April 2002
UK Transmission Date: 30 June 2002
Terrestrial UK Transmission Date: 7 July 2002
Writer: Maurice Hurley
Director: Frederick K Keller
Cast: Carlos Bernard (Tony Almeida), Penny Johnson Jerald (Sherry Palmer), Xander Berkeley (George Mason), Daniel Bess (Rick), Tanya Wright (Patty Brooks), Vicellous Reon Shannon (Keith Palmer), Jude Ciccolella (Mike Novick), Željko Ivanek (Andre Drazen), Misha Collins (Alexis Drazen), Henri Lubatti (Jovan Myovic), Navi Rawat (Melanie), Vincent Angell (Dr Phil Parslow), David Franco (Morgan), Edoardo Ballerini (Frank), Kirk Baltz (Teddy Hanlin)

5:02: Jack discovers that Alexis had a payoff meeting in 45 minutes with the red-capped man. Nina finds a suitcase containing bearer bonds. She tells Jack that she intends to come with him to co-ordinate backup. Mason asks Tony if he has any leads on Teri and Kim. Tony notes that Paulson and Breeher were probably killed whilst trying to protect the women. Kim and Rick search through Dan's books, much to the consternation of Melanie. Kim hopes that Dan has Gaines's number, which could help the police to track down her mother. Melanie notes that Dan will be furious when he finds out that they went through his stuff. Kim asks Rick why he didn't tell Melanie about Dan's death. Rick says that Melanie would freak. As would Dan's brother, Frank. He, Rick notes, is on his way over.

FASHION VICTIMS Jack changes his bloodied white shirt with a tasteful dark blue one worn by another agent, Jake. Luckily, they're exactly the same size.

5:05: Parslow refreshes Teri's memory about her husband, Jack, and her daughter, Kim.

BACK STORY Teri and Jack were separated about six months ago and that's when she and Parslow met. When Teri asks who *he* is, Parslow replies that he's a friend, although he wanted to be more than that. Parslow continues that he doesn't know why Teri decided to go back to Jack, but he does know that she asked Parslow never to call her again. Teri says that she can't remember any of this.

5:06: Parslow says that he needs to take Teri to a hospital. Isn't he, himself, a doctor, she asks? Parslow says that he's a surgeon, not a neurologist, which he feels she needs. Teri snaps that she doesn't want to go to hospital. Ignoring what he's just said, Parslow asks if he can examine her here. Teri agrees.

LOGIC, LET ME INTRODUCE YOU TO THIS WINDOW Just why is Teri so keen to be examined by a person who, not a moment earlier, told her that he wasn't qualified to do so? Is she stupid? Okay, silly question... Having given her a cursory physical examination, Parslow then comes up with a brilliantly definitive, and accurate, psychological diagnosis. Not at all bad for a *surgeon*.

5:08: Palmer plays Keith's tape for the benefit of Sherry and Mike and reveals his intention to put the tape in the public domain. Sherry says that today can either be about Palmer winning the election or it can be about a political scandal. It can't be about both. She orders David to destroy the tape, or bring the entire Democratic party down with him. Palmer has no intention of destroying the tape, suggesting that the position will be much worse if someone else brings the facts that it contains to light first. Mike advises that the tape has the potential to be the tastiest piece of blackmail that a US President could ever hope for against some of the most powerful people in the country. Jack calls Tony, because he needs to speak to Mason. Tony begs Mason to tell Jack the truth about his family. Mason refuses. Jack explains what he and Nina are about to do and requests backup at Connies, a restaurant in the California Plaza, within 15 minutes. Jack convinces Mason that waiting for Alexis to pull through - *if*, indeed, he survives - is a futile exercise. Mason tells Jack that he has recently spoken with Paulson who told him that Teri and Kim were sleeping. Jack, satisfied, asks that Mason have them call him when they wake up.

LOGIC, LET ME INTRODUCE YOU TO THIS WINDOW Both Mike and Sherry offer the opinion that the tape Keith made, of Carl talking about the death of Ferragamo, isn't evidence. *Of course* it is. It's admissibility into any criminal proceedings *might* be open to question (as Mike notes), although secret tape recordings of confessions *have* certainly been used in court cases before. But the fact remains that it is a boasting, and pretty damning, confession concerning a conspiracy to commit murder and implicate someone else.

5:16: Jack asks Nina what Teri said in the safehouse. Nina tells him and says that she handed the debriefing over to Paulson believing that her presence would be awkward for Teri. Jack doesn't blame Nina for this. He should have told Teri himself, he notes. Nina recommends that he call her now. Jack says that Teri is still probably asleep, but asks Nina to call Paulson to find out. When Nina's call won't go through, Jack assumes that this is because of the area they are in. Mason asks Tony if he thinks that Jack and Nina still have feelings for each other. Their discussion erupts into a shouting match.

QUOTE/UNQUOTE Mason: 'Know what? There's entirely too much personal business going on around here... It seems to me Nina Myers is a big part of that problem.'

5:19: Before he gives Keith's tape to the District Attorney, Palmer wants Keith to understand about the people that they are up against. Keith tells his father that when he said Palmer wasn't there for him, it wasn't true. He is ready to face the consequences of his actions. Andre Drazen calls Jovan to see if he has heard from Alexis whom, he says, is meeting Morgan in 20 minutes. Jovan himself is somewhat preoccupied in his search for Teri and Kim. When asked where he plans to look for the women, Jovan says that he intends to return to the Bauer house.

L.A. STORY The California Plaza is situated on Grand Avenue in Downtown L.A.

5:22: Melanie demands that Rick get Kim out of her house before Frank arrives. Kim doesn't particularly want to hang around where she isn't welcome. She tells Rick that she plans to go to a park that her parents told her to go to in the event of an earthquake. Rick thinks that she should go home instead, but Kim believes that the terrorists will know where she lives. Rick notes that he is on probation. If he's arrested for Kim's kidnapping, he will be going to jail for a long time. Kim understands and says that she wishes they had met under different circumstances. Dan's menacing brother, Frank, arrives. Noticing Rick's black eye, Frank interrogates Rick about how things went last night. Rick says that things went fine and that Dan will be back soon. Frank stops Kim from leaving until Dan returns with the money.

CIGARETTES AND ALCOHOL There are a couple of empty beer bottles in Rick's front room. Later, Frank gives Rick a can whilst having one himself.

5:30: Nina explains to Jack where the CTU teams are stationed in the plaza. Mason calls Jack with some bad news: Teddy Hanlin is in charge of the backup. Hanlin is someone that Jack does not want to work with. Mason apologises, claiming that Division have assigned Hanlin and asking that Jack try to avoid a confrontation.

BACK STORY Nina remembers Hanlin as the former partner of Seth Campbell, one of the dirty agents whom Jack previously busted.

5:31: Hanlin greets them on arrival, noting what good connections Jack must have to have screwed up as many times as he has today and not 'get spanked' by the agency. Hanlin continues that he hopes he doesn't have a bad aim and accidentally shoot one of his own people. Tony tells Mason that a woman matching Teri's description was spotted walking around Griffith Park, near the safehouse. Agent Williams has been sent to check on this.

LOGIC, LET ME INTRODUCE YOU TO THIS WINDOW When, exactly, was Teri 'seen wandering around Griffith Park?' Presumably, Tony means that she was seen on that short stretch of Mulholland before Tanya picked her up, which does, at least, border Griffith Park. One car did, indeed, drive past her at this time. But why would the driver report Teri to the authorities? She wasn't acting particularly suspiciously. In several shots, Rick's facial bruise disappears only to reappear again later. Where did Palmer get a second tape from so quickly to pull the stunt he does on Sherry?

5:32: Parslow, having examined Teri, believes that someone may have assaulted her. He also thinks that her amnesia could be disassociative, which happens when a person suffers severe emotional trauma.

POINTS AT WHICH TERI NEEDS A SLAP When Parslow insists that she go to hospital, Teri has a completely over-the-top panic attack, flapping her arms around like a wounded albatross and whimpering miserably. Parslow who, let us remember, is still desperately trying to get into Teri's knickers, manages *not* to supply a time-honoured medicinal cure for hysteria by slapping her.

5:34: Noticing Palmer leaving for a meeting with Mike, Sherry also spots Patty putting an envelope into a wall safe. Sherry sneaks into the room, retrieves the envelope, which is addressed to the D.A., and then quickly hides it when her burglary is interrupted by Patty. Once she's alone again, Sherry opens the envelope and removes Keith's tape.

5:41: Sherry is still sitting in the room when Palmer returns. Palmer opens the safe, and sees that his envelope is missing. Sherry flatly tells him that she has destroyed the tape. Palmer replies that it breaks his heart for him to discover that he was right about her. He then pulls the *real* tape from his shirt pocket. Sherry says that she will do whatever it takes to protect her family. She asks if that makes her a bad person. Palmer orders Mike to schedule an immediate press conference.

BACK STORY Hanlin asks if Jack remembers Seth Campbell's wife, Judy, who recently hanged herself. She didn't even leave a suicide note, Hanlin continues. She probably didn't bother to because it was obvious why she was doing so, with her husband in prison, his pension gone, and four kids to feed. And all of this, because Jack led the internal investigation on Seth. Jack offers to sit down with Hanlin and tell him his side of the story some day when it's more convenient.

QUESTION Nina rings Mason and begs him to stop Hanlin's baiting of Jack which is in danger of undermining the operation. Is this, in fact, a subtle way of making the Jack/Hanlin situation even worse?

5:53: Jovan is about to break into the Bauer house when he spots their alarm system. Agent Williams arrives and does a cursory check outside the house. Frank tells someone over the phone that Dan will be home soon. He notes that they will need the money by seven o'clock. Kim asks Rick what will happen when Frank figures out that Dan isn't coming home. Rick says that *he's* not about to tell Frank. Kim notes that Rick has so much going for him; he's smart, good-looking and funny. She begins to tell him about her foster-home friend, Todd, who got a scholarship to Stanford. Rick admits that Kim is probably right, but unfortunately they are in the middle of a drug deal about to go very wrong and he believes that this probably isn't the best time to deal with his own shortcomings.

SEX AND DRUGS AND ROCK 'N' ROLL Kim asks Frank what *deal* Rick is referring to. Frank replies that he's taking the 20,000 dollars that Dan made last night and using it to buy a large quantity of Ecstasy.[56] He then intends to resell this for upwards of 50,000 to some idiots from Redondo Beach.

5:55: Morgan arrives at the plaza, meets Jack and asks for the money. First, Jack says, he would like to go over what Morgan is supposed to do. Morgan reveals that he will be shutting off the power on Grid 26GG at 7:20, and then turning it back on at 7:25. Morgan suddenly seems to realise that he is being set-up and he makes a run for it. Jack chases Morgan through a crowd of people, as Hanlin announces over the radio that he's got the target in his line of fire. Jack tells Hanlin that Morgan isn't a threat. Hanlin ignores Jack and coldly shoots Morgan, who crashes through a glass wall on a bridge and lands on the concrete pavement below. Parslow

5PM

- -

56 Ecstasy, or E, is the hallucinogenic drug *methylenedioxymethamphetamine* (MDMA). The name refers to the extreme feeling of euphoria it induces in its users. Because of this, intoxication with the drug is often referred to as being *loved-up*. First synthesised in 1960 as a slimming pill, use of Ecstasy became widespread during the mid-80s (initially under the street-name *Adam*, taken from the DC comic-book character Adam Strange). It is most associated in the media with the late 80s rave and acid house culture.

and Teri arrive at the Bauer house. In the bushes, Jovan lies in wait for them beside Williams's dead body.

LOGIC, LET ME INTRODUCE YOU TO THIS WINDOW Why doesn't Morgan notice much earlier that the supposed Serbian terrorist he is dealing with sounds strangely like an American? Come to that, why doesn't Jack, who has worked quite extensively in the Balkans, at least *try* to put on a fake accent?

'YOU MAY REMEMBER ME FROM...' Edoardo Ballerini's movies include *Romeo Must Die*, *The Last Days of Disco* and *The Pest*. Kirk Baltz appeared in *Rave Macbeth*, *Bulworth*, *Dances With Wolves*, *Face/Off* and *Reservoir Dogs*.

BEHIND THE CAMERA The creator of the Borg on *Star Trek: The Next Generation*, writer Maurice Hurley also worked on *The Proposal*, *Baywatch*, *Diagnosis Murder*, *Kung Fu: The Legend Continues*, *The Equalizer*, *Miami Vice* and *Pointman*.

Fred Keller has directed episodes of *The Pretender*, *She Spies*, *Angel*, *Roswell*, *Inner Sense* and *Veronica Clare*, and the movies *My Dark Lady*, *Vamping*, *The Eyes of the Amaryllis* and *Tuck Everlasting*. He also wrote *Columbo Goes to College*.

NOTES 'Why don't we let the electorate decide on that?' Another awkward, fractured, very long-winded episode, albeit slightly better than the last couple. One or two of the subplots have now become pure padding. Kim and Rick's brush with the seamier side of the L.A. underworld is almost as annoyingly silly and stereotypical as Teri's continued amnesia. Not only that, but the production was really milking the *black widow* aspect of Sherry's character for all it was worth at this point. Even Jack's tense stakeout at the restaurant is almost ruined by the introduction of the completely over-the-top character of Hanlin, a little piece of backstory intended to add tension but which merely ends up getting very dull very quickly. At least a couple of things manage to save this episode from being a complete disaster. Chiefly, it's the interplay in the scenes between Nina and Jack that hold it all together.

Kim has an aunt named Ethyl. Presumably she's Jack's sister (or the wife of Jack's brother) since it's impossible to believe that Teri is anything other than an only child, and a spoiled one at that. Rick tells Frank that Kim is a friend of his from San Diego. The envelope that Sherry takes from the safe is addressed to one Jim Lapidus, named after *24*'s costume designer. Zach Grenier's voice is heard on Keith's tape when dialogue is replayed from '3:00 P.M.-4:00 P.M.' This is the first episode that specifically identifies David Palmer as a Democrat. Well, you didn't seriously expect a black man to be in with a shout of getting the Republican nomination did you? Agent Williams's car licence-plate number is G13 23846. Parslow's car-plate number is 4IBY911. Some fans have suggested that the latter (911) was a pointed, and somewhat tasteless, jibe at the date of the events which caused the postponement of the first episode of *24*. This seems to be highly unlikely, however.

SOUNDTRACK 'Winter Notes' by Picastro, 'Remain' by John Frusciante and the excellent 'As Sure as the Sun' by Black Rebel Motorcycle Club.

CAST AND CREW COMMENTS 'Part of the appeal of the show is the real time conceit,' notes Howard Gordon. 'We're not *ER* but we're certainly improving,' added Gordon concerning the show's slow climb in the ratings. 'We all feel that the amnesia [storyline] at some level may have been stepping our toe over the line. It may not have been our finest moment. I think it's a given that everybody is tired and hungry and probably in need of a shower by now.' But for a show that Gordon calls a 'turbocharged soap opera,' such liberties can, perhaps, be excused. 'Some of the implausibilities are kind of the things that [add to] the show's charm,' he adds. 'Someone once said art aspires to improbable possibility. I think that's sort of where this is trying to be.'

DID YOU KNOW? 'I feel lucky that my agent got me in here,' noted director Frederick Keller. 'It is one of the best experiences of my professional life. The ensemble cast was unbelievable.' Keller added that the cast's dedication to the series was exemplified by Kiefer Sutherland. One day, Kiefer came all of the way in to the studio to voice the unseen end of a telephone conversation. 'He had only one line,' says Keller. 'And it was "yup."'

5PM

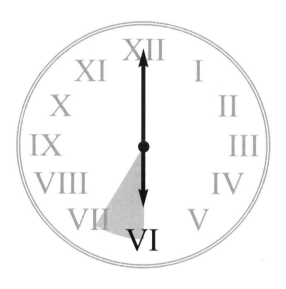

6:00 P.M. – 7:00 P.M.

12:00 1:00 2:00 3:00 4:00 5:00 6:00 7:00 8:00 9:00 10:00 11:00 12:00 1:00 2:00 3:00 4:00 5:00 **6:00** 7:00 8:00 9:00 10:00 11:00 12:00

19   6:00 P.M. – 7:00 P.M.

US Transmission Date: 2 April 2002
UK Transmission Date: 7 July 2002
Terrestrial UK Transmission Date: 14 July 2002
Writers: Joel Surnow, Michael Loceff
Director: Frederick K Keller
Cast: Carlos Bernard (Tony Almeida), Penny Johnson Jerald (Sherry Palmer), Xander Berkeley (George Mason), Daniel Bess (Rick), Vicellous Reon Shannon (Keith Palmer), Megalyn Echikunwoke (Nicole Palmer), Zach Grenier (Carl Webb), Željko Ivanek (Andre Drazen), Henri Lubatti (Jovan Myovic), Navi Rawat (Melanie),Vincent Angell (Dr Phil Parslow), Edoardo Ballerini (Frank), Darin Heames (Krugman), Jenn McCullough (Elaine), Randy J Goodwin (Security Guard), Noel Guglielmi (Craig), Jason Matthew Smith (Chris), Lew Dauber (Jorgensen), Mariah Pasos (Elaine's Partner), Kirk Baltz (Teddy Hanlin)[57]

> **6:00:** Jovan watches as Teri and Parslow enter her home. When the alarm sounds Teri, still having amnesia, doesn't know how to turn it off. Whilst she's busy wailing and panicking two guards from the alarm company arrive. Teri looks for her purse to show them some identification. She notices photographs of Kim and Jack in the living room. The guards notice them too, recognise Teri from the photos, and turn off the alarm for her.

LOGIC, LET ME INTRODUCE YOU TO THIS WINDOW Can this flaming amnesia plot get any more contrived or ridiculous? Sorry, that's another silly question, yes *of course* it can. The first time that Teri invited Parslow back to her home, she left her keys in his car and, because it was raining, she conveniently showed him where she kept a hidden spare (under a rather obvious piece of garden furniture). Does Jack know about this moronic example of a lack of security in his household? How do the guards from the Superior Alarms security company arrive within, at most, two minutes of the alarm first sounding. Unless of course they were, literally, stationed next door? And why do they accept photographic evidence as proof of Teri's identity and that she lives there?

Kim's bedroom and, indeed, much of the Bauer house, looks little like the location used in the first episode.

> **6:05:** Nina tells Jack that the man whom Hanlin shot is named called Alan Morgan. Jack notes that he was supposed to turn off the electricity in a section of the city of Saugus's power grid at a specific time. Nina heads back to CTU. Jack gets a call from Palmer, who has uncovered the missing Drazen file from a source in the Pentagon. It contains an address in Saugus. Jack alerts Tony, who finds that the address falls within the grid co-ordinates that were going to be blacked out. Mason arrives at the Plaza and tells Jack that he will accompany Jack to Saugus.

6PM

QUOTE/UNQUOTE Mason, to Jack: 'Have you noticed how there's always a body count wherever you go?'

● ●

57 Credited as appearing in this episode, but does not.

LOGIC, LET ME INTRODUCE YOU TO THIS WINDOW When Jack apologises to Mason for having shot him the previous night with a tranquiliser, he explains his actions by saying that he was pretty wound-up. But now, he continues, he feels a lot better knowing that his family is safe. When Jack shot Mason, however, Jack had only just discovered that Kim had sneaked out of the house. At that stage, he had no idea that she had been kidnapped or, indeed, done anything other than gone to a party or to a friend's house. Jack shot Mason, specifically, to get some blackmail information. Jack tells Mason that Victor Drazen was behind all of the ethnic cleansing operations in Kosovo, Sarajevo and Bosnia. Sarajevo *is* in Bosnia - it's the capital.

6:09: Frank is furious that Dan has not yet arrived with his money. When Frank is out of the room, Kim tries to escape, but Melanie stops her. Kim blurts out that Dan isn't coming back. Rick is forced to admit that Dan was killed by Gaines. Frank is, seemingly, more concerned that he doesn't have the money for the drug deal than with his brother's death.

QUOTE/UNQUOTE Mason: 'So, correct me if I'm wrong. What this day basically boils down to is a personal vendetta against you and Palmer by the sons of Victor Drazen?' Jack: 'Today is the second anniversary of the death of Victor Drazen.' Mason: 'Happy anniversary.'

6:15: Sherry is angry with Keith for causing her so much pain. During the ensuing argument, Nicole begins to hyperventilate. She apologises to her father, saying that everything is her fault. At CTU, Nina discovers that the address in Saugus is a wildlife reserve. Parslow tells Teri that he, personally, never met Kim. He says that Teri told him she had asked Jack to move out because he had become too removed. Parslow had hoped for a relationship to develop between himself and Teri, but she was afraid of losing her family.

LOGIC, LET ME INTRODUCE YOU TO THIS WINDOW Saugus is about 20 miles north of Los Angeles (it's near Santa Clarita). Yet Mason and Jack drive there from downtown in less than half an hour. Impossible. There are, actually, several illogical elements to the entire Saugus plot. Palmer says he's never heard of the town when he clearly should have. He mentions that the address 21911 Kipling features in the missing Drazen file. Yet, subsequently, Jack asks Tony to look up 21911 Kipling *Avenue*. Why is this address mentioned in the Drazen file at all? When we subsequently discover exactly what the address is, we also learn that it's one of dozens of similar facilities dotted around the country to which the mysterious prisoner is relocated every few days. So why is this one, specifically, mentioned in the file? Also, what does a secret underground prison need to have an actual postal address for? It's not like they're going to be getting much mail. Jack says that Saugus is all industrial. It isn't, it's a town, like any other town, and has non-industrial areas.

6:22: Frank's drug-buying associates arrive with a bag full of lethal looking guns. With no money to deal, they intend to rob the drug dealers. After a doctor checks Nicole, Palmer asks his family for their support when he makes his announcement. Teri looks through her diary in the hope of jogging her memory. Meanwhile Parslow has invited a friend, Chris, over to help him protect Teri. Teri is frightened when she sees that Chris has a gun. Parslow assures her that he is only trying to look after her best interests. Jovan tells Andre that Teri is in the house. He is merely waiting for the right opportunity to kill her.

DOWN THE PAN Chris asks to use the bathroom. This is, remarkably, the first time in more than 18 hours that anyone on the show has displayed the slightest desire for a pee.

6:33: Palmer divulges to the media that he misjudged the intentions of some of his campaign backers. They, he says, acted without Palmer's consent or knowledge in conspiring to murder George Ferragamo. Palmer has turned over the confession tape to the D.A. He then tells reporters that Keith will surrender himself to the authorities and that Palmer will stand fully behind his son. Palmer is convinced that Keith will be found guilty of, at worst, failing to report an accidental death. He asks the press to respect his daughter's privacy. Carl watches the press conference with three of the financiers. Although Carl vows to take care of the situation, Jorgensen says that it's too late.

6:40: Nina learns, from Tony, that Teri and Kim are missing. She calls Mason and asks why he hasn't told Jack yet about his family. Mason gives neutral answers so that Jack, in the car with him, will not overhear anything prejudicial. Arriving at the wildlife reserve, George and Jack walk into the woods. Jack tells Mason that Victor Drazen worked directly for Serbian dictator Milosevic and that he was the man behind most of the ethnic cleansing campaigns in Eastern Europe. Jack's unit killed Drazen and now his sons are, seemingly, seeking revenge with a group of exiled Serbs. Jack and Mason stumble upon a power transformer in the middle of the field. Jack becomes suspicious when he realises that this wildlife reserve appears to be devoid of both water and animals.

6:46: The drug dealers arrive, and question Frank as to why Kim and Rick are present. Frank demands the Ecstasy. The dealers notice Frank's gun and there is an armed stand-off. As Frank disarms one of the dealers, he hits Rick in his injured shoulder, saying, 'All this because you couldn't keep my brother alive.' One of the dealers, Krugman, tells Frank that he has the right to remain silent, revealing that he is an undercover cop. A SWAT team bursts through the doors and arrest Frank and everyone in the room who isn't a cop, including Rick, Melanie and Kim.

6:55: Palmer continues his press conference, explaining that he bears full responsibility for not knowing about what was going on within his own family. He closes by asking the voters to consider electing him, noting that he is not the first person in public office to make a mistake. At the Bauer house, Teri notices a box with 'Mom' stencilled on it. She remembers that Kim made it for her. She is staring at it when Jovan enters the house and shoots both Chris and Parslow. Jovan demands that Teri tell him where her daughter is so that he can kill them both. Teri has no idea. As Jovan is about to execute her, he is shot from behind by Tony. Teri begins to cry and, in a moment seemingly unique in medical science, she remembers that she saw Kim die in a car crash.

6PM

COMPLETELY POINTLESS CLIFFHANGER #3 Jack and Mason are in a Saugus field when a helicopter approaches. Jack is convinced that someone knows that they are there.

Randy Goodwin appeared in *Down 'n Dirty*, *Girlfriends* and *Hyperion Bay*. Noel Guglielmi was in *The Fast and the Furious* and *Training Day*. Darin Heames appeared in *Buffy the Vampire Slayer*, *Rough Riders*, *Dr Giggles* and *Baywatch*. Lew Dauber's CV includes *Jingle All the Way*, *Dangerous Women*, *Quantum Leap*, *Murder She Wrote* and *Matlock*. Jason Matthew Smith appeared in *Airborne*.

NOTES 'You still think this is just about you.' Well, thankfully Teri's amnesia is over. Not only that, but isn't it great that smug, full of himself Phil Parslow has been shot. Even better, Kim's been and gone and got herself arrested. It's almost as though all of the writers simultaneously woke up from a two and a half episode snooze and wearily asked 'How the hell did we get ourselves into *this* mess?' From here, things quickly start to pick up. Jack and Mason's intriguing little double act out in the country is a rediscovery of the clever, witty dialogue that helped to make *24*'s early episodes so enjoyable. Having said that, the Palmer family dinner table row is a ghastly miscalculation that just goes on and on and on until you wish that they'd all choke on something and die. Frankly, it resembles the kind of thing that *The Simpsons*' writers can do in two or three lines and then move on to something else.

According to Parslow, Teri is a freelance interior design consultant. Yes, that sounds like just the kind of 'non-job' job that Teri *would* have. She has a work colleague called Kitty. Recent entries in Teri's diary include:

Yvonne's birthday.

Kim in Cambria for the weekend.

Dinner with Phil. Ivy on the Shore.

Parslow remembers the latter, noting that they had to wait for an hour at the restaurant so they decided to walk along the pier and get hot dogs instead. He also mentions that Teri then beat him at air hockey. This seems to suggest that the location he's describing is Pacific Park, the famous funfair on Santa Monica pier. Parslow has two young daughters by his previous marriage: Emily (aged 11) and Jennifer (aged 9). Teri has never met the girls. Morgan works for the Pacific Electric Company in Saugus.

SOUNDTRACK 'Ny Batteri' by Sigur Rós, 'Fix and Destroy' by The Dirtmitts. Another of Kim's bedroom posters is just visible, this one for nu-metal band Linkin Park.

CAST AND CREW COMMENTS Part of what makes *24* unique, notes Fred Keller is 'Like that old [Jean-Luc] Godard line - "The cinema is truth 24 frames per second." When you do something in exact time, it creates tremendous tension. It's marvellous.'

'This show is absolutely a child of the cellphone age,' Howard Gordon notes. 'But I said the same thing about *The X-Files*, and I did *The X-Files* for four years. The split screen has been a way to answer what traditionally has been something people are scared of. [Namely], the phone call as a dramatic device.'

DID YOU KNOW? It was around this point - April 2002 - that Fox first began to make noises suggesting that *24* would more than likely return for a second season. (The actual renewal decision wasn't taken until May, however.) Initial press reports seemed to indicate that the series' innovative format may change in any hypothetical second season, with certain producers quoted as saying they were not sure whether they could sustain another year of real time action. Joel Surnow told the *New York Daily News* 'We all love the format, but there are problems with it. It asks the viewer to tune in every week to follow the story. That's not what research says are the viewing habits of the American public.' As a result, the newspaper noted, each episode next season could have a more traditional format. But, many viewers and industry professionals were compelled to ask what's the point of changing a winning formula? Given that the heart-thumping, clock-ticking premise of *24* had been the hook that had brought in many loyal viewers in the first place, why would Fox Entertainment President Gail Berman, or Chairman Sandy Grushow - the two executives ultimately charged with making the decision - want to abandon the idea? 'It's not going to be as unique, but I do think it will open it up to a larger range of viewers,' noted Stacy Lynn Koerner, senior vice-president and director of broadcast research at the US-based media-buying firm Initiative Media. 'But they have to keep the suspense of every single episode.'

6PM

20 7:00 P.M. – 8:00 P.M.

US Transmission Date: 16 April 2002
UK Transmission Date: 14 July 2002
Terrestrial UK Transmission Date: 21 July 2002
Writers: Robert Cochran, Howard Gordon
Director: Stephen Hopkins
Cast: Lou Diamond Phillips (Mark DeSalvo), Carlos Bernard (Tony Almeida), Penny Johnson Jerald (Sherry Palmer), Xander Berkeley (George Mason), Daniel Bess (Rick), Tanya Wright (Patty Brooks), Megalyn Echikunwoke (Nicole Palmer), Jude Ciccolella (Mike Novick), Željko Ivanek (Andre Drazen), Vincent Angell (Dr Phil Parslow), Darin Heames (Krugman), Jenn McCullough (Elaine), Christian Hastings (Harris), Melanee Murray (Lucy), Rick Garcia (Reporter), Dennis Hopper (Victor Drazen)[58]

7:02: Mason thinks that he and Jack are wasting their time, but Jack knows that Alexis wouldn't have paid Morgan to shut off the power for no reason. Mason receives a call and is told that Alexis is out of surgery. He believes they should be there when Alexis wakes up. Jack wants to continue looking until 7:20, at which point Mason can send a car to pick him up. Tony helps a sobbing Teri and a wounded Parslow to his car. Teri can't stop crying about Kim dying in the explosion.

7:06: Nina tells Tony to take Parslow to the clinic, but recommends that he bring Teri to CTU.

POINTS AT WHICH TERI NEEDS A SLAP Tony tells Teri that Kim is, actually, alive and not dead as Teri believed. Instead of her being, you know, relieved or something, whilst Tony is struggling valiantly to get the injured Parslow into the car, Teri merely returns to her neurotic, terminally-irritated state and prattles on and on with a series of inane questions. Where is Kim now? Why doesn't Tony know? What's being done to find her? For God's sake just *SHUT UP, WOMAN* and be grateful that you're still alive.

7:08: At the police station Kim begs for a phone call. Melanie tells Krugman not to listen to Kim, whom she calls a pathological liar. Rick asks Kim if she trusts him. Kim says that she's aware he *is* trying to help her. Rick says that he will back up anything that Kim tells the police. Kim warns him that he will get in trouble.

REAL WORLD JUNCTION Sherry tells Palmer that she isn't in the mood to celebrate his election concession. Palmer feels that she's being hasty in her prediction. She asks if he really believes the public want a President who acts like a guest on a cheap afternoon TV chat show and reminds Palmer that it is Mike's job to tell Palmer what he wants to hear. She hopes Palmer's conscience will be there for him when this is all over. All *very* Hillary Clinton.

7:09: Jack finds a set of steps that lead into an underground tunnel. Meanwhile, from a covert camouflage tent, Andre Drazen receives a call from a man named Harris, who tells him that

Jack has found the location. Jack descends the stairs, but two armed men appear and shoot Jack with tasers.

7:16: Jack wakes up in a cell and is violently sick. Jack's new host introduces himself as DeSalvo from the Department of Defense. This is a Class Three Detention Centre, and DeSalvo asks Jack what he's doing there. Jack hurriedly explains how a man named Morgan was bribed to shut off the power at 7:20. DeSalvo's reaction suggests that something important is due to happen at that time. DeSalvo notes that a prisoner is being flown in though he, personally, has no idea of the prisoner's identity. DeSalvo asks Jack what terrorists could want with the prisoner. Since neither know who the prisoner is, Jack can only speculate that they either want to kill him or free him. Jack tells DeSalvo to call for backup. After some debate, DeSalvo makes the call. Andre announces to his accomplices that they've got three minutes. Harris worries that Andre still hasn't heard from Alexis. Andre says that if there was a problem, Alexis would have called.

As a helicopter arrives, Harris counts how many men they are dealing with. Eight, including Jack. Yet Andre implied that there would be only three guards. Andre tells him not to worry about it as they will be disoriented when the power is shut off. The helicopter lands and the team take the prisoner to the compound. The lights remain on. A furious Andre wants to go in anyway, but Harris suggests that this is not a good idea.

REFERENCES There are dialogue allusions to *A Few Good Men* ('You're not qualified to tell me the truth') and *Poltergeist* ('They are here'). One of the girls in the holding cell with Kim wears a Queen T-shirt. A criminal *and* an overblown pomp-rock fan? God certainly dealt *her* a rotten hand in life, didn't he?

7:27: Krugman interrogates Kim. She tells him that her father is Jack Bauer. The name means nothing to Krugman who says that he wants information on Frank Allerd and his plan to buy and distribute a thousand hits of Ecstasy. Kim doesn't know anything about Frank. She mentions the assassination attempt on David Palmer. Krugman notes that this has been all over the news for the past 12 hours. Kim says that she wasn't aware of this since she's been kidnapped all day by the same people who tried to kill Palmer. She gives him CTU's number and demands that Krugman call it and tell whomever answers that he's got Jack Bauer's daughter. Krugman leads her back to the cells.

Jack warns DeSalvo that the terrorists will be working on a contingency plan. Jack asks to talk to the prisoner. DeSalvo refuses, saying that he is under explicit orders. Jack is welcome to go over his head, he notes. Jack asks to use DeSalvo's phone.

7:34: TV news are reporting that not only is Palmer's lead in the election holding steady, but in some states, it's actually increasing. An America's Choice poll reveals that 60% of the people who voted don't care about the shenanigans involving Palmer's family. Only 18% felt that it made them less likely to vote for him. An aide tells Palmer that Jack Bauer is on the phone. Jack needs Palmer's help in getting to DeSalvo's superior. Palmer says that he'll do what he can. Jack finds himself in a room full of monitors. Idly he pushes a few buttons until one of the monitors shows a CCTV picture of the cell in which the prisoner is being held. DeSalvo arrives just as Jack gets a glimpse of the prisoner's face.

Bauer: 'It's Victor Drazen.' DeSalvo: 'Who's he?' Jack: 'A man I killed two years ago.'

7:43: Jack says that he wants the prisoner moved as soon as possible. DeSalvo goes to make a call to his superiors. Andre tells Harris that they should assume Alexis is dead. He initiates a new plan, involving the electricity substation that powers the compound. Harris tells him that the plan was not to attract the attention of the authorities. Andre corrects him; the reason for the operation is to get his father out of prison. Nina is surprised to see Mason back at CTU without Jack. Mason says that Alexis has regained consciousness.

Mason, on Alexis: 'He hasn't talked yet. But I cut off his morphine supply so he should be pretty chatty in about an hour.'

7:45: Nina realises that Mason *still* hasn't told Jack that Teri and Kim are missing once again. Mason replies that the last time he checked he wasn't required to explain himself to a subordinate like Nina. He won't be telling Jack about his wife and daughter's abduction, if he can possibly help it, until Palmer is safe.

In the worst scene of the episode, if not the entire series, there's a victory party going on at Palmer headquarters. Yet Palmer, himself, locked away moodily in a side room, doesn't appear to be in the mood to celebrate. When Sherry arrives and finds him sitting on his own, Palmer notes that Sherry is a woman who knows what she wants. He isn't confident that she wants *him*. She dismisses this as nonsense. Palmer says that after all of those years lying to him, he simply cannot trust her. And if he can't do that, then he can't love her either. Sherry suggests that though this may be true, Palmer will never leave her and demands that he get out and greet his workers who have spent every day of the last year 'helping to put us into office.' When Palmer questions her use of the word *us*, she tells him that when he is being sworn into office she intends to be standing by his side. Yawn. So, anyway, back to the important stuff...

7:54: Krugman leaves a nervous Kim in a cell full of scary-looking women. Given permission to interrogate his nemesis, Jack tells DeSalvo that someone must have realised that Drazen was more valuable alive than dead. Jack enters Drazen's cell and introduces himself. He asks that Drazen excuse his surprise as it appears rumours of Victor's death have been greatly exaggerated. Jack acknowledges that no one could survive being blown up and adds that he had no intention of killing Drazen's wife and daughter. He would, therefore, appreciate it if Drazen would reciprocate. He suggests that Drazen is in danger of losing his two sons. Drazen says that his sons are soldiers. DeSalvo tells Jack that they have received permission to move the prisoner. Drazen is frog-marched towards the exit, but the column comes to an abrupt halt when the lights in the compound are suddenly shut off. With satisfaction, Drazen tells Jack: 'They are here.'

7PM

Nina asks Tony how far away from CTU he is. He replies between 20 and 30 minutes. Yet it's already been well established (several times) that the Bauer house is within a five minute drive from CTU. Indeed, in the previous episode Tony himself was *at* CTU with eight minutes of the episode to go. Yet, by the end credits, he'd had the time to arrive at Jack's house *and* shoot Jovan. The sun sets *remarkably* quickly over Saugus, it appears. One moment it's twilight, but still reasonably bright. The next, boom, it's pitch black. Meanwhile, 25 miles south in Santa Monica, and a few minutes later, there's still bright sunlight. Jack recovers consciousness from three very nasty taser blasts in a little under three minutes, with only a mild case of nausea to show for his harsh treatment.

So, let's just confirm this; a 'class three detention facility' (i.e. a *high security prison*) has ... just *three* guards staffing it? Why isn't Kim's interview with Krugman being tape recorded, or at least attended by a second officer? Any information given in such uncorroborated circumstances would surely be inadmissible in court and could cause a major drug trial to collapse on a technicality. A mobile phone that works underground? Yeah, right, sure... The headlights of a car can be seen in the middle-distance behind Jack as he investigates the, supposedly deserted, wildlife reserve in Saugus. Harris doesn't seem to be a very Serbian-type surname, yet he's got a Central European accent. And it isn't, seemingly, an alias as Andre calls him by this name. A little over half an hour after Palmer has ended his speech, there is a television news report stating that voting figures from across the country suggest that the revelations about Palmer's family are not having a significant effect on his campaign. No way has there been enough time for any sort of even remotely accurate assumptions to be drawn on this. Firstly, the polls on the East Coast had already closed when Palmer made his speech. Short of a huge last minute rush of people who hadn't already voted in the other three time zones to the ballot box to register their angry protest at Palmer's duplicity, there's little difference that any announcement made at that time would have been *likely* to make. In 13 minutes, Sherry notes, Palmer has destroyed what it took them 25 years to build. But, his speech actually lasted over 20 minutes.

'YOU MAY REMEMBER ME FROM...' *'Don't you fuckin' look at me!'* With this one, immortal, line Dennis Hopper, whose movie career had floundered throughout the 70s and 80s, was reborn as the apotheosis of middle-American urban menace in David Lynch's classic thriller *Blue Velvet*. Hopper's mesmerising performance as Frank Booth led to a slew of similarly over-the-top psychomaniac roles (some of them very good, like the character he played in *Speed*, others less successful, such as *Waterworld*). But it also announced the comeback of a truly gifted actor whose talents had too often been under-utilised (by both himself and others). As a young man Hopper appeared in the final movies made by his friend and mentor James Dean, *Rebel Without a Cause* and *Giant*. A committed method actor, Hopper was often pegged as 'difficult' by various studio bosses and spent much of the next decade working either in TV (*The Time Tunnel*, *Gunsmoke*, *Bonanza*, *The Twilight Zone*, *Naked City*) or with maverick outsiders of the Hollywood system like Roger Corman (*The Trip*). Off-screen, Hopper was an active part of the era's pop-art explosion, both as a savvy man-about-town partygoer, hanging out with all the rock groups in Laurel Canyon and on Sunset Strip, and as a fine photographic chronicler of the mid-60s L.A. scene. In 1969 he directed, co-wrote, and starred in *Easy Rider*, the ultimate counterculture movie. Flush with its astounding success, he went on to make the daring, self-reflective and wilfully anti-commercial *The Last Movie*, the crushing failure of which alienated him totally from Hollywood's establishment.

Actually, the drug-crazed abandon of the movies' shooting, in Peru, was far more interesting than the film itself. By his own admission, Hopper then wandered in a morass of drugs and drink through much of the next decade (and, watching his manic performance in Coppola's *Apocalypse Now*, you can *easily* believe it). Since *Blue Velvet*, he has worked steadily (including an Oscar-nominated performance in *Hoosiers* and playing a burned-out ex-hippie in *Flashback* opposite Kiefer Sutherland). He's also become a noted director (showing a solid understanding of the mainstream in *Colors* and a wry appreciation of *noir*-irony in the erotic thriller *The Hot Spot*). Other important movies of this genuine Hollywood legend include *True Romance* ('you know something is wrong when Dennis Hopper plays the most "normal" character in a movie' noted one contemporary reviewer), *Cool Hand Luke, Hang 'em High*, the outstanding *Out of the Blue* (which he also directed), *True Grit, Paris Trout, Rumble Fish* and *Tracks*. Five times married, and still raging after all these years, Hopper was recently quoted as saying: 'Like all artists I want to cheat death a little and contribute something to the next generation.' *Shine on*, you crazy diamond.

Before making his name as the ill-fated teenage rocker Ritchie Valens in *La Bamba*, Lou Diamond Phillips had already co written and starred in *Trespasses*. Phillips's subsequent movies have included *Stand and Deliver, Young Guns* (and its sequel, co-starring with his friend Kiefer Sutherland), *A Show of Force, Malevolent, Route 666, Hangman, Brokedown Palace* and *Teresa's Tattoo*. He continues to work successfully on both sides of the camera, producing *Dakota*, writing *Ambition* and directing *Sioux City* whilst starring in the series *Wolf Lake* as Noah Cassidy. Melanee Murray appeared in *Judging Amy* and *K-PAX*.

'Just because they haven't attacked yet, doesn't mean they're not going to.' Dennis Hopper *Dennis freakin' Hopper!* You know, there's *good* casting, and then there's *inspirational* casting. Having Mad Bad Dennis in *24* is, definitely, an example of the latter. This is, actually, a super episode. It sees the series finally having struggled free of the straitjacket that it's been in for the last couple of hours, and flexing its dramatic muscles once again. There's loads of good lines (Mason, in particular, gets a bunch of them), and the action around the prison complex is fast and furious. The only thing letting it all down here is the Palmers's marital strife. How many times do we have to sit through variations on, basically, the same conversation to work out that David and Sherry are falling apart?

Sherry and David have been married for 25 years. Tony's licence plate is 4IZK505.

'My Night' by Pet Shop Boys.

'Getting Dennis Hopper was a real coup,' noted Stephen Hopkins, and inevitably, the sudden appearance of Hopper grabbed most of the media attention during this period. Hopper was signed for his *24* role shortly before Kiefer Sutherland won the Golden Globe in January. Sutherland himself had actually suggested Hopper, his co-star in two previous movies, for the part of Victor Drazen, Howard Gordon later noted. When Hopper agreed to appear, he hadn't seen any of *24* because he was out of the US making a movie. But, once given a taster, he immediately professed his love for the show's flashy, split-screen look and its real time storytelling.

'When I was in my 20s, Vincent Price said, "You should be playing bad guys,"' Hopper told the press. 'He was right.' Dennis also noted that, during the period when he was making movies with James Dean, he also carved out a small niche for himself playing psychotic bad guys on the small screen. He often appeared as a guest star on some of Warner Brothers' hugely popular roster of TV Westerns like *Cheyenne*, *Sugarfoot* and *Maverick*. 'The guest star was usually either the crazy psychopath or the young gun-fighter that comes into town and is getting into trouble,' said Hopper. 'I was always the troubled person because the good guys were already in place.'

CRITIQUE

'Characters drive from one location to another far too quickly for crowded Los Angeles highways. The body count of those killed stands at nearly 30, but no major characters have spent much time under arrest or in questioning. You rarely see characters shower, sleep, eat or use the restroom,' wrote Eric Deggans. 'While many shows avoid scenes showing characters on the telephone (because it's boring), cellular telephone calls have become integral in spicing *24*'s narrative - adding excitement to real time car trips and hospital waiting-room scenes.'

CAST AND CREW COMMENTS

'We would never have had the incredible year we did if it wasn't for critical support,' notes Kiefer Sutherland. He also says that he's happy that Jack might actually be allowed to eat and go to the bathroom next season, two things he was not seen doing at all during the first year.

'I love the split screen, and the use of hand held cameras,' Dennis Hopper noted. 'I love the idea that it's in supposed real time. It's a marvellous format and an imaginative show. It's a fun show to work on. I don't know how I end up, but I hope badly,' he added. 'I don't think this guy should be around long.'

DID YOU KNOW?

Sherry Palmer has become something of a TV icon. She makes the relatively innocent deceit of Stockard Channing's Abby Bartlet, the First Lady on *The West Wing*, look like a lightweight choir girl by comparison. Not since the glory days of Larry Hagman's J.R. in *Dallas* have television fans fallen so completely in love with a character who is so unredeemably, and gloriously, bad. 'People *love* to hate her,' notes Penny Johnson Jerald. She goes on to describe Sherry as 'a passionate, loving family person [but] driven by ambition that will stop at nothing. The show's writers intentionally threw in many parallels to both Shakespeare's Lady Macbeth and, more obliquely, Hillary Clinton, she continues. But Penny - who credits the writers with creating the most fascinating role of her career - is quick to point out that her character is not one-dimensional. 'I don't want people to think [that] she's a monster without feeling.' Howard Gordon confirmed that such multi-layered characterisation *was* intentional. 'Sherry was benign at the beginning, but the more we made her capable of greater treachery we said: "Let's take her further." There's definitely a very operatic quality to her.'

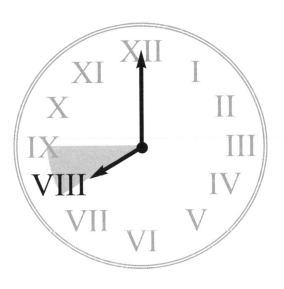

12:00 1:00 2:00 3:00 4:00 5:00 6:00 7:00 8:00 9:00 10:00 11:00 12:00 1:00 2:00 3:00 4:00 5:00 6:00 7:00 **8:00** 9:00 10:00 11:00 12:00

21   8:00 P.M. – 9:00 P.M.

US Transmission Date: 23 April 2002
UK Transmission Date: 21 July 2002
Terrestrial UK Transmission Date: 28 July 2002
Writers: Joel Surnow, Michael Loceff
Director: Stephen Hopkins
Cast: Dennis Hopper (Victor Drazen), Lou Diamond Phillips (Mark DeSalvo), Carlos Bernard (Tony Almeida), Penny Johnson Jerald (Sherry Palmer), Xander Berkeley (George Mason), Tanya Wright (Patty Brooks), Jude Ciccolella (Mike Novick), Željko Ivanek (Andre Drazen), Jon E Epstein (Al), Paul Schulze (Ryan Chappelle), Navi Rawat (Melanie), Darin Heames (Krugman), Jenn McCullough (Elaine), Christian Hastings (Harris), Angelo Pagan[59] (Drake), Pete Antico[60] (Barnes), Gwen Stewart (Female Officer), Lisa Joyner (Reporter), Melanee Murray (Lucy)[61]

8:02: The polls close in California. A television reporter announces that Palmer appears to have swept the state.

SUPER TUESDAY   This episode confirms that these events take place on Super Tuesday in which several states cast their votes in the primaries on the same day. The first Super Tuesday election took place during 1998. The aim of this is to encourage the support of the southern states and, at the same time, to downplay the importance of the New Hampshire primary which takes place some months before most of the rest. In the 2000 election primaries, 12 states took part in Super Tuesday, including, for the first time, California. In the *24* universe, 11 states are holding their elections on this day. And, when Palmer rejoins his staff's party he receives congratulations from Mike for sweeping all 11.

8:03: An officer pushes Melanie into the holding cell. Melanie walks over to Kim and tells Kim that she is in her seat. Kim gets up and sits elsewhere. Melanie then saunters to Kim's new position and repeats this. Depressed, Kim goes to stand by the bars.

BULLIES   Unfortunately Kim hasn't yet realised that Melanie is nothing more than a bully and that if you stand up to such people they usually crap their pants and run a mile.

LOGIC, LET ME INTRODUCE YOU TO THIS WINDOW   Palmer's press conference to announce his revelations about Keith, Lyle Gibson, Ferragamo, Carl and his backers ended at exactly 6:57. At 8:04 *Fox News* announce the results of a poll which suggests that 83% of voters approve of the way in which Palmer handled the Ferragamo crisis. How on earth did

59 Angelo Pagan played an unnamed FBI agent sent to dust for prints in '1:00 P.M. - 2:00 P.M.' Here, he plays Drake, a member of the CTU. It's probably best to assume that these are two different characters.
60 On the other hand, Pete Antico played one of the nameless CTU commandos in '12:00 Noon - 1:00 P.M.' Here, he is a CTU field officer called Barnes. It is quite possible that these are intended to be the same character.
61 Uncredited.

they get any sort of representative sample for such a poll and collate the results in an hour? Palmer's opponent, Hodges, is mentioned again. That's only about the third time in 24 hours. One might have thought that he would be slightly higher up the agenda on today of all days. Why is there a huge map on one of the CTU monitors which seems to be highlighting the results of the election? We know that their main *raison d'être* is in keeping David Palmer alive. But is whether or not he wins the democratic nomination to run for President part of their mandate?

8:05: Palmer asks Mike if they've heard from any of the financial backers. Mike says that they're probably laying low. Palmer stops the party to tell his staff that although this has been a very difficult day for all of them, he is confident that honesty was the best policy. Mason tells Nina that Division will consider the threat to Palmer to be minimal now that Alexis Drazen has been captured. Jack calls Mason and says that he needs a field unit to be sent immediately. Mason says that he will have to call Division. Jack makes it clear that Andre and his men are not going to wait whilst the request goes through the proper channels. Mason orders an assistant to dispatch a field unit which, he says, he will clear with Chappelle later.

Tony arrives at CTU with Teri who asks if they have any word on Kim's or Jack's location. Nina asks Teri to join her and Tony in the conference room for a debriefing.

8:08: At gunpoint, Jack orders Drazen to open the door and step out into the corridor. Andre and his men blast a hole through the wall. Jack, DeSalvo and Drazen are forced to make a hasty retreat into the prison.

POINTS AT WHICH TERI NEEDS A SLAP She visits Mason and says that neither Nina nor Tony will tell her anything about Kim. Mason notes that since Jovan asked Teri where Kim was, then it stands to reason that the terrorists are still looking for Kim too. Mason stresses that Jack means a lot to CTU and that he, personally, will do everything that he can to make sure that Kim is found. Mason continues that when they hear from Jack, he will let Teri know. He then asks his assistant, Rebecca, to keep Teri out of his hair.

8:17: Patty notices that Palmer seems distant and asks if he is feeling all right. Palmer says that he's just had a long day. Patty says that she admires him for standing by his principles. Mason calls the leader of the field unit, Barnes, who says that it appears the facility has been breached. As the smoke clears Andre orders Jack to let his father go and shows Jack that he has taken DeSalvo hostage. Jack drops his weapon and puts his hands in the air. Andre promptly shoots DeSalvo dead. Having been reunited with his son, Victor grabs a gun and prepares to execute Jack. Harris interrupts noting that there are a dozen well-armed men outside. Drazen orders the collapse of the corridor immediately. They take Jack with them as they may need him for bargaining purposes.

QUEEN BITCH Kim watches a violent struggle over a ciga- **8PM** rette in the prison cell. Seeing Kim cowering in the corner, Melanie confidently sits down next to her and begins to bait her. Kim asks Melanie what her problem is. Melanie tells Kim that *she* is her problem. Kim reminds Melanie that the only reason she's in this situation is because Melanie told the cops that Kim was part of the drug deal. The pair continue to bicker for several minutes, mostly about Rick. Kim finally gets fed up and, in a thoroughly satisfying moment, tells a, suddenly speechless, Melanie what a rotten day she's had. You *go*, girl!

QUOTE/UNQUOTE Kim, angrily to Melanie: 'Last night I was kidnapped, tied up in the back of a trunk and then I got to see your friend, Dan, get shot in the head... You take all of the bad luck you've had in your entire life, it wouldn't fit into half of what's happened to me in the past 24 hours. So messing me up may not be as easy as you think. But, you wanna try? Bring it on!'

8:28: As his men search for an alternative exit, Victor Drazen scolds Jack for believing that he is a monster simply because he wants revenge. Jack tells Drazen that he was a monster long before Jack met him. Drazen notes that Jack's opinion of him was formed by reading biased reports. Victor has called CTU and speaks to Mason. Drazen asks if Mason is the person that will be conducting negotiations. Mason replies that he is willing to listen to Drazen's concerns.

8:31: Mason breaks the bad news to Nina and Tony. Nina asks how Jack sounded. 'Alive,' notes Mason. He adds that Nina knows the situation may not have a happy outcome, and he suggests putting somebody else on the job who is less emotionally involved. Nina refuses the offer.

QUEEN BITCH (THE REMATCH) Back at the jail, there's further tension when the butch Lucy demands that Melanie take Lucy's spliff as a guard is about to enter the cell. Melanie refuses, and the drug falls to the floor. The guard demands to know who the culprit is. Melanie denies that it's hers, but she seemingly isn't believed by the screws. Well, she lacks credibility, for one thing. For reasons best know to herself, Kim blurts out that Melanie is, honestly, telling the truth. This once, anyway. Kim then boldly stands up for herself yet again as the furious Lucy attacks her. Lucy promptly knocks Kim to the floor.

BULLIES: A SECOND THOUGHT Okay, so it doesn't *always* work to stand up to bullies. Particularly not if they're the size of a small Third World country. However, having seen this display of brave stupidity, Melanie has one of those sudden changes of character motivation that only seem to happen in the movies. She tells the guard that she wants to speak to Krugman.

BACK STORY Jack asks Victor Drazen about the lookalike who must have gone into the building before Jack's crew blew it up. Jack says that since Drazen was using a body double, he knew that he was a likely target. Since he also let that target get near to his family, Victor himself put his family in danger. Sounds like Jack trying to weasel out of taking responsibility for his actions, in all honesty. But Drazen responds that his wife and daughter were supposed to be away that day and, unbeknown to him, they came back earlier than expected. He agrees that he should have been more careful. As he says this, Jack viciously kicks Drazen in the leg, steals his weapon and prepares to make his getaway. But Andre stops him and Jack promptly receives a severe punishment kicking.

8:40: Patty apologises because today has gone so spectacularly wrong for Palmer. He asks her not to feel bad for him, Keith and Nicole are the ones who have been really suffering. Patty tells Palmer that he worries about other people too much. Chappelle returns Mason's call. He's angry with Mason for allowing Jack to blunder into a Defense Department operation. Mason tells Chappelle that he doesn't particularly like Jack either, but at least he gets results. Chappelle should be grateful to Jack, he notes, for not allowing Victor Drazen to escape custody. Chappelle asks Mason how Victor Drazen could have escaped when he isn't, *technically*, a prisoner, or even *alive*? Mason is told to end the hostage situation one way or another, and to end it quickly. Mason apologetically tells Nina that he is ordering a full assault from the field unit.

8:45: Tony calls Teri, who is being kept in the examination room, to say that Kim has been found. Relieved, Teri asks if she can speak to Kim. Tony says that he will put Kim through as soon as that's possible. Nina arrives shortly after Teri has received this good news. But Nina has to temper it with some bad, telling her what has happened to Jack. The field unit are about to launch their assault on the facility. Mason is asked what to do about Jack. Mason has no advice on that, his only orders are to make sure that they get Drazen.

8:53: Krugman rushes to the holding cell to tell a relieved Kim that she is being released having spoken to someone at CTU. He offers to drive Kim there himself where her mother is waiting.

POWER POLITICS As Palmer and Mike prepare for Palmer's victory speech, Mike recommends that David forget his troubles. He's won, after all. Palmer feels his troubles are only just beginning. Mike explains that in the White House the office comes first and the President's home life second. There will be plenty of time for him to sort out the Sherry situation once he's elected.

8:56: The field unit storm the complex and find DeSalvo's body. They discover an escape tunnel, but it has been rigged with laser mines. Outside, Victor Drazen prepares to shoot Jack yet again, consoling Jack with the thought that Teri and Kim will soon be joining him. Jack tells Drazen that CTU have Alexis. Drazen and Andre bundle Jack into the back of their vehicle. In a police car, Kim asks to borrow Krugman's phone.

POINTS AT WHICH KIM NEEDS A SLAP On the telephone Teri and Kim each express relief that neither of them are dead. Kim says she will be with her mother soon, and returns the phone to Krugman. As she does this, a van smashes headfirst into the side of their car. Armed terrorists rush out of another vehicle, shoot Krugman and Kim is kidnapped yet again. Did your mother never warn you about speaking too soon?

LOGIC, LET ME INTRODUCE YOU TO THIS WINDOW How, exactly, *has* Victor Drazen been keeping in contact with his sons to allow them to set up the plan to rescue him? How, for instance, did he know to which facility he would be taken on this particular day? When Drazen is talking on his cellphone to someone at CTU and then hands the phone to Jack so that he can confirm that he is alive, Jack somehow knows that he's talking to Mason. How? Drazen never told Jack to whom he would be speaking. It could, just as easily, have been Nina or Tony or someone else entirely. One of the Serbian soldiers says 'Let's hustle, men.' So, he's a starting quarterback for the San Francisco 49ers in his spare time, is he? Could the collection of street-whores, druggies, psychos and the like in the hold-

8PM

ing cell be any more stereotypical? Particularly as they include a pot-smoking big butch mama who is *down* on all the white girls. Come on, this isn't *Prisoner Cell Block H.*

Jack knowing that Alexis had a meeting with Elizabeth Nash at 4:30 in no way proves that Alexis is still alive. Merely, that CTU have blown Alexis's cover and found out about his movements. Andre suspected this anyway since he's been working under the assumption that Alexis is dead. It's *very* surprising that Victor and Andre fall for this particular ruse. Kim uses Krugman's phone to ring Teri at CTU. Teri answers, not on her mobile, but on an internal CTU phone. How, therefore, did Kim know the specific number in CTU to ring and to speak to her mother direct? Remember that no operator puts her through and that, also, Teri is in a conference room and not in Jack's office which Kim would probably know the number for. As we've seen, there doesn't appear to be a switchboard at CTU suggesting that there are separate lines going to specific work stations so, is this just a lucky guess on Kim's part to get directly through to Teri instead of, say Tony or Nina?

Why does Nina tell Teri that Jack has been captured by the terrorists? Once again, as with the Alan York information all those hours ago, there really doesn't seem any reason for her to divulge this other than the purely sadistic. Was Nina hoping that Teri would cause a huge fuss, run crying and shouting into Mason's office and distract him from ordering the field unit to go in take out the terrorists? If so, then her plan fails miserably. Or, alternatively, was this merely a bit of mean spirited payback for Teri who was so incredibly nasty to Nina at the safehouse? If Andre's and Victor's plan was to kill Jack at this point - as they are very definitely intending to do at least twice in the episode - then *how* were they intending to kill Palmer? Jack seems to be a key element of *that* part of their plan. If, indeed, they've actually *got* a plan. Let's be honest, they're making it up as they go along, aren't they? At least Gaines had a scheme. An incompetent, overcomplicated scheme, possibly, but still...

Gwen Stewart appeared in *Down to Earth.* Lisa Joyner was in *Bounce.* She's also an entertainment correspondent for *Fox News.*

NOTES 'Enjoy the rest of the evening.' Just when you thought that two of the three Bauers were safe and sound, something comes along and proves you wrong. Indeed, a running joke on several *24* websites around this time was 'Do any members of the Bauer family meet any *other* members of the Bauer family during this episode?' The answer was, invariably, no. It had to be said that, this is mostly another *nothing* episode. There's little that is actually wrong with it, *per se*, but the plot does not advance an inch during the course of it. Some of the little side-alleys that various characters go down are quite fun. (Kim in jail, particularly. *That's* really good for a laugh.) Ultimately, however, Teri is at her most irksome here, and there's not much common sense being shown in many of the activities of the Drazen family. Still, if only for the brief moment where Jack gets a good hard shoeing from Andre, the episode is a valuable lesson never to take things at face value.

Palmer has won the nomination in 11 states today although, he reminds Mike, America has 39 others. However, not all of these hold primaries. In New York, Palmer won 64% of the vote against Hodges's 36%. In Ohio, the result was 69% Palmer, 31% Hodges. Maryland is said to have had an 80% turnout. Governor Hodges has had 25 years experience in government. The Drazen's getaway Ford transit van has the licence plate 4DEQ797.

CRITIQUE '24 was unique because it unfolded in real time,' noted Tim Goodman. 'That forced the writers to keep a lot of plates spinning at once, a harrowing feat that engendered applause all by itself. But the inherent problems cropped up quickly. Namely, Teri had to have a series of dramatic events come down on her head - she was raped, she was kidnapped (twice!), she was forever running from gunmen and, in the season's biggest leap of logic, she got temporary amnesia after seeing her daughter, Kim, apparently die in a car explosion. Only Kim didn't. That would have meant the end for one of television's most in-trouble teens. When 24 got weak, it was because Teri and Kim kept fumbling into harm's way, often in unbelievable fashion.'

CAST AND CREW COMMENTS 'Kiefer, on screen, projects a certain darkness,' notes Robert Cochran. 'He's played a lot of villains. So to take a guy like that and make him a hero, you get all of the good things about being a hero [like] the nobility and the courage. But underneath it, there's an edge, that darkness, those demons that he's fighting against.'

DID YOU KNOW? The producers were, reportedly, amused by questions from reporters about what would have happened if the show had been cancelled short of its 24-show premise. Did the 24 hour concept and, indeed, the series *title* put pressure on the network to keep the show on after it had passed its sell-by date? If that were the case, noted Joel Surnow wittily, 'We should have called it *110*, shouldn't we?'

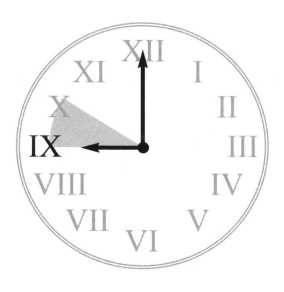

9:00 P.M. – 10:00 P.M.

12:00 1:00 2:00 3:00 4:00 5:00 6:00 7:00 8:00 9:00 10:00 11:00 12:00 1:00 2:00 3:00 4:00 5:00 6:00 7:00 8:00 **9:00** 10:00 11:00 12:00

22   9:00 P.M. – 10:00 P.M.

US Transmission Date: 7 May 2002
UK Transmission Date: 28 July 2002
Terrestrial UK Transmission Date: 4 August 2002
Writers: Joel Surnow, Michael Loceff
Director: Paul Shapiro
Cast: Dennis Hopper (Victor Drazen), Carlos Bernard (Tony Almeida), Penny Johnson Jerald (Sherry Palmer), Xander Berkeley (George Mason), Tanya Wright (Patty Brooks), Željko Ivanek (Andre Drazen), Misha Collins (Alexis Drazen), Christian Hastings (Harris), Endre Hules (Serge), Juliette Dudnik (Mila), Christina Moore (Dana), Eugene Lazarev (Nikola)

9:00: The kidnappers put Kim in their van. Palmer enters the hotel's banquet room to give an inspirational speech. Jack is given a cellphone by Andre, calls Nina, and asks her to get Alexis on the line so that Victor can confirm his son is alive. Victor offers to trade the life of Jack for that of his son. During Palmer's speech, Sherry tells Patty that she cannot travel with her husband to Dallas the next day because of a prior commitment. She asks Patty to keep him company.

9:08: Mason tells Nina that Chapelle would never allow the trade. Any dealings with Drazen would be an acknowledgement that he is still alive. Nina breaks the terrible news to Teri.

9:15: Andre and Victor bring Jack to the basement of a Slav restaurant. Drazen warmly greets the owner, Nikola, and his daughter, Mila. Mason is battling with his superiors to save Jack when Teri interrupts him. Teri demands to know what he is doing about the situation.

POINTS AT WHICH TERI NEEDS A SLAP Barging into Mason's office and demanding that he stop patronising her Teri, finally, gets at least a verbal dose of what she's deserved for much of the last 21 hours.

QUOTE/UNQUOTE Mason, to Teri: 'I'll tell you exactly what I'll do. I'm gonna call up Division and ask them to reconsider one more time. They're gonna say "No", and that'll be the end of it. Anything else?' Nice one, George.

9:17: Teri begs Nina for help. Nina claims that she is attempting to get in touch with someone who could possibly aid Jack and asks Teri to trust her. Palmer is talking to his supporters when he receives a call from Nina who informs him that Victor Drazen is alive and is holding Jack hostage. Palmer promises to help. Tony is alerted that Kim has been kidnapped from the police car.

FANCY A SNACK, JACK? Drazen offers Jack something to eat, but he refuses. Must be tempting, though, since Jack hasn't been seen to eat *anything* since Midnight.

BRIBERY AND CORRUPTION Palmer calls Mason and demands that he complete the trade. Mason is reluctant noting that this does not fall under the Senator's sphere of influence. He will, Mason notes, be reprimanded for exceeding his authority. Palmer assures Mason that when he becomes President, he will instate Mason to a position of power. Mason questions what will happen if Palmer does not get elected. 'That's not going to happen,' Palmer replies.

9:28: Despite being tied up, Jack is still able to knock down his guard and grab a knife. Jack then holds the knife to Mila's throat and orders the terrorists to drop their weapons. Everyone does, except Victor who shoots Mila in the head, killing her. The guards apprehend a shocked and appalled Jack.

CIGARETTES AND ALCOHOL Drazen drinks some red wine with his meal. Palmer and Patty share a glass of champagne as she flirts with him. There's also an 'open bar' at the Senator's victory party.

9:29: Andre calls Mason again and George agrees to the trade. Andre instructs him to bring Alexis to an address on Grand Avenue. Tony finds that the address is a repair garage.

QUOTE/UNQUOTE Mason: 'We're going to do the swap on our terms.' Andre, sarcastically: 'Yeah, *that's* an interesting dream.'

9:32: Sherry chastises Palmer for stepping away from his victory party to take Nina's call. Patty informs Palmer that she has prepared a series of answers to possible questions that may arise dealing with the Keith situation. Palmer wants to go over them immediately, and arranges to meet her upstairs in five minutes. Nikola grieves over his dead daughter, as Victor consoles him. Suddenly, Nikola turns his anger on his guest. Drazen shoots Nikola. With the restaurant now resembling a bloodbath, Kim is dragged in. A guard puts a hood over Jack's head and carries him up the stairs. Kim is left in the basement with the dead bodies.

9:39: Teri is relieved to learn that a trade will be made for Jack. When she asks about Kim, Nina says that she will look into it. Teri thanks Nina for being honest with her. Nina admits to Tony that she just couldn't tell Teri the truth. In the van, Jack begs for his daughter's life. He tells Andre that if they kill innocent people, it will be harder for them to leave the country alive. Patty questions whether Palmer has had any past indiscretions. Palmer asks if Patty is flirting with him. She responds that yes she may well be. Palmer shrugs this off and they go back to the party.

REFERENCES *The Wall Street Journal* is mentioned.

9:45: The van parks in a field close to an oil rig. Andre handcuffs Jack to a fence, warning that if Alexis is not delivered, then Jack will die. Andre puts a cellphone into Jack's pocket and leaves. Sherry asks Patty if she went upstairs with Palmer. Patty tells her that she did what Sherry told her to, but that she feels uncomfortable about deceiving Palmer. Sherry assures Patty that *this* is what Palmer needs, whether he realises it or not. Her actions, Sherry continues, are for the good of the campaign.

9:54: Mason brings Alexis Drazen in an ambulance to the meeting place. Harris alerts Andre over a phone that Alexis is in far worse shape than they thought. Mason demands that Jack be turned over immediately. Harris says that once they are satisfied that they are not being followed, they will provide Mason with Jack's location. Mason asks about Kim, but Harris is only concerned with Jack. Mason allows the green SUV to leave the garage. He calls Nina, and she tells him that she has the SUV tracked.

L.A. STORY The garage where Alexis is taken is located at 2127 Grand Avenue. This runs parallel to the 110 from South L.A. ending at the junction of the 101 right in the heart of Downtown. Interestingly, the filming location used for this wasn't on Grand at all. In fact, it looks like they are back in the Valley. At the end of the episode, Jack is told by Andre to drive towards Century City. With its towering office blocks and giant boulevards, Century is one of L.A.'s most egregious examples of style over substance. Originally part of the 20th Century Fox studio lot,[62] the residential city began to take shape in the 1960s, just as nearby Beverly Hills was starting to acquire its reputation for being the in-place for the international jet-set to have homes. Despite Century's dreary concrete plazas and singular lack of charm, the area remains a very popular location for movies and TV shows. Much of *Die Hard* was filmed there, for instance.

9:58: Harris waves a signal detector over Alexis and discovers the tracking device. He smashes it on the ground. Nina realises that her trace is gone. At the oil rig, a shot rings out from the darkness. The restraint is blown off, freeing Jack. The cellphone in his pocket rings. Andre tells Jack that if he ever wants to see Kim alive again, he should go to a nearby-parked car and drive.

LOGIC, LET ME INTRODUCE YOU TO THIS WINDOW It has to be asked, why is Nina so desperate to get Jack released? She goes to some extraordinary lengths (including ringing David Palmer directly). Is it because Jack needs to be free to deliver the bomb that will kill Palmer? Yeah, okay, that sort of makes sense. But then, if that's been the terrorists' plan all along, why were Victor and Andre about to kill Jack just ten minutes ago before he revealed that Alexis was still alive? Sorry, all this thinking is giving me a headache.

The rifle shot that breaks Jack's handcuff chain and frees him is one of the finest pieces of marksmanship since the JFK assassination. Allegedly.

'YOU MAY REMEMBER ME FROM...' Endre Hules appeared in *The Seventh Sense, 8 Heads in a Duffel Bag, Diagnosis Murder, Zoolander, The Craft, China Beach* and *Apollo 13*. Eugene (Yevgeni) Lazarev is one of the foremost Russian stage-actors of his generation. He has also appeared in *The Saint, The Agency, Alias* and *The West Wing*. Christina Moore was in *Second Skin, Friends* and *Just Shoot Me*.

BEHIND THE CAMERA Paul Shapiro's CV includes *Smallville, Dark Angel, Roswell, What We Did That Night, Millennium, Robocop, Avalanche, The Lotus Eaters, The X-Files, Kung Fu: The Legend Continues, The Commish, Mom P.I., Rookies, Hockey Night, Clown White* and *Miracle at Moreaux*.

9PM

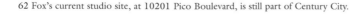

62 Fox's current studio site, at 10201 Pico Boulevard, is still part of Century City.

'Jack's like all the rest of us. Expendable.' Ooo, it's getting really exciting now. The subplots have mostly been shed and we're back to the original handful that we started with: can Jack save his daughter and avoid killing Palmer? And who is the mole? Dennis Hopper's over-the-top moments of ranting pyschomania occasionally threaten to derail the carefully built tension and suspense. But then you get a moment like his sinister ice-cold stare as he shoots the girl whom Jack is attempting to hold hostage, and you remember what a bloody great actor this bloke is. A quick word, too, about some of the supporting work. Carlos Bernard, Xander Berkeley and Željko Ivanek, in particular, are never really given much in the way of background to work with throughout the series. But all three manage to bring elegant touches of characterisation to their vastly different roles. They contrive to turn Tony, Mason and Andre into much more than the cardboard cyphers that they could, so easily, have been in lesser hands.

There was a time when Palmer was 10 points behind in the polls. But, even then, David was confident of victory. Palmer offers Mason a deal in return for his help in freeing Jack. Mason must exceed his CTU authority to do this and will, Palmer speculates, be reprimanded and probably demoted because of it. Mason sarcastically notes that it sounds *great* so far. In nine months, Palmer continues, he will be in the White House. Within the first month of his presidency, he promises, Mason will be given a high level position in Washington thus bypassing five years of middle-management. It *is* interesting to note that, in the first episode of the second season, Palmer has been President for approximately seven months already and Mason is *still* stuck at CTU. Perhaps, like many politicians, Palmer is really just an incorrigible liar and all this integrity is pretence? The Senator refers to the people for whom Carl works as 'The Latham Group' (named after the series' Editor David Latham). Sherry is committed to attending a National Youth Service Day event in L.A. tomorrow. Sherry likes cherries. Mason's contact with LAPD is Chris Porterfield, named after *24*'s Production Co-ordinator. Doctors Brian Chasim and Darrell Maines from UCLA are currently working with some success in the field of AIDS research.

Palmer's victory party includes ghastly musak-instrumental cover versions of a trio of cheesy 80s disco favourites: 'We Are Family' by Sister Sledge, 'I'm So Excited' by the Pointer Sisters and the turgid, 'Celebration' by Kool and the Gang. What a total nightmare.

'Undermining *24* more than anything was Sept. 11,' noted Frazier Moore. 'Already stricken for real by the unexplainable, many viewers may have looked askance at any TV show designed to keep them in the dark for months. The hopped-up sense of dread that ensnares *24* may have struck many viewers not as sleek escapism, but as an echo of their own altered world. Familiar rhythms are absent from *24*. There is never a break. No sleep, no awakening. Just the fearsome rush of time, often flashing on the screen like a digital compulsion. As a wild ride, *24* has been a resounding success, even if the things that make it right seemed wrong to some viewers after Sept. 11. It surely isn't comfort-food TV.'

'After its early days, American TV opted for the open-ended series form,' noted David Thompson. 'In a series, you establish the endless situation and the ageless characters (think *Friends*) and then turn that engine over so that the viewers are immediately at home with any episode. The idea of "story", on the other hand, is based on the confidence that says: we can hook you, you are going to be smart enough to keep up and clamour for every new episode, you won't go away. If you think of it like this, then *24* is not so much revolutionary as a return to a more challenging past.' Along with *The Sopranos*, Thompson continued, *24* is also a sign of 'how far cable TV is pushing network shows into being more interesting. Of course, in America, where it showed on the Fox network, each episode of *24* filled an hour – with commercial breaks – but they only run 45 minutes in the UK. Purists may say that Britain gets the better side of the deal. I disagree; the commercial breaks, the bumpers, the digital clock, all worked very well together, and many of the adverts set up fascinating interplays with the show itself, for they were trying to sell the comfort, the peace of mind and the absence of betrayal that it scorns.'

CAST AND CREW COMMENTS 'The day will be over, the story will come to an end, it's not a cliff-hanger,' pledged Kiefer Sutherland shortly before the season concluded. 'It's a hard ending, but I think it will be satisfying on a lot of different levels.' Not that, even *he*, knew how the final episode would look until a fortnight before transmission. 'Various endings were being considered, and when we started shooting, I said, "Look, which one are we committing to?" They said, "We *think* this one." But I [did voice-overs for] three different endings.'

DID YOU KNOW? President Josiah Bartlet may rule *The West Wing* universe, but next year he will be required to share Air Force One with President David Palmer. One of Dennis Haysbert's inspirations for his portrayal of Palmer is Sidney Poitier's defiant declaration in *Guess Who's Coming to Dinner?* that, whilst his father still saw himself as a black man, the son sees himself as a *man*. 'I no longer call myself an African American,' says Haysbert. 'I call myself an American of African descent. My parents were American, my grandparents were American. And so on, all the way back until you get to those ancestors who *did* come over on that boat.' Whilst that sensibility was developed over a lifetime, it crystallised, notes Haysbert, after the events of September 11. Staying in a New York hotel just blocks from ground zero while filming the movie *Far From Heaven* reinforced Haysbert's sense of community. 'For a brief moment I didn't feel any racism. I felt a sense of unity like I'd never seen or felt in the city before,' he said.

9PM

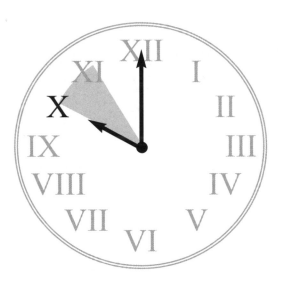

10:00 P.M. – 11:00 P.M.

12:00 1:00 2:00 3:00 4:00 5:00 6:00 7:00 8:00 9:00 10:00 11:00 12:00 1:00 2:00 3:00 4:00 5:00 6:00 7:00 8:00 9:00 **10:00** 11:00 12:00

23 10:00 P.M. – 11:00 P.M.

US Transmission Date: 14 May 2002
UK Transmission Date: 4 August 2002
Terrestrial UK Transmission Date: 11 August 2002
Writers: Robert Cochran, Howard Gordon
Director: Paul Shapiro
Cast: Dennis Hopper (Victor Drazen), Carlos Bernard (Tony Almeida), Penny Johnson Jerald (Sherry Palmer), Xander Berkeley (George Mason), Tanya Wright (Patty Brooks), Željko Ivanek (Andre Drazen), Misha Collins (Alexis Drazen), Paul Webster (Agent Ron), Josip Kuchan (Serbian Doctor), Yvette Fernandez (Reporter), Emile Williams (Secret Service Agent)

10:02: Jack calls CTU and notes that he has been freed and must find Kim. Mason and Nina simultaneously realise that the only reason Jack would be set free is if the terrorists were going back to their original plan to use Jack to kill Palmer. The Senator gives Patty a room key and tells her to meet him in 20 minutes. Victor and Andre Drazen reunite, briefly, with Alexis. Then he dies from internal bleeding.

10:14: The manipulative Sherry tells Patty to report back to her after she has slept with the Senator. Tony discovers that the plans to the Saugus detention facility had been tampered with. Nina orders him to find out who has had access to them in the last month believing there may be a second dirty agent within CTU.

POINTS AT WHICH TERI NEEDS A SLAP Nina tells Teri that Jack has been freed, but that he is not yet ready to return to CTU. She reveals that Jack has gone to find Kim whom, she admits, the terrorists have captured yet again. Needless to say, Teri can't handle this information.

10:17: Jack calls Palmer and tells him that the Drazens want their $200,000,000 of frozen assets. Patty makes her way to the Senator's room. Palmer promptly fires her for collaborating with his wife. Patty pleads that it was all Sherry's idea but Palmer will have none of her excuses.

QUOTE/UNQUOTE Patty, on Sherry: 'She can be pretty scary sometimes.'

10:27: Tony discovers that Mason accessed the facility plans four days ago. Nina suggests they shut down Mason's network access. Palmer confronts Sherry and tells her that he has fired Patty. Sherry's plan to compromise him with a honey-trap has failed. Jack arrives at the hotel and asks Palmer to transfer the money. Palmer insists that even if he wanted to he couldn't as the money has been long spent. Furthermore, Drazen *must* know this. The phone given to Jack by Andre rings, and Palmer agrees to keep the terrorists on the line for as long as possible. Jack suddenly realises that they have been set-up. The phone is a bomb. Jack throws it through the window and pulls Palmer down as it explodes. Victor and Andre share a smile of satisfaction as, they believe, their revenge is finally complete.

10PM

There's a direct allusion to *Die Hard* ('everything that happened today was because of money?'). At CTU, the agents watch the breaking news of Palmer's 'death' on the news station KRLH. There is a misquotation of the biblical text concerning 'the sins of the father' (alluded to in Exodus 20, Leviticus 26, Psalm 79, Isaiah 65 and Daniel 9, amongst others).

10:37: Jack searches the rubble for clues. Palmer tells the Secret Service agents to report that they don't yet know if he survived the blast. Jack tells Sherry that the world has to believe that the Senator was killed in the attack. Though Sherry is furious, Palmer agrees. Mason asks Tony to find out when Palmer will leave for Dallas. Nina tells Tony to restore Mason's access but to redirect everything to her so that she can monitor what he is viewing. The news breaks on television that Senator Palmer is dead. Andre calls Jack to check whether Jack survived the blast. Jack offers to trade himself for his daughter.

CLUE Andre agrees, and tells Jack that if he tries to involve CTU, that the terrorists will know immediately. That's virtually telling Jack *we have someone working for us in CTU*.

10:46: Jack calls Nina and tells her that he's going to get Kim. Nina hands the phone to Teri.

POINTS AT WHICH TERI NEEDS A SLAP Knowing that something may go wrong even without her husband telling her how dangerous a situation he's about to leap into, Teri takes the wholly inappropriate opportunity to finally tell Jack that she is pregnant. This, obviously, makes Jack cry like a girly-man.

L.A. STORY The Drazen's warehouse is located at Dock 11A, part of the Port of Los Angeles in Long Beach.[63]

10:51: At their new location, on the docks, Andre tells Kim why she is being held. Mason calls Nina and Tony into his office and tells them that Palmer is still alive.

CLUE The camera lingers for a few vital seconds longer on Nina registering her obvious shock at this news, than on Tony.

10:52: Mason asks if Jack has called in. Nina says that he hasn't. Outside, Nina tells Tony that Jack has, indeed, called and what he intends to do. Kim makes a daring escape, only for Andre to corner her on the edge of the pier. Kim jumps into the ocean.

LOGIC, LET ME INTRODUCE YOU TO THIS WINDOW Kim throws scalding hot coffee into the face of the terrorist who is guarding her. Yet about 20 seconds later, this man is joining his

63 Most of Long Beach's more interesting sights - including the location of the anchored cruise liner *Queen Mary* - are grouped together well away from the actual port itself. Once the stomping ground mainly for off-duty naval personnel, Long Beach's numerous porn shops and sleazy bars combined to give the area an extremely seedy reputation. In the last decade, a billion-dollar cash injection, and the construction of a convention centre, several swanky shopping malls and the restoration of some of the harbour's 19th century buildings, has somewhat changed this image.

colleagues in the chase for her, instead of lying, clutching his face on the floor whimpering for his mommy as most people would be. Cor, *he's* hard.

THE MISSING SCENE At this point, as everybody watching the overseas print will know, there is an extra scene, and it's a really important one, foreshadowing a key revelation made a few moments later. Nina goes to see if Teri needs anything. Teri, in one of her finest moments, tells Nina that the past is the past. Whilst, up until today, Nina has for the most part been merely a voice on the other end of the phone to her, Teri says that she has nothing but total respect for Nina. She adds that she, Kim and Jack all probably owe Nina their lives. Nina looks a bit uncomfortable at this suggestion. Then, Teri drops her bombshell. She tells Nina, as she told Jack moments earlier, that she is pregnant. There is a look on Nina's face that's pitched midway between horror and disgust. Of course, you *think* it's because Nina still loves Jack. Who knows, maybe she really does...?

LOGIC, LET ME INTRODUCE YOU TO THIS WINDOW Mason makes it back from Grand Avenue to CTU in Santa Monica in under 12 minutes. That's goddamn *impressive*. Jack joins in with the 'faster than a speeding bullet' routine later, doing Sunset Boulevard to Long Beach in slightly over 20 minutes. (It should take double that time, at least.) Does Jack have the authority to order high ranking members of Palmer's Secret Service detail to do anything? He may have helped to save the Senator's life twice today, but he's still a pretty lowly agent in national terms.

10:59: Kim manages to untie her ropes and swims under the dock. Andre's phone rings. His call is from a woman identifying herself as Yelena. She tells him that David Palmer is not dead. There is one final revelation. Yelena is Nina.

DOES NINA'S TRUE IDENTITY MAKE SENSE? So, the series' second most popular character, true-blue seven year veteran CTU agent (and Jack's former lover) Nina Myers is, seemingly, also known as Yelena. And, she's really a Serbian/German-speaking international terrorist working with the Drazens. Sarah Clarke, herself, told the press after this revelation was broadcast, that *she* didn't learn until late December - around the shooting of episode 14 - that she was to be the mole. From that point onwards, in little glances, stray remarks and subtle elements of the plot, Nina's true role, in hindsight, makes more or less complete sense. But, what about before that?

Howard Gordon, within days of the broadcast of this episode, was claiming to several newspapers, that the show's writers had planned it this way all along.[64] The production office even produced an extensive document for journalists to explain many of the apparent contradictions within the plotlines of the earlier episodes. So, basically, the question is, does Nina's story tie-up? Here is a recap of some of the more important points:

Walsh gave Jack the keycard that he got from Baylor in episode two. He told Jack that whomsoever's electronic signature was on the card was a double agent within CTU. Jamey (*herself*, let's remember, a double agent) subsequently finds Nina's details on the card. It is, therefore, fair to say that for a good proportion of the first three episodes, or

10PM

64 This was subsequently contradicted by Robert Cochran: See the **Did You Know?** section for episode 24.

thereabouts, Nina looks a very likely candidate for the mole within Jack's team. It is also worth noting that, on the 'My Name is Jack Bauer...' recap at the start of most episodes, when Jack says 'and the people that I work with may be involved', this is always followed by a brief shot of Nina glancing up and looking rather furtive. That could, one suppos- es, have been a subtle clue that was there all along for anyone to see who knew what they were looking for.

When Jack confronts Nina about the card, she deflects his suspicions by pointing out that she was with him in Santa Barbara on the day that her computer was used to produce the card. Of course, Nina could easily have altered the date on the card to cover her tracks. Or she could have got somebody else, like Jamey for instance, to use her computer thus giving herself a cast iron alibi. Or, is this all a double-bluff to deliberate- ly make Jack initially suspect her, so that when she produces her alibi, for the rest of the day, he will believe that she is one of the few people whom he very definitely *can* trust? The dead Dunlop Plaza assassin's thumb, removed by Jack, cannot be identified. The spec- ulative explanation is that 'either this guy doesn't exist or he has friends in high places.' Nina could certainly *be* that friend, erasing any records of him from the database. There are a cou- ple of further examples of files or evidence going missing or information being incorrect or incomplete as the day progresses, all of which Nina could be responsible for.

Nina calls Teri and tells her that the dead body Jack found in Penticoff's car was one Alan York. Thus, she alerts Teri to the fact that the man claiming to be Janet York's father, in whose car she's currently sitting, is an impostor. This is possibly the most tricky of Nina's actions to rationalise with hindsight. Nina has absolutely no reason to do this. Except that she may be unaware of the exact details of Ira Gaines's end of the conspira- cy, and thus not recognise any significance in the man's identity. She, also, later gives the same information to Jack himself, a further indication that she is unaware that the name Alan York means anything to the Bauers.

Jack subsequently kidnaps and shoots Nina, on Gaines's instructions. This suggests that whilst Nina may know, roughly, who Gaines is and what he's doing, Gaines does not know about Nina or her place in the conspiracy.

Nina, aided by Tony (whom several people tell during the course of the day that Nina is blatantly using him), catch Jamey spying for Gaines. This is a perfect opportuni- ty for Nina to deflect her own actions by fingering Jamey who, it seems, was as unaware of Nina's true allegiance as Gaines was. Jamey's death makes Nina's cover virtually complete.

Nina suggests to Jack around episode 14 that there may be a second mole within CTU. Having framed Jamey so successfully, there doesn't seem any reason for her to do this. But it's something that Jack may have figured out himself anyway and, by Nina giv- ing him her opinion on the matter, it reinforces his trust in her. She clearly appears at various points during the day to be attempting to set up George Mason as a potential fall guy, sowing the seeds of doubt in Jack's mind about him.

Nina brings Teri and Kim to the safehouse, essentially setting a trap for them to be recaptured or killed. She then manipulates Teri into realising that Nina and Jack were recently lovers, thus turning Teri against her and giving Nina a perfect excuse to leave before the assassins arrive. An excuse that even Jack is able to understand.

Once Alexis Drazen is stabbed and taken into custody, why doesn't Nina tell Andre? It could be that she considers telling him about his brother's wounding could, ultimately, deflect Drazen from his *real* objective - ensuring that Palmer is assassinated. There is, also, a delicious possibility that Nina deliberately manipulated Elizabeth Nash *into* stabbing Alexis (hopefully to death). Whilst it would mean the death of an important member of the terrorist group, and the son of its *leader*, it does remove any chance of the tracking device that Elizabeth is about to plant leading CTU to Andre and, ultimately, Victor. Note that Nina is the one who is left alone with Elizabeth and, from the few bits of their conversation that we see, she seems to be talking a great deal about how Alexis *used* Elizabeth so callously. Hell has no fury like a woman scorned.

Nina then accompanies Jack to the meeting with Morgan and, although she does it *very* subtly she is, certainly, a factor in the barbed interplay between Jack and Hanlin. This, ultimately, results in Morgan's death before he can give away too much incriminating information.

Nina then has to return to CTU where she, desperately, tries to let Jack know that Kim and Teri have both disappeared from the safehouse and have possibly been recaptured by the terrorists. As Jack is about to blunder into what Nina knows to be the rescue from captivity of Victor Drazen, keeping his mind occupied with his family would be highly advantageous. Thankfully, Mason doesn't let her speak to Jack.

Nina then tells the terrorists where to find Kim, thus providing them with a further element of leverage to force Jack into killing Palmer.

But why is Nina so desperate for Mason to exchange Jack for Alexis? She tells Teri about Jack's capture, possibly in the hope that Jack's frantic and annoying wife will be able to put pressure on Mason. (The alternative is that she's just playing sadistic mindgames with Teri whom she must *really* hate after the way she was treated earlier in the day.) When that plan doesn't work, she goes directly to Senator Palmer to ensure Jack's release by appealing to Mason's ambition. What's all that about? Given that Victor's and Andre's plan (*eventually*) is that Jack will be given the booby-trapped mobile phone that is intended to kill Palmer, Nina knows that Jack must be free to deliver this. Plus, it would hardly be in-character for Nina to meekly surrender her former lover to the fates. Rather than, as she does, make quite a show of being trying to help him in his darkest hour. But all of this is another point at which if you start to examine Nina's motivation too closely you end up in the windmills of your mind going wibble, wibble...

The Drazens want Jack and his family dead. So, why doesn't Nina kill Kim, or Teri, or both on the numerous occasions when she has the chance? Again, that could be because *Nina's* objective, and the objective of the people whom she *really* works for, is Palmer's assassination. The deaths of Jack's family, and indeed of Jack himself, may seem

10PM

indulgent to Nina. She may well consider that this is an incidental bit of revenge-scenario for the Drazens benefit and mere window-dressing to the *real* task in hand.

The big question: aside from those occasions when we can, with hindsight, tell that she's sending him off down blind avenues (the entire adventure with Penticoff gets Jack not an inch closer to the main plot, for instance), why does Nina help Jack so loyally throughout the day? It's probably simply because Nina knows that she is more powerful when she's in Jack's total confidence than she would be if he didn't trust her. That's a position that both Mason and Tony find themselves in at various points throughout the day.

All of this ignores the fact that Nina doesn't ring the Drazens as soon as she finds out that Palmer is still alive, but she *does* contact them immediately after she finds out that Teri is pregnant. This is because what hell *really* hath no fury like, is The Other Woman finding out that her bloke's wife has just got herself a useful weapon in hanging onto him.

Once again, it's worth stressing that just about everything regarding Nina's actions, from around episode 14 or 15 onwards, do make a kind of sense if you think hard and long enough about the context. Before that, however, it's up to the viewer to see if they can spot the mole within.

'YOU MAY REMEMBER ME FROM...'

Josip Kuchan was in *Fall*. Paul Webster appeared in *Innocent*.

NOTES

'We have decided the sins of the father need not be visited on her.' It is the final scene of this episode that will live in the memory. A quite brilliant moment of pure unbridled drama that is guaranteed to leave every viewer staring blankly at their TV screens shaking their head and muttering 'but... but...' Sadly, the Nina revelation conspires to cover for much of the rest of the episode which is actually, in places, rather disappointing. With the exception of the Palmer bomb-blast, once again little of any consequence happens. The episode looks great - there's that fabulous opening aerial shot of L.A. at night, for instance. But apart from aesthetics like this, it's all talk, talk, talk. There's much exposition, bluff and many moody shots of Jack driving his car. They were obviously saving up all the tension for the next episode.

Mason's CTU ID is 226-005-57951. He had level 8 security. Work station names at Division include Taunton, Porter, Titan and Babel 5. Andre's sister, Martina, was a photographer.

THE FINAL TRAILER

'*After 23 hours on the edge of your seat, the most thrilling, the most powerful, the most shocking hour... will be the last. The season finale of 24, next Tuesday at nine (eight Central) on Fox.*' So, not much hype there.

CRITIQUE

'Many people have noted that *24* is the first great work driven by the cellphone,' wrote *The Independent*. 'It often seems to be a portrait of a world in which hushed neurotics are talking to themselves. But the cellphone isn't just a gear system for the story - it's a paradigm of a world in which we can always break in on others (and be broken into). These telephones aren't just linking systems, tender and warm. They're bugs, parasites eating their way out from inside the wounded head.' The piece also noted that: 'By chance alone, the show's view of the US security agencies coincided fruitfully with the slowly emergent understanding that the events of 11 September might have been identified and averted. We live in a world where even the good news is bad, if you shift the light in which you see it. No one really gets tired - this is a new version of the American dream. Don't die: keep awake.'

On the Nina revelation, Channel 4 newsreader Khrishnan Guru-Murthy spoke for many fans when he described his feelings: 'It really undermines your sense of what humanity is all about.'

CAST AND CREW COMMENTS 'It has been quite a day,' Leslie Hope noted as everybody prepared for the finale. In fact, she was even happy to suggest that Teri's brief bout of amnesia was, conceptually, just what the doctor ordered. 'As difficult as [the amnesia] storyline was to process as an actress, it was also a huge relief. I didn't have to carry 14 shows' worth of drama behind me. Teri could forget for a while!' Hope also noted that this was the first time that she had ever been involved in a series that was likely to be considered for Emmy recognition. 'Creatively and personally, 24 has been one of the best experiences I've ever had. I've done shows that I thought were crap where I had to reach for an answer, but I haven't had to lie for this show... Except about what I know!'

'Once you start watching the show, I think the time frame element, combined with the fact that it's a thriller, you just get hooked into wanting to see the end,' added Kiefer Sutherland. 'The fantastic thing about our show is in the nature of the concept. It has a conclusion. This day does end and there is a result.'

On *24: The Post Mortem*, Carlos Bernard revealed that he had thought for most of the series filming that the mole was likely to be either his own character, or George Mason. He also said that he had believed throughout the season that Richard Walsh wasn't really dead and would make a surprise return in the final episode. It was an assistant director who told him the *real* ending. 'That was when my jaw hit the ground,' he noted.

THE BRITISH ANGLE 'The beer's on ice, the pizza's been ordered, and the VCR is poised for action,' wrote *The Independent*. After nearly six months, the most talked-about US import since *Twin Peaks* was finally due to reach its dramatic climax in front of a British audience of more than three million. And, there was more good news as, following weeks of behind-the-scenes negotiations, the BBC revealed just prior to the finale that it had won the rights to screen the forthcoming second series, fending off prospective rivals including Sky One. Though confined to the relative minority of BBC2 and the even more obscure digital channel, BBC Choice, 24 had steadily built up a loyal and vocal British following since it started airing in the UK in March 2002. The final episode was originally scheduled to be shown on BBC Choice a week prior to BBC2, but the corporation took a last-minute decision to cancel this, fearing that those viewers who had seen it would spoil the *denouement* for everyone else forced to wait for the terrestrial broadcast.

Indeed, it's not inconceivable to say that the British success of 24 may have contributed in no small way to 24 gaining a second season in the US. 'Our sales department *loves* this show,' noted Fox's Sandy Grushow. 'This series is making money. The international revenues are immense.'

10PM

Kiefer Sutherland was so impressed with the way that the BBC screened *24* that he helped to persuade his bosses to go commercial-free in America. The first episode of the second season was shown in the States without any advert breaks - an experiment virtually unique on American television. 'We're ecstatic about it,' Sutherland told a BBC website. 'I think its success in England was phenomenal. It was the biggest show the BBC's ever had.[65] It was the number one DVD, knocking *Lord Of the Rings* off the top... It's unheard of for a television show DVD to knock out every feature DVD available.[66] That's because they showed it without commercials. Eventually I think it's going to be the way of television. I don't know exactly how they're going to figure out how to advertise, because they will. Whether it's product placement in the show itself... I know we're all driving Fords this year. But, we're very grateful to Ford for doing it. Grateful that, for at least for the first hour, we get to do [an episode without adverts] here.'

●●●

65 Oh, no it wasn't!

66 That's not quite true either. Both *Buffy the Vampire Slayer* and *The X-Files* regularly top the British DVD and video charts.

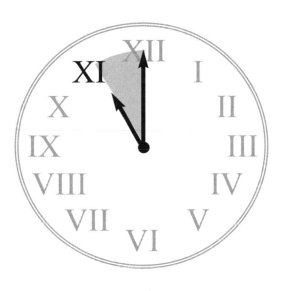

SEASON I

12:00 1:00 2:00 3:00 4:00 5:00 6:00 7:00 8:00 9:00 10:00 11:00 12:00 1:00 2:00 3:00 4:00 5:00 6:00 7:00 8:00 9:00 10:00 11:00 12:00

24 11:00 P.M. – MIDNIGHT

US Transmission Date: 21 May 2002
UK Transmission Date: 18 August 2002[67]
Writers: Joel Surnow, Michael Loceff, Robert Cochran, Howard Gordon
Director: Stephen Hopkins
Cast: Dennis Hopper (Victor Drazen), Carlos Bernard (Tony Almeida), Penny Johnson Jerald (Sherry Palmer), Xander Berkeley (George Mason), Jude Ciccolella (Mike Novick), Željko Ivanek (Andre Drazen), Endre Hules (Serge), Kevin Chapman (Coast Guard Officer), Terrell Tilford (Paul Wilson), Karina Arroyave (Jamey Farrell), Rey Gallegos (Sergeant Devlin), Tico Wells (Karris), Jane Yamamoto (Field Reporter)

11:02: As Jack races to the docks, Kim gets out of the water, climbs over a fence, she is able to flag down a passing truck. Sherry is still very pissed at her husband for continuing the public charade that he is dead. Palmer tells her that he will not blow his cover until he knows that Kim is safe. Mason gets a call from the highway patrol saying that they have found Kim. She tells George that the terrorists are at the pier.

11:07: Jack arrives at the pier. Andre calls him and demands to know where he is. Jack asks to speak with Kim but Andre refuses, suggesting to Jack that the terrorists no longer have his daughter. Jack phones CTU and tells Nina that someone within the agency must have tipped off the terrorists that Palmer is alive.

11:17: Nina calls Victor and tells him that Kim is safe. Victor orders Nina to tell Jack that his daughter is dead. Drazen hopes that this will enrage Jack enough to come after the terrorists. Nina makes the call. Having momentarily grieved for his lost daughter, Jack hotwires a van and drives it through the front of the warehouse. Victor and Andre attempt to flee to their boat. In a wild frenzy of gun fire, Andre is shot. Victor has Jack in his sight, but he is out of ammunition. Jack shoots Victor repeatedly until the Serbian's body falls into the water. Then he shoots Victor a couple more times just for good measure.

QUOTE/UNQUOTE Mike, to Palmer: 'I think this last day has been about finding out who you really are.'

LOGIC, LET ME INTRODUCE YOU TO THIS WINDOW Jack has a First Aid box in his briefcase along with his gun. Is that supposed to be satire or something? Cos, you know, an Elastoplast could come in really useful if he gets shot. We are given a brief look at the face of the man whom Kim threw the coffee at in the last episode. Astoundingly, there's not the slightest trace of third degree burns. Tony's stubble was much more prominent in the last episode than here, yet it's unlikely he would have found time for a quick shave. Why does Nina speak to Andre in English the second time she calls yet Serbian the first time?

67 Simultaneously broadcast on both BBC2 and BBC Choice. On the latter, the episode was followed by an amusing 50 minute studio discussion programme, *24: The Post Mortem*, hosted by Claudia Winkleman. This included some exclusive interviews from the cast and crew along with contributions from a lively studio audience of fans, together with journalist Charlie Brooker and author Jim Sangster.

How many bullets do those two handguns that Jack has contain? He goes through almost two minutes of non-stop shooting at anything that moves. It's like something from D-Day. This culminates in him pumping five slugs, one by one, into Victor. And through all of this, he doesn't have to reload once. Isn't the car Jack drives back to CTU the same one that he's been driving for the last two episodes (i.e. the one that Andre left for him at the oil field)? It seemingly is. So why does it feature a monitor device (see **Cool Gadgets**) on which Jack can receive and view incriminating CTU videos?

11:28: Sherry tips off the press that Palmer is still alive. Palmer is incandescent with rage and comes very close to attacking his wife, having to be held back by Mike. The Senator is forced to make a statement to the media regarding reports of his death having been premature. Mason gets the call from the tactical team who say that Jack went in guns blazing, eliminating seven terrorists including both the Drazens.

POINTS AT WHICH TERI NEEDS A SLAP Teri stumbles in on this conversation but everyone is too busy to talk to her. She decides to find Nina to ask what, exactly, Jack had been involved with. Stupid woman, don't you realise she's the traitor? No? Okay, fair enough.

11:30: Nina, realising that her cover either has been blown, or will be very soon, enters a storage room and guns down a surprised maintenance worker. As Nina is busy downloading information from her computer to a CD, Teri finds her talking on the telephone in German. When Nina sees Teri, she ends the call and says that she has been speaking to the Frankfurt division. Nina continues that Teri shouldn't worry, everything is fine and Jack is alive.

THE MISSING SCENE (SLIGHT RETURN) Once again, British viewers got a bit more of this scene than their American counterparts. Nina tells Teri that as soon as all of this is over she plans to have herself transferred to another department so as not to be in the way between Teri's and Jack's future happiness.

11:35: Teri is, once again, filled with the milk of human kindness towards Nina ... until she notices the dead body of the maintenance girl in the corner. Teri tries to run but Nina pulls a gun on her. Jack contacts the harbourmaster and asks to claim Kim's body. He's relieved, if somewhat confused, to learn that Kim is in fact alive. Jack calls Mason to inform him that Nina must be a traitor.

QUOTE/UNQUOTE Mason, to Jack: 'As usual, I don't know whether to congratulate you, or demand your resignation.'

REFERENCES *The X-Files* ('don't trust anyone'). Mike and Palmer watch the public revelation that Palmer isn't dead on *CNB News*. Jack's handling of two guns during the climactic battle is a clear visual tribute to the movies of John Woo.

11:42: Jack asks Paul Wilson at CTU to find him the security footage of the room where Jamey committed suicide. The tapes, Jack is told, were erased but they should have digital backups. Sherry meets Palmer in the deserted hotel ballroom. Palmer tells her that she has lost touch with what it's like to be a wife. He adds that he will be seeking a divorce, noting that she is not fit to be First Lady.

QUOTE/UNQUOTE Sherry, to Palmer: 'David, you just don't walk away from me. You can't do this without me.'

11:45: Wilson calls Jack after finding the footage. He patches a download of it through to Jack's car. Jack then forwards the video, which shows Nina killing Jamey and then staring menacingly at the security camera, to Mason. George says he will lock down the building.

COOL GADGETS Jack has a Rosen Unlimited Vision monitor in his car (however, see **Logic, Let Me Introduce You To This Window**).

11:53: Nina leaves Teri slumped in the corner and makes her escape via the car park. Taking out a couple of CTU officers, she gets into a car and heads for the exit just as Jack drives in. An elaborate game of 'chicken' follows which culminates in Jack stopping Nina before she can get out. Mason and Tony manage to get to Jack before he can kill Nina. An injured Nina is taken into custody. Her parting shot is to tell Jack that she didn't work for the Drazens. Jack rushes inside. There, he finds Teri tied to a chair, shot dead.

'YOU MAY REMEMBER ME FROM...' Kevin Chapman was in *Blow*, *Vig*, *In Too Deep*, and *Snitch*. Terrell Tilford appeared in *Guiding Light*. Tico Wells was in *The Relic*, *The Dream Team*, *Universal Solider* and *The Cosby Show*. Jane Yamamoto can be seen in *American Sweethearts*. She's also a reporter for *KTTV Fox 11 News* in Los Angeles.

NOTES 'I was just doing my job.' Well, *that* was emotional. As good a finale episode as it was possible to do given the circumstances and the amount of loose ends that required tying up. Once again, however, the astoundingly effective last few scenes shouldn't mask some earlier glaring faults. In particular, it's completely clear by the end of the episode that, far from having a single vision of what, exactly, the terrorists' plan was, the writers are just as confused as the rest of us. The Drazen gang have, indeed, seemingly been blundering around in the dark as much, if not more, than Jack himself. Still, a word of real and genuine praise for the production team for taking the difficult decision to end the series in the only way that they could and killing a major character. As has been noted elsewhere, fan reaction was decidedly mixed and, in some cases rather hysterical. But to have ended Jack Bauer's longest day with a crass happy ending would have rendered much of the previous drama worthless. For *24* to have the impact that it did, it needed this. Of course, you'll never satisfy all of the people all of the time, but this author likes to believe that, in years to come, when people remember the first season of *24*, they'll remember it as a brave experiment that continued to, mostly, make the right choices, even if they weren't the *easy* choices, up to and including its final shot. We can forgive all of the amnesia plotlines in the world if, in return, we get realism that is, for once, truly realistic. Life's a bitch and then you die, right?

The clearance code that Jack gives to Paul Wilson to get the digital backup of the security tape is C22717. Amongst the server names to have accessed the CTU video logs today are: Spartan, Mosher, CTU-int05 (which appears to be Nina's reference), CTU-AK, LAPD-act and Hunter08.

The original US broadcast aired with a viewer discretion warning about the violence in the episode. Because the previous 23 episodes didn't feature any violence at all, did they?

CRITIQUE 'Is [24] taking itself seriously or what?' asked Howard Rosenberg in the *Los Angeles Times*. 'The show's writers have issued a document resembling a diplomatic white paper, replete with bullet points explaining, in detail, "Why Nina is the mole." Not needed. As if even huge fans of the show were expecting *logic* from *24*. Not that I won't return to *24* next season, even though it became about the most illogical drama after those tight early scripts that drew me in irrevocably.'

'Episode 24 has a killing scene - done from the point of view of a dead-eyed CCTV camera - that is one of the great shots in film,' noted David Thompson. 'When the killer gazes up at the camera it's as if those eyes have seen the back wall of our soul.'

'It came as a slight disappointment that all roads led to Dennis Hopper affecting a chronic Eastern European accent,' wrote *TV Zone*. 'In a sense, this highlighted the main problem of the show. Yet the first 10 or 12 episodes rank amongst the most compelling US television ever broadcast.'

EVERYONE'S A CRITIC It was somewhat inevitable that Teri's death, and to a lesser extent Nina's treachery, would draw complaints about a betrayal of The Sisterhood: 'I was left with the same sense of disgust I felt at the end of *American Beauty*,' wrote one outraged *Radio Times* reader. 'Another beautifully produced bit of film whose mature women characters were either neurotic or zombified.'

SOMETIMES, YOU'VE GOT TO LAUGH Shortly after this episode aired in the US, a range of *South Park*-influenced T-shirts hit the streets. These featured the slogan *Oh My God! They Killed Teri!*

THE ALTERNATE ENDING Three different endings were shot, two of them decoys, in an attempt to discourage leaks. One of the alternates, in which Teri survives, was included as an extra on the final disc of the Region 2 DVD release. In this authors opinion it is, whilst well acted, dramatically rather weak and I'm very glad they went with the ending that they did.

One other point about the DVD extras: Considerable prominence is given on the cover to what is described as a 'Season Two Preview'. This actually turns out to be a three minute Kiefer Sutherland monologue about how exciting and challenging making the *first* season had been over numerous clips *from* the first season. It ends with Kiefer saying that they'll soon be coming back to do it all over again. So, *that*'s it? *That's* the 'Season Two Preview'? It's to be hoped that nobody splashed out forty quid for the DVD box-set purely for *that*.

THAT REGION 2 DVD DEBACLE! IN FULL! Due to the extraordinary success of *24* in the UK, Fox rush-released a Region 2 six-DVD box-set featuring all 24 episodes, plus some extras (see above). This came out in August 2002, just weeks after the season finale had aired on the BBC. That was, however, merely the beginning of a saga almost as complicated as the series itself. Within days of the release, bemused purchasers were noting that some of the episodes appeared to have been edited. Initial reports appeared on BBC teletext stating that the discs had suffered numerous cuts from the originally broadcast episodes. The article quoted a Fox spokesman as being 'aware of the problem.' It also noted that the UK VHS box-set, which came out at around the same time had, seemingly, *not* been cut. Two immediate edits were highlighted: One, a brief shot of Jack on the dock in the final episode, taking cover behind a post. The other, a more significant omission, the scene in episode 23, in which Teri tells Nina that she is pregnant. What subsequently emerged was that the episodes on the UK DVD release were actually those as broadcast in *the US*, Fox having copied the discs directly from the original master videotapes. The BBC, it was discovered, had exclusive rights to some untransmitted material as the US broadcast versions of some episodes had some scenes removed or shortened to make way for more adverts. The UK VHS box-set *had* used the episode prints sent to the BBC, though many potential purchasers were put off from buying this as an alternative to the DVDs by the fact that the episodes were not presented in widescreen. Amongst the missing scenes highlighted were:

7PM - 8PM: Andre threatening Harris with a knife.

10PM - 11PM: Teri telling Nina that she is pregnant.

11PM - Midnight: The shootout between Jack and the Drazens is approximately a minute longer. Nina's conversation with Teri after she catches her on the phone in the control room is also, significantly, extended.

Fox subsequently issued a statement which noted that the Region 2 DVD release *had*, indeed, been taken from the shorter US transmission print. These, therefore, did not contain some footage unique to the UK broadcasts during the last five episodes (Fox claimed it amounted to no more than 90 seconds in total). If consumers wished to replace discs 5 and 6 of their box-set, Fox continued, they could do so by returning their original ones. Replacements would be made, free of charge.

This author still has his original, cut, DVD set and is desperately clinging on to it in the hope that it is going to be a collectors item one day.

CAST AND CREW COMMENTS Devoted fans of 24 weren't the only ones who had to pluck their jaws from the floor when Teri Bauer was killed. Elisha Cuthbert couldn't believe it either. 'I was in shock. It was sprung on us quite quickly. We got the script only a couple of days before we shot it. But, that's television and that's the life of an actor. I thought [that the storylines] started getting repetitive,' she continues. 'I kept thinking: I just want to get out of this mess. I don't want to get kidnapped anymore. I guess I'm lucky to still be alive and going on to next season.'

'All my friends were calling, almost as if this was my life,' added Sarah Clarke. 'They were really disappointed in me. They had been so proud and impressed that I could work at the CIA and now, "How could you do it, you let us all down!"' Sarah noted that a huge turning point in a plot is never a safe move. 'You always run the risk of losing your audience. The viewer initially tends to be in shock and then needs to be convinced. There's a little adjusting time.' But she added that she was thrilled with the surprise character shift. 'It gave me something very specific to play and something very serious to contribute.'

DID YOU KNOW? Shortly after the season ended, Robert Cochran confirmed to *Entertainment Weekly* that the writers had decided that Nina was the mole only about halfway through the season. He also noted that they hadn't always intended to kill Teri, but that they ultimately felt that someone *had* to die in the finale to bring true closure to this most dramatic of days.

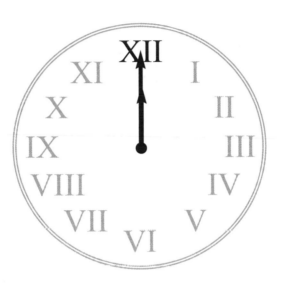

CONCLUSION

12:00 1:00 2:00 3:00 4:00 5:00 6:00 7:00 8:00 9:00 10:00 11:00 12:00 1:00 2:00 3:00 4:00 5:00 6:00 7:00 8:00 9:00 10:00 11:00 12:00

TOMORROW IS JUST ANOTHER DAY

'Sometimes, the men sworn to keep us safe are the most dangerous of all.'

In its debut season, *24* ended with a very literal bang - the gunshot that killed Teri Bauer. As several commentators felt compelled to ask, what could the producers possibly do for an encore? Once you've saved a presidential candidate from an assassination plot that reaches into the heart of secret government agencies and international terrorism, how can you top that?

24, as this book has hopefully shown, wowed the critics right from the beginning. They raved about the show's innovative format, relentless pace and sleek visual branding. But the series was *always* a much tougher sell to the viewers. *24* eventually ranked as the 74th best watched show of the season in America. It averaged around 8.5 million viewers per week.[68] Even so, with such highly-regarded Fox series as *The X-Files* and *Ally McBeal* having recently reached their conclusion, the network simply could not afford, in artistic if not commercial terms, to lose such a distinctive newcomer. Not only did Fox renew *24*, but the network insisted that the real time format that had made the first season such an intellectual winner should not, under any circumstances, be changed. Trade publications had, previously, predicted that season two would see each episode encapsulating one 24-hour day in stand-alone stories. Fans were horrified. One Internet wag even pointed out that, should this happen, it would need to be reflected in a change of title. *Month*, perhaps. Joel Surnow and Michael Loceff did, indeed, write a sample stand-alone script that took place over the course of one day. It was, said Surnow, 'Fine. But it was just like *any other* TV show.' This script was presented to the network by the producers along with their proposed real time storyarc for a second season. There was never much doubt which road Fox and *24* would ultimately take. 'You cannot take the incredible push that the media gave the producers for creating this idea and then say "Thanks for all your help, now we're gonna change it so [the series is] easier to syndicate"' Kiefer Sutherland noted perceptively. 'The backlash would not only be justified, but it would wipe out the show.'

Fox Entertainment's President Gail Berman announced in May 2002 that the second season would again consist of 24 episodes chronicling another day in the life of Jack Bauer. 'We ultimately concluded that *this* was the show,' she told the *Cincinnati Enquirer* enthusiastically. The producers had, she added, 'laid out a storyarc for next season that totally blew us away.' But before they could start on that, there were some issues left over from last year that needed be laid to rest. Quite literally, in the case of Jack's wife. Yes, Teri Bauer really *is* dead, Robert Cochran confirmed in late May. There would be no miraculous resurrection for Teri as some of the more fanatical fangroups had suggested was probable. Howard Gordon noted that everyone connected with the show had wished to retain the real time element. 'We [wanted to] keep all the stuff that makes the show unique and compelling. To do another day in Bauer's life.' He certainly wasn't alone. 'Thank God that they're going to keep the format,' Leslie Hope told *TV*

68 In comparison, a top ten-rated series like, for instance NBC's *The West Wing* has an average weekly audience of somewhere in the 14-16 million range - double *24*'s average. The US's current top-rated series, *C.S.I*, regularly attracts 20 million plus.

Guide in a bittersweet interview in June. 'I know it's difficult for the writers, but it [takes] the show to another level. Without [the real time element], it's reduced to being just an ordinary TV drama.'

So, tomorrow really *is* another day. The 24 hours depicted in the season two would take place approximately 16 months after the traumatic events of the first season.[69] The show, numerous press reports noted, would be keeping its Tuesday 9PM, timeslot on the Fox network, meaning that it would once again do battle for ratings with popular shows like *Frasier* and *Smallville*. '[The series is] something that all of us are incredibly proud of,' Kiefer Sutherland told *FoxNews*, allegedly fresh from signing a five year contract. 'It's very unconventional for television. The satisfaction in doing this, compared to a film, is the amazing response you get on the street.' Insomniac fans of *24* had much reason to celebrate during the summer. The Fox cable network, FX, aired the entire first season back-to-back during 24 straight hours over the Labor Day weekend. The marathon kicked-off at midnight on Saturday, 31 August 2002, and ran throughout Sunday, culminating with the finale at 11PM.

By this time 'spoiler' websites were, literally, falling over themselves to bring their readers every titbit that they could uncover concerning the second season: Everybody wanted to know whether David Palmer would become the President. Yes he, seemingly, would. 'I'm honoured. I know there's a great deal of responsibility that goes along with the job,' noted the man destined to play fictional drama's first African-American President, Dennis Haysbert. 'I will try to bring as much integrity and dignity to [the position] as I can.' Another hotly debated topic was whether Jack Bauer would be consumed solely with avenging his wife's murder? It soon became apparent that he would not. Jack, although still obviously grieving for Teri, would be spending his day trying to track down a terrorist-controlled nuclear device set to explode in Los Angeles. It could be powerful enough to destroy 100 square miles of Southern California. Not to mention the entire US film and TV industry along with it. 'Whatever boundaries Jack had last year are pretty much gone now,' Sutherland told *Entertainment Weekly*. 'Last year's promo was great: "I'm federal agent Jack Bauer and today is the longest day of my life." Now, maybe, it's "I'm federal agent Jack Bauer and today is the most violent day of my life."'

The producers seemed to have looked to the real world for their inspiration for the second season's ongoing storyline. A real world, it should be remembered, that almost screwed-up their carefully crafted premiere a year previously. As with the third season of NBC's acclaimed political drama *The West Wing*, the events of 11 September 2001 have had a major impact on the *24* universe and its storylines. One report suggested the plot would focus on a Muslim Fundamentalist terrorist named Mahmud Rasheed Faheen, a member of Hezbollah, who had been planning a nuclear attack on L.A. for over two years. Faheen is also involved with a splinter group called Second Wave,[70] whose training camps were said to be based in Eastern Iraq.[71] 'If you do a show about terrorism and avoid what's happening in the real world, I don't know what your show's about,' Robert

- -

69 Given the levels to which *Die Hard* is a very obvious, and acknowledged, influence on *24*, one of John McClane's lines from *Die Hard II* seems rather appropriate at this juncture: 'How can the same shit happen to the same guy two years running?!'

70 'You just hope Second Wave won't prove to be an angry Beach Boys cover band' noted *Entertainment Weekly*'s Ken Tucker.

71 As it subsequently transpired, in the first episode of the second season, the name of the Arab country in which Second Wave's camps are located is not actually revealed, merely that they have a Prime Minister.

Cochran noted when asked about this subject. 'It's like doing a cop show and saying you're not going to deal with serious crimes. It's not as though we're saying the religion of Islam is made up [entirely] of terrorists. But there *are* people who are believers of Islam and who are also terrorists... You *have* to do something that is grounded in the real world.' But that real world had one more go at biting *24* in the ass, when a carefully co-ordinated media campaign of posters and adverts for the second season was caught in the metaphorical crossfire of the very real Washington D.C. sniper drama. Fox received public complaints about the ads, which depicted a rifle sight's cross-hairs over Kiefer Sutherland's face. 'We're pulling the ads,' a Fox spokeswoman told MSNBC, noting that they had been designed many weeks earlier before the sniper's attacks began in October 2002.

The series, it was widely reported, would begin its drama at 8AM one morning, with the now-President Palmer at Lake Oswego in Oregon on a well-earned fishing trip with his son, Keith. Before the first act was concluded, however, Palmer would be safely 200 feet below ground in the government's Northwest Regional Operations Complex. Several other casting questions were quickly answered. Both George Mason and Tony Almeida would still be working hard at CTU. The former has been demoted from Division to take Jack's place at CTU. He is still, impatiently, waiting for President Palmer to fulfil his promise and move him to a cushy job in Washington. Tony, meanwhile, is doing Nina's old job. The first episode would also see Kim now working as a live-in nanny, looking after pretty nine year old Megan Matheson (played by Skye McCole Bartusiak). Popular actress Tracy Middendorf would be joining the cast as Carla, Megan's unhappy mom. We soon find out the reason for her unhappiness. Carla's husband, Gary (Billy Burke), is an abusive, violent thug.

Kim, seemingly a much more mature and level-headed young lady than last year, is nevertheless somewhat estranged from her father. Not that she blames him for her mother's untimely death, she is quick to stress, but she *is* very mixed-up emotionally by the whole turn of events. (Kim tells Jack, at one point, 'Every time I see you, I think of mom'.) There will also be, to complicate matters, a new woman in Jack's life later in the season, Kate Warner (played by Australian actress Sarah Wynter). Other new faces will include Reiko Aylesworth, who previously starred in UPN's *All Souls*. Reiko appears as Michelle Dessler, a new member of the CTU team who works closely with Tony. She will be joined at CTU by former *Roseanne* star Sara Gilbert playing the computer expert Paula Schaeffer. Also featuring will be characters like Eric Rayburn (Timothy Carhart), the hawkish head of the NSA and Jenny Dodge (Tamlyn Tomita), Palmer's press secretary. One of Palmer's closest aides, Lynne Kresge, is played by former *Star Trek: The Next Generation* and *Kalifornia* actress Michelle Forbes whilst veteran character actor Harris Yulin (Quentin Travers in *Buffy the Vampire Slayer*) will play Roger Stanton. We will also meet Kate Warner's wealthy family; her likeable father, Bob (John Terry), a successful businessman, and her younger sister, Marie (Laura Harris). Marie is due to be married this evening to Reza (Phillip Rhys), a London-born Arab who works for Bob and whom Kate discovers may have links to terrorism.

By August, the spoilers were piling up: In an echo of the popular series *Alias*, the first scene would take place in Seoul, where South Korean intelligence agents would be shown torturing a suspected terrorist. Having extracted the information that they require, one of them tells several American military personnel in a nearby room: 'It's happening today.' Jack is initially reluctant to have anything more to do with CTU and refuses to take Tony's calls, but President Palmer telephones Jack personally, and tells him about the nuclear threat to L.A. On compassionate leave from the CTU, Jack was said to be looking quite scruffy and this was confirmed when the first trailers for the new season appeared in September 2002 showing Sutherland sporting a rather shaggy beard. Nevertheless, by the end of the first episode, after a necessary shave, everybody was delighted to find that the old Jack Bauer was, well and truly, back.

The first episode aired, without commercial interruption, courtesy of a sponsorship by Ford, on Tuesday 29 October 2002. The episode ran to 51 minutes and 43 seconds[72] with the rest of the hour being filled by two extended-length Ford commercials and Fox promos for the series *John Doe* and for the next episode of *24*.[73]

'There is an incredible amount of pressure going into this season,' Kiefer Sutherland noted. 'Last year, we created a pilot and were told by the network: "Now go make the next 23 episodes as good as the pilot." The Emmys didn't help. The newspapers actually liked us, and our viewership grew.' Sutherland does admit that he has wondered more than once if he should quit whilst he's ahead. Rarely in his career has the actor had this much critical acclaim. 'If we do this season badly, then we take away from what we did the first year.' Dennis Haysbert, however, is confident and upbeat that the production can produce the magic all over again. 'It's going to be every bit as riveting as it was last year,' he told the *Detroit Free Press* in July. On person who *did* enjoy the season opener was *TV Guide*'s respected critic Matt Roush, a long-time champion of the show: 'Whenever Sutherland is on screen,' he wrote enthusiastically, '*24* is *electrifying*. You might grow a bit impatient when the focus is elsewhere... Especially with Jack's daughter, Kim, whose damsel-in-distress act wears thin as she flees a more homegrown form of terror. Even so, *24* is irresistible, entertaining, compelling... I'm counting the hours already.' On the other hand John Ruch felt that 'There is a price for post-Sept. 11 realism. Disturbingly, *24* appears to justify torture, murder and the illegal arrest of journalists in the fight against terrorism. Reasonable, perhaps, if a nuke were about to go off in Los Angeles, but not very reflective of the more complex real world that the series is based on.' Several reviewers felt compelled to comment upon the wedding subplot. 'A possible terrorist, who is an Arab, marrying a white blonde woman, seems to be taking fears of terrorist cells into the territory of classic racist hysteria,' noted the *Boston Herald* with some justification. 'They've come for our women!' Critic Scott Pierce suggests that this moderate example of dumbing-down may be for a very good reason: 'If the storytelling seems a bit more straightforward [this year], that may have something to do with the fact that, while a critical darling, *24* never became a mainstream hit during its first season.' And, ironically, although the decision to broadcast the episode without advert breaks was applauded by most reviewers, Rob Owen noted that 'Without the breaks, the hour feels bloated and less relentless.'

By episode two, it was announced, Jack would be going undercover as a recent

72 Subsequent repeats of this episode in the US removed or shortened several scenes to bring the episode's running time down to approximately 43 minutes.

73 Helped by massive pre-publicity, the opening episode achieved *24*'s highest ever viewing figures with an audience of 13.5 million viewers. 'We have always believed in the show, but *24*'s return was beyond my wildest expectations,' Gail Berman told *The Hollywood Reporter*. The series was also given the benefit of a regular repeat slot, on Monday nights, filling a hole left by the cancellation, after just two episodes, of David E Kelley's legal series *Girls Club*.

parolee, attempting to infiltrate the complex levels of the conspiracy. One aspect of this involves Jack working with some very unpleasant white middle-class Timothy McVeigh-type urban guerrillas.[74] A gang of alleged patriots who are anxious to see the US government overthrown and who intend to blow up a Los Angeles target as part of their plan that Jack has good reason for wanting to protect. There will also be a spectacular return for the former Mrs Palmer around episode six of the season. 'Penny has the most fun part to play,' notes Howard Gordon. 'Her Lady MacBeth is a really delicious character. We motivated her properly.' Nina is also scheduled to make a welcome return to the show, initially from her prison cell, around episode five. 'The hardest thing this year,' Gordon told *St Paul Pioneer Press*, 'was finding the emotional centre of the show. Last year, it was clear - Jack Bauer was trying to put his family back together. This year, we drew from the same emotional well.'

What the writers have in store for later in the season, we'll have to wait and see. But this certainly looks like it could be an even longer day in the life of Jack Bauer.

74 Timothy James McVeigh (1968-2001): Born in Pendleton, New York. An army veteran who took part in Operation Desert Storm, McVeigh became internationally infamous when he was charged with bombing the Alfred P Murrah US government building in Oklahoma City in 1995, in which 168 people died. At his trial in 1997, a Denver jury found him guilty of conspiracy and murder, and he was sentenced to death by lethal injection. McVeigh was executed on 11 June 2001, at the federal penitentiary in Terre Haute, Indiana.

12:00 1:00 2:00 3:00 4:00 5:00 6:00 7:00 8:00 9:00 10:00 11:00 12:00 1:00 2:00 3:00 4:00 5:00 6:00 7:00 8:00 9:00 10:00 11:00 12:00

SELECTED BIBLIOGRAPHY

The following books, articles, interviews and reviews were consulted in the preparation of this text:

Adalian, Josef, and Schneider, Michael, 'Plots are hot-spots for Net', *Daily Variety*, 23 September 2001.

Alter, Ethan, '*24* entering a darker day', *Media Life*, 29 October 2002.

Atherton, Tony, 'Fantasy TV: The New Reality', *Ottawa Citizen*, 27 January 2000.

Ausiello, Michael, 'Backstage Scoop at the Emmys', *TV Guide*, 5 November 2001.

Barney, Chuck, 'The perils of playing at-risk roles', *Contra Costa Times*, 19 June 2002.

Barnhart, Aaron, '*24* is best new show of the year', *Kansas City Star*, 5 November 2001.

Battaglio, Stephen, '*24* may get new format', *Toronto Star*, 11 April 2002.

Betts, Hannah, 'And now, ladies, just for yourselves... When Harry met Garry', *The Times*, 7 July 2001.

Bianco, Robert, 'A bad day gets a good *24* off to a great start', *USA Today*, 28 October 2002.

Bloom, Jonathan, 'Hopper's on *24*. He's the villain (duh!)', *Boston Herald*, 16 April 2002.

Boedeker, Hal, 'Dennis Hopper plays TV villain', *Knight Ridder Newspapers*, 17 April 2002.

Bone, James, 'Declaration of Ignorance as American teenagers flunk July 4 Quiz', *The Times*, 4 July 2001.

Bottomley, Suzette, 'Conspiracy Theory', *Herald and Post*, 26 October 2001.

Brooker, Charlie, 'Screen Burn', *The Guide*, 20 July 2002.

Carlin, Peter Ames, '*24* may not be landmark TV, but it's cool', *The Oregonian*, 10 April 2002.

Carmen, John, '*24* promos try viewers patience', *San Francisco Chronicle*, 26 October 2001.

Caro, Jason, 'Season One Review', *TV Zone*, Special #48, November 2002.

Carr, Coeli, 'She's So Bad', *New York Post*, 19 May 2002.

Carr, Coeli, 'Final hour of *24*', *New York Post*, 20 May 2002.

Carter, Kelly, 'Sutherland makes time for *24*', *USA Today*, 25 February 2002.

Collins, Monica, 'Time sensitive: Grim themes of *24* and *NYPD Blue* premieres are painfully familiar', *Boston Herald*, 6 November 2001.

Cornell, Paul, Day, Martin, and Topping, Keith, *X-Treme Possibilities: A Comprehensively Expanded Rummage Through the X-Files*, Virgin Publishing, 1998.

Cozens, Claire, '*24* sponsorship deal spells trouble for BBC', *The Guardian*, 29 October 2002.

Crichton, Michael, 'Could Tiny Machines Rule The World?', *Parade*, 24 November 2002.

Cuthbert, Elisha, 'Most Wanted!', interview by Jake Bronstein, *FHM*, issue 153, September 2002.

Deggans, Eric, '*24* gets help from Hopper's evil ways', *St. Petersburg Times*, 16 April 2002.

Deggans, Eric, '*24* stands its ground', *St. Petersburg Times*, 28 October 2002.

Dickey, Jeff, *The Rough Guide to Los Angeles*, Penguin Books, 2000.

Dickson, E Jane, 'Beat the clock', *Radio Times*, 8 June 2002.

Dudek, Duane, 'President takes lead in *24*, his career', *Milwaukee Journal Sentinel*, 29

October 2002.

Duffy, Mike, 'Fabled bad guy Hopper punches in for *24* role', *Detroit Free Press*, 16 April 2002.

Duffy, Mike, '*24* finish tough day with a bang', *Detroit Free Press*, 21 May 2002.

Duffy, Mike, '*24* star hails chance to the chief', *Detroit Free Press*, 25 July 2002.

Farhi, Paul, 'TV concept that bears repeating', *Washington Post*, 19 March 2002.

Flaherty, Mike, 'Man Of The Hour', *Entertainment Weekly*, 23 November 2001.

Flaherty, Mike, 'The Longest Day', *Entertainment Weekly*, 8 March 2002.

Feran, Tom, 'Drama shows politics can succeed on TV', *Cleveland Plain Dealer*, 22 September 1999.

Fiore, Faye, 'Washington cast an eye on Hollywood', *Los Angeles Times*, 15 July 2001.

Gilbert, Matthew, '*24* continues to be time well spent', *Boston Globe*, 29 October 2002.

Goodman, Tim, 'Both *24*, *Alias*, deliver no-brainer thrills', *San Francisco Chronicle*, 19 February 2002.

Goodman, Tim, 'Fox's *24* buys itself some time', *San Francisco Chronicle*, 3 April 2002.

Goodman, Tim, 'White-knuckle tension grips fans of *24*. Show's sophomore season promises to be another wild ride with Jack Bauer', *San Francisco Chronicle*, 28 October 2002.

Graham, Alison, 'Today's Choice', *Radio Times*, 2 March 2002.

Graham, Alison, 'Today's Choice', *Radio Times*, 18 August 2002.

Haysbert, Dennis, 'Having the time of his life', interview by John Naughton, *Radio Times*, 16 March 2002.

Hope, Leslie, 'The Wife that Jack Loved', interview by Ian Hockley, *TV Zone*, Special #48, November 2002.

Hill, Michael E, 'It's a new day for hour one of *24*', *Washington Post*, 4 November 2001.

Kaplan, Don, 'More of *24* girl', *New York Post*, 3 September 2002.

Keck, William, 'Office Politics', *Entertainment Weekly*, 12 October 2001.

Kiesewetter, John, '*24* is worth every minute', *Cincinnati Enquirer*, 11 February 2002.

Kiesewetter, John, '*24* fans speculate on final hour', *Cincinnati Enquirer*, 21 May 2002.

Kruger, Henrik, *The Great Heroin Coup: Drugs, Intelligence & International Fascism*, South End Press, 1980.

Levin, Gary, 'Another "perilous day" for Fox's *24*', *USA Today*, 22 July 2002.

Levin, Gary, '*24* premiere terrorizes competition', *USA Today*, 30 October 2002.

Littleton, Cynthia, '*West Wing* premiere postponed to address attacks' *The Hollywood Reporter*, 21 September 2001.

Littleton, Cynthia, '*24* return kick-starts Fox just in time for Nov. sweeps', *The Hollywood Reporter*, 31 October 2002.

MacDonald, Ian, *Revolution in the Head* [Second Edition], Fourth Estate Ltd, 1997.

Maltin, Leonard [ed], *Maltin's 2002 Movie & Video Guide*, Signet Publishing, 2001.

Marrs, Jim, *Crossfire*, Pocket Books, 1993.

McDaniel, Mike, 'Jack be nimble, Jack be quick: New season of *24* promises bad day', *Houston Chronicle*, 27 October 2002.

Moore, Frazier, 'What fun *24* could have been', *Deseret News*, 21 May 2002.

Moore, Frazier, 'The clock strikes 12 in *24* finale', *Associated Press*, 22 May 2002.

Morrison, James, 'Millions tuned to final *24*', *The Independent*, 18 August 2002.

Morrow, Terry, 'Another day, another season: Sutherland feels the pressure at the dawning of another *24*', *Knoxville News-Sentinel*, 26 October 2002.

Mosby, John, 'Clock Watching', *Impact*, issue 127, July 2002.

Naughton, John, '24 hours to go - and the clock is ticking', *Radio Times*, 2 March 2002.

Ogunnaike, Lola, 'With *24*, Kiefer becomes Man of the Hour', *New York Daily News*, 11 March 2002.

O'Hare, Kate, '*24* recounts Jack Bauer's second longest day', *St Paul Pioneer Press*, 27 October 2002.

Owen, Rob, 'Groundwork and no commercials cut into tension of *24* premiere', *Pittsburgh Post-Gazette*, 29 October 2002.

Pergament, Alan, 'Work on *24* was No. 1 thrill for Buffalo's Frederick Keller', *The Buffalo News*, 5 June 2002.

Pierce, Scott D, '*24* is back with a bang', *Deseret News*, 28 October 2002.

Pompa, Frank, 'A Nation Ablaze with Change', *USA Today*, 3 July 2001.

Poniewozik, James, 'The Time of Their Lives', *Time*, 12 November 2001.

Rackman, Jane, 'Today's Choice', *Radio Times*, 16 March 2002.

Rice, Lynette, 'Kiefer Madness', *Entertainment Weekly*, date unknown.

Rohan, Virginia, 'Viewers seem to be gravitating towards "comfort programs"', *St Paul Pioneer Press*, 28 October 2001.

Rosenberg, Howard, 'Working Overtime, *24* ticks down', *Los Angeles Times*, 20 May 2002.

Rosenberg, Howard, '*24* is the most suspense we've had in hours', *Los Angeles Times*, 28 October 2002.

Rosenthal, Phil, 'How the mole stayed secret', *Chicago Sun-Times*, 21 May 2002.

Rosenthal, Phil, 'Death and taxis. The fall season so far', *Chicago Sun-Times*, 30 October 2002.

Roush, Matt, 'Reality Check', *TV Guide*, 20 October 2001.

Roush, Matt, '24 Things I Love About 24', *TV Guide*, 3 November 2001.

Roush, Matt, 'Hours of Power: On *24*, the dawn of a suspenseful new day', *TV Guide*, 26 October 2002.

Ruch, John, 'Thrills work overtime on *24*', *Boston Herald*, 28 October 2002.

'Rush Hour', *Entertainment Weekly*, 7 June 2002.

Rutenberg, Jim, 'Expletives? more coming on fall TV', *New York Times*, 3 September 2001.

Salem, Rob, 'Next *24* series now Hope-less', *Toronto Star*, 23 May 2002.

Sangster, Jim and Bailey, David, *Friends Like Us: The Unofficial Guide to Friends* [revised edition], Virgin Publishing, 2000.

Scales, Tom, '*24* building suspense by the hour', *Washington Post*, 6 November 2001.

Schneider, Mike, 'High school friend turns into sexy star on *24*', *Detroit News*, 25 December 2001.

Schulte-Peevers, Andrea and Peevers, David, *Los Angeles*, Lonely Planet Publications, 1999.

'Second season lets *24* renew ratings quest', *Rocky Mountain News*, 20 May 2002.

Stone, Oliver & Sklar, Zachary, *JFK - The Book of the Film, a documented screenplay*, Applause Books, 1992.

Summers, Anthony, *Conspiracy*, McGraw-Hill, 1980.

Susman, Gary, 'Shot Down', *Entertainment Weekly*, 18 October 2002.

Sutherland, Kiefer, 'The Man with the Golden Globe', interview by Andrew Duncan, *Radio Times*, 6 April 2002.

Thompson, David, 'At the end of the day: The *24* finale', *The Independent*, 15 August 2002.

Topping, Keith, *High Times: An Unofficial and Unauthorised Guide to Roswell High*,

Virgin Books, 2001.

Topping, Keith, *Hollywood Vampire: The Revised and Updated Unofficial and Unauthorised Guide to Angel*, Virgin Books, 2001.

Topping, Keith, *Slayer: An Expanded and Updated Unofficial and Unauthorised Guide to Buffy the Vampire Slayer*, Virgin Books, 2002.

Topping, Keith, *Inside Bartlet's White House: An Unofficial and Unauthorised Guide to The West Wing*, Virgin Books, 2002.

Topping, Keith, *Beyond the Gate: The Unauthorised and Unofficial Guide to Stargate SG-1*, Telos Publishing, 2002.

Tucker, Ken, 'Kiefer Madness', *Entertainment Weekly*, Issue 624, 9 November 2001.

Tucker, Ken, 'Rush Hour', *Entertainment Weekly*, Issue 680, 1 November 2002.

'*24* debut gets quick return', *Seattle Times*, 1 November 2002.

Waxman, Sharon, 'Around-the-clock role model', *Washington Post*, 29 October 2002.

Webb Mitovich, Matt, '*24* Star: Glad clock is still ticking', *TV Guide*, 21 May 2002.

Weeks, Janet, 'Secrets & Spies', *TV Guide*, 3 November 2001.

Weinraub, Bernard, 'It's Been a Long Day', *The Observer*, 3 March 2002.

Weintraub, Joanne, 'Real world may prove too much for *24*', *Milwaukee Journal Sentinel*, 6 November 2001.

Wells, Matt, 'Media stereotypes upset stars of *24*', *The Guardian*, 8 July 2002.

Wloszcyzna, Susan, 'Tear down those walls, Mr President', *USA Today*, 18 October 2002.

Wolk, Josh, 'The Day After', *Entertainment Weekly*, issue 697, 25 October 2002.

Wyman, Mark, 'A Fable For The Internet Age', *Shivers*, issue 68, August 1999.

Zinn, Howard, *A People's History of the United States*, Harper & Row, 1980.

Zoller-Seitz, Matt, 'Moral Action', *All TV*, 19 February 2002.

ABOUT THE AUTHOR

12:00 1:00 2:00 3:00 4:00 5:00 6:00 7:00 8:00 9:00 10:00 11:00 12:00 1:00 2:00 3:00 4:00 5:00 6:00 7:00 8:00 9:00 10:00 11:00 12:00

GOODNIGHT, HOLLYWOOD BOULEVARD

Rockin' Keith Topping is a freelance journalist, and author. His previous work includes co-editing two editions of *The Guinness Book of Classic British TV* and writing more guides to television series as diverse as *The X-Files, The Sweeney, Doctor Who* and *Roswell* than he cares to remember. He's also written four novels (including the award-winning *The Hollow Men*), and a novella (Telos's own *Ghost Ship*). His other books include *Beyond the Gate* and the best-selling volumes *Slayer, Hollywood Vampire* and *Inside Bartlet's White House*. He remains a regular contributor to numerous genre magazines, including *TV Zone* and *Shivers*, and is a former Contributing Editor of *DreamWatch*. He specialises in coverage of US television.

A notorious troublemaker, and *geezer*, Keith was born on the roughest estate on Tyneside on the same day in 1963 that his beloved Newcastle United lost 3-2 at home to Northampton Town. He prefers 'Can You Dig It?' by the Mock Turtles to 'Can U Dig It?' by Pop Will Eat Itself, and Joy Division's 'Atmosphere' to Russ Abbot's 'Atmosphere'. Perversely, he considers the Talking Heads' version of 'Take Me To The River' to be the definitive one, and not the Reverend Al Green's. But then, Keith was always *weird*. He regularly appears on local radio and has also contributed to the BBC television series *I♥ the 70s*. He has recently co-scripted, with Martin Day, a proposed TV series format for an independent production company. His hobbies include socialising with friends, foreign travel, loud guitar-based pop music, trashy British horror movies of the 60s and 70s, football, comedy and lots of other stuff. *A Day in the Life* is his 28th book. No, *honestly*, it is ...

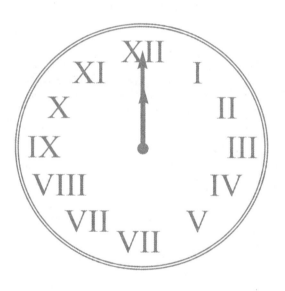

DOCTOR WHO: NIGHTDREAMERS
By Tom Arden
Perihelion Night on the wooded moon Verd. A time of strange
sightings, ghosts, and celebration. But what of the mysterious
and terrifying Nightdreamers? And of the Nightdreamer King?
An adventure featuring the third Doctor and Jo.
Featuring a foreword by Katy Manning.
Deluxe edition frontispiece by Martin McKenna.
£10 (+ £1.50 UK p&p) Standard h/b
ISBN: 1-903889-06-5
£25 (+ £1.50 UK p&p) Deluxe h/b
ISBN: 1-903889-07-3

DOCTOR WHO: GHOST SHIP
By Keith Topping
The TARDIS lands in the most haunted place on Earth, the
luxury ocean liner the Queen Mary on its way from
Southampton to New York in the year 1963. But why do
ghosts from the past, the present and, perhaps even the
future, seek out the Doctor?
An adventure featuring the fourth Doctor.
Featuring a foreword by Hugh Lamb.
Deluxe edition frontispiece by Dariusz Jasiczak.
SOLD OUT Standard h/b
ISBN: 1-903889-08-1
SOLD OUT Deluxe h/b
ISBN: 1-903889-09-X

DOCTOR WHO: FOREIGN DEVILS
By Andrew Cartmel
The Doctor, Jamie and Zoe find themselves joining forces
with a psychic investigator named Carnacki to solve a series
of strange murders in an English country house.
An adventure featuring the second Doctor, Jamie and Zoe.
Featuring a foreword by Mike Ashley.

Deluxe edition frontispiece by Mike Collins.
SOLD OUT Standard h/b
ISBN: 1-903889-10-3
£25 (+ £1.50 UK p&p) Deluxe h/b
ISBN: 1-903889-11-1

DOCTOR WHO: RIP TIDE
By Louise Cooper
Strange things are afoot in a sleepy Cornish village. Strangers
are hanging about the harbour and a mysterious object is
retrieved from the sea bed. Then the locals start getting sick.
The Doctor is perhaps the only person who can help, but
can he discover the truth in time?
An adventure featuring the eighth Doctor.
Featuring a foreword by Stephen Gallagher.
Deluxe edition frontispiece by Fred Gambino.
£10 (+ £1.50 UK p&p) Standard h/b
ISBN: 1-903889-12-X
£25 (+ £1.50 UK p&p) Deluxe h/b
ISBN: 1-903889-13-8

DOCTOR WHO: WONDERLAND
By Mark Chadbourn
San Francisco 1967. Summer has lost her boyfriend, and
fears him dead, destroyed by a new drug nicknamed Blue
Moonbeams. Her only friends are three English tourists: Ben
and Polly, and the mysterious Doctor. But will any of them
help Summer, and what is the strange threat posed by the
Blue Moonbeams?
An adventure featuring the second Doctor, Ben and Polly.
Featuring a foreword by Graham Joyce.
Deluxe edition frontispiece by Dominic Harman.
£10 (+ £1.50 UK p&p) Standard h/b
ISBN: 1-903889-14-6
£25 (+ £1.50 UK p&p) Deluxe h/b
ISBN: 1-903889-15-4

Other Titles

URBAN GOTHIC: LACUNA & OTHER TRIPS
Edited by David J. Howe
Stories by Graham Masterton, Christopher Fowler, Simon Clark, Debbie Bennett, Paul Finch, Steve Lockley & Paul Lewis.
Based on the Channel 5 horror series.
SOLD OUT

THE MANITOU
By Graham Masterton
A 25th Anniversary author's preferred edition of this classic horror novel. An ancient Red Indian medicine man is reincarnated in modern day New York intent on reclaiming his land from the white men.
£9.99 (+ £1.50 p&p) paperback
ISBN: 1-903889-70-7
£30.00 (+ £2.50 p&p) signed and numbered hardback
ISBN: 1-903889-71-5

CAPE WRATH
By Paul Finch
Death and horror on a deserted Scottish island as an ancient Viking warrior chief returns to life.
£8.00 (+ £1.50 p&p)
ISBN: 1-903889-60-X

TELOS PUBLISHING
c/o 5a Church Road, Shortlands, Bromley,
Kent, BR2 0HP, UK
Email: orders@telos.co.uk Web: www.telos.co.uk

To order copies of any Telos books, please visit our website where there are full details of all titles and facilities for worldwide credit card online ordering, or send a cheque or postal order (UK only) for the appropriate amount (including postage and packing), together with details of the book(s) you require, plus your name and address to the above address. Overseas readers please send two international reply coupons for details of prices and postage rates.

BEYOND THE GATE
THE UNOFFICIAL AND
UNAUTHORISED GUIDE TO STARGATE SG-1
KEITH TOPPING

Stargate SG-1 has, like a fine wine, matured over six seasons from a basic movie spin-off into the best science-fiction show on television. And one that includes, within its impressive arsenal of strengths, a sly and laconic humour - heavily pushed by the personality of its leading man and executive producer, Richard Dean Anderson. The series is witty, inventive, surprising in all sorts of ways, and massively popular across the globe. It has tackled some very serious issues, but it's also loads of fun - full of pithy dialogue and knowing winks to its audience.

In *Beyond the Gate*, an indispensable unofficial and unauthorised guide to the *Stargate* universe, acclaimed author Keith Topping breaks down each of the series' 100-plus episodes, analyses the elements and recurring themes that make it so popular, uncovers possible influences, acknowledges the moments when logic simply flies out of the window and provides trivia for use at dinner-parties and conventions.

288pp. A5 paperback original
ISBN 1-903889-50-2   £9.99 UK $17.95 US $24.95 CAN

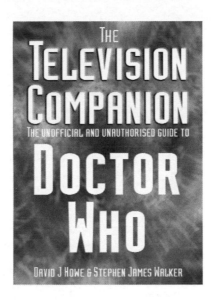

THE TELEVISION COMPANION
The Unofficial and Unauthorised Guide to Doctor Who
David J Howe & Stephen James Walker

Everything you ever wanted to know about the cult BBC television series *Doctor Who* which celebrates its 40th anniversary in 2003.

Every story is covered in depth in all aspects of production, including plot details, cast and crew lists, episode endings, transmission dates, memorable quotes and popular myths. In addition there is a comprehensive analysis of every adventure, utilising reviews both contemporary and retrospective from a wide variety of sources.

This book is the essential companion for every trip you will ever take into the TV universe of *Doctor Who*.

550pp approx. A5 paperback; also available as a signed (by Howe & Walker) and numbered, limited hardback edition
ISBN 1-903889-51-0 (pb)   £14.99 UK $29.95 US $35.95 CAN
ISBN 1-903889-52-9 (hb)   £30.00 UK $59.95 US $64.95 CAN

HOWE'S
TRANSCENDENTAL TOYBOX
THE GUIDE TO DOCTOR WHO COLLECTIBLES
DAVID J HOWE & ARNOLD T BLUMBERG

David J Howe and Arnold T Blumberg present the definitive collector's guide to *Doctor Who* merchandise. From activity books to wallpaper, everything is covered. From the rare and obscure to the commonplace and disposable, every facet of *Doctor Who*'s penetration into the merchandise marketplace is detailed. As well as including factual material, descriptions, photographs and a guide to current prices, *Howe's Transcendental Toybox* also helps the beginner in what to get and what to ignore and what to look out for especially. The book covers *Doctor Who* merchandise around the world, including items released in America, France, Portugal, Canada, Hungary and Australia as well as the many UK-produced items. *Howe's Transcendental Toybox* is both a fascinating tour through the many ways that *Doctor Who* has been presented over the years and an entertaining guide to the world of *Doctor Who* collecting. Fully revised and updated from the first edition, this new edition covers all items released up to the end of 2002.

750pp approx. A5 paperback
ISBN 1-903889-56-1 (pb)   (Prices to be determined)
PUB: SEPTEMBER